D0479506

PolicePrep's Comprehensive Guide to Canadian Police Officer Exams

COMPREHENSIVE GUIDE TO CANADIAN POLICE OFFICER EXAMS, published by:

PolicePrep
http://www.policeprep.com
info@policeprep.com

Authors:
Deland Jessop, Kalpesh Rathod, and Adam Cooper.

ISBN 10: 0-9735151-0-4
ISBN 13: 9-780973-515107

Printed and bound in Canada

Table of Contents

Introduction

Welcome to PolicePrep. As former police officers, we understand the situation you're in and the challenges you face ahead. This study guide was developed to help you prepare for the police exams used by forces across Canada.

By purchasing this guide, you have taken an important step - you have moved from thinking about doing something to improve your chances of being hired to taking action. Police services are looking for action-oriented individuals. Your dedication to preparing for your police exams demonstrates that you are just this type of person.

If you are looking for more practice tests and further preparation materials, visit our website at WWW.POLICEPREP.COM. We offer a special discount of 25% for those who have purchased this guide. If you're interested in taking advantage of this offer, input the following code into the Referral Code section when registering on our website (note the code is case sensitive):

ppdc1320

Please do not hesitate to contact us if you have any questions, concerns or comments about this book, our website, or the application and testing process. We will be happy to assist you in any way that we can.

Email: info@policeprep.com
URL: http://www.policeprep.com

Preparation Material

Resume Building

A resume is a tool used to demonstrate your suitability for the job-specific requirements of a career. This holds true with policing. Few people have received instruction on building a resume, or had much experience writing them. They don't understand what should or should not be included to present themselves in the best manner they can.

Resume building does not start at the writing stage. If you are serious about becoming a police officer, you should have a long list of volunteer experience, academic achievements, languages, computer skills and other highlights to place on your resume. If you don't, begin today. Many organizations, including food banks, charity organizations and Children's Aid Societies are desperate for volunteer help. Languages are vital to police forces, as are computer skills and any other life skills.

The main purpose of your resume is to frame your experiences, skills and knowledge in a manner relevant to the police service to which you are applying. You have to not only demonstrate what you've done, but also show that you have done it well. It is crucial to present information clearly and concisely so the person reviewing your resume can quickly find what they require. Three principles should be followed:

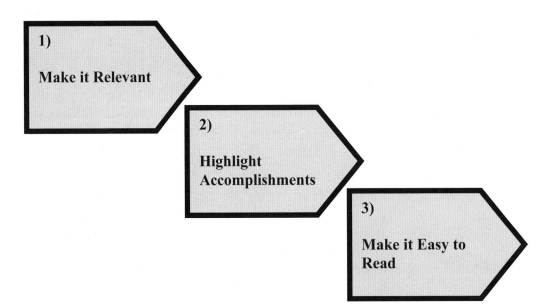

1) **Make it Relevant**

2) **Highlight Accomplishments**

3) **Make it Easy to Read**

Principle One: Make it Relevant

Police forces want to fill positions with people who fit their needs. It is important to determine what competencies are required for the job. Below is a list of core competencies that police forces are searching for.

Analytical Thinking	The ability to analyze situations and events in a logical way, and to organize the parts of a problem systematically.
Self – Confidence	A belief in your capabilities and recognition of personal limitations.
Communication	You must have the skills to effectively communicate using listening skills and verbal and written communications skills.
Flexibility / Valuing Diversity	As a police officer, you will have to work with a wide cross-section of the community that includes diverse backgrounds, cultures and socio-economic circumstances. You must have the ability to adapt your approach to each situation.
Self - Control	Policing can be extremely stressful. You must establish that you can control your emotions actions when provoked.
Relationship Building	Developing contacts and relationships both within and outside the police service is extremely valuable.
Achievement Orientation	You must demonstrate a desire for continuous improvement in service and accomplishments.
Information Seeking	The ability to seek out and analyze information from various sources before making decisions.
Concern for Safety	The ability to exercise caution in hazardous situations in order to ensure safety to self and others.
Assertiveness	The capacity to use authority confidently and to set and enforce rules appropriately.
Initiative	Demonstrated proficiency to be self-motivated and self-directed in identifying and addressing important issues.

Cooperation	Willing to act with others by seeking their input, encouraging their participation and sharing information.
Negotiation / Facilitation	The ability to influence and persuade others by anticipating and addressing their interests and perspectives.
Work Organization	The ability to develop and maintain systems for organizing information and activities.
Community Service Orientation	Proven commitment to helping or serving others.
Commitment to Learning	Demonstrated pattern of activities that contribute to personal and professional growth.
Organization Awareness	A capacity for understanding the dynamics of organizations, including the formal and informal cultures and decision-making processes.
Developing Others	Commitment to helping others improve their skills.

Many people squeeze everything into a resume hoping that something will click. Any material on your resume that does not exhibit traits from the list of core competencies the police service is looking for is a waste of space.

Do not include every employer on your resume unless you are specifically asked to provide that information. Many police services require an employment history application. Pick out the most relevant positions you have had and focus on demonstrating the qualities. Any additional information such as Activities, Volunteer Experience, Education, or Special Skills should also demonstrate your competencies.

Principle Two: Highlight Accomplishments

Accomplishment statements should give the police service an indication of how well you performed. It should reveal not only what you did, but also how well you did it. Each statement should include the following:

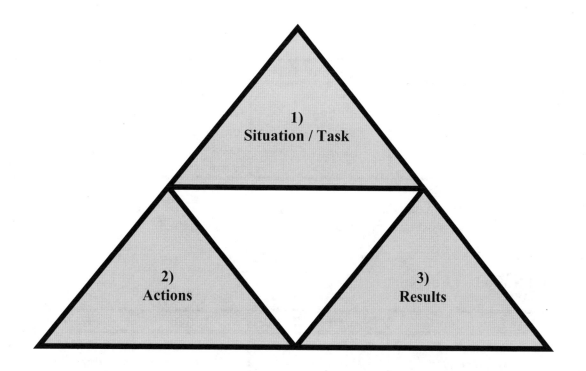

Each accomplishment statement should describe skills relevant to the police service. Practice writing these statements. Typically, accomplishment statements fall under the Work Experience, Volunteer Experience, or Education sections of your resume.

Each statement should use action verbs that emphasize and empower your accomplishment statements. Quantifying your results when you can will add impact.

Example Action Statements

1) Day Camp Counsellor

Core Competency	Situation / Task	Action	Result
Developing Others, Cooperation, Concern for Safety, Assertiveness, Community Service, Communication.	Field trips as a day camp counsellor.	Instruction and supervision.	Ensured safety of 60 children with fellow counsellors.

"Supervised and instructed 60 young children on field trips, ensuring their safety and enjoyment with a team of fellow counsellors."

2) Retail / Grocery

Core Competency	Situation / Task	Action	Result
Work Organization, Communication, Negotiation / Facilitation	Controlling Inventory.	Organized units and placed orders (quantified)	Diverse customer needs anticipated and satisfied.

"Organized shelving units and placed orders in excess of $20,000, ensuring diverse customer needs were anticipated and satisfied."

3) Post-Secondary Education

Core Competency	Situation / Task	Action	Result
Initiative, Achievement Orientation, Analytical Thinking, Commitment to Learning, Communication	Attending post-secondary education.	Studied sociology (or any other major)	Graduated with a strong standing, developing a core set of skills.

"Developed analytical, presentation, computer and XXXX skills by studying sociology, graduating with a 75% average."

4) Volunteer Work

Core Competency	Situation / Task	Action	Result
Initiative, Communication, Cooperation, Work Organization, Developing Others, Self-Confidence, Flexibility / Valuing Diversity, Negotiation / Facilitation, Community Service Orientation	Food drive at work.	Organized and implemented.	Raised $2,000 for needy people in the community.

"Organized and implemented a Food Drive with a team of volunteers, effectively raising $2,000 for needy people in the community."

Action Verbs to be used for your Accomplishment Statements

Accelerated	Displayed	Negotiated	Saved
Accumulated	Documented	Ordered	Scheduled
Accomplished	Effected	Organized	Selected
Acquired	Enforced	Performed	Separated
Analyzed	Engineered	Perpetuated	Served
Applied	Evaluated	Planned	Set
Arranged	Facilitated	Prepared	Shared
Assessed	Filed	Prescribed	Showed
Authorized	Financed	Presented	Solved
Approved	Founded	Problem-solved	Strengthened
Began	Generated	Processed	Succeeded
Bought	Hired	Produced	Supplied
Budgeted	Identified	Promoted	Taught
Coached	Implemented	Provided	Team-built
Collected	Invented	Questioned	Trained
Combined	Launched	Raised	Translated
Communicated	Learned	Read	Tutored
Conducted	Made	Realized	Uncovered
Convinced	Maintained	Reorganized	Unified
Coordinated	Managed	Repaired	Utilized
Developed	Marketed	Researched	Vitalized
Directed	Minimized	Revised	Won
Discovered	Monitored	Risked	Wrote

Principle 3 - Make it Easy to Read

Police recruiters look at thousands of resumes each year. They do not necessarily spend a lot of time on each one. This means your resume has only a few minutes to prove that you are a good fit for their police service. The information presented has to be immediately pertinent and easy to read. Key things you should be mindful of when finishing up your resume are:

- use high quality bond paper
- incorporate as much white space as possible so the reader is not overwhelmed
- highlight only key words or positions to attract attention
- use bullet points rather than paragraphs
- keep font sizes between 10 and 12 pt

Language and grammar are very important on a resume and the following should be observed:

- make every word count
- use short, simple and concrete words that are easily understood
- use strong nouns and vital verbs to add action, power and interest
- avoid personal pronouns
- spell check the document and always have someone proof read the material
- double check the meaning of easily confused words, i.e.:

>
> affect (influence) vs. effect (result)
> personal (private) vs. personnel (staff)
> elicit (draw forth) vs. illicit (unlawful)
> discreet (showing good judgement) vs. discrete (distinct or separate)
> allude (indirect reference) vs. elude (to evade)

A few rules-of-thumb

- months do not need to be included in dates when the length of employment is greater than six months
- part-time and full-time descriptors are generally not included
- do not include names of supervisors
- Check with the police service you are applying to about disclosing full employment history

Review the copy of the sample resume below.

Resume Components

Name	Address Telephone Number E-mail

Education

Educational Institution Location Degree	Date
Educational Institution Location Degree	Date

Work Experience

Company, Geographic Location   Date
Position title
 - Descriptive Statement if needed
 - Relevant Accomplishment Statement
 - Relevant Accomplishment Statement

Company, Geographic Location   Date
Position title
 - Descriptive Statement if needed
 - Relevant Accomplishment Statement
 - Relevant Accomplishment Statement

Company, Geographic Location   Date
Position title
 - Descriptive Statement if needed
 - Relevant Accomplishment Statement
 - Relevant Accomplishment Statement

Examples of Optional Section Headings

- Professional Development	- Awards
- Computer Skills	- Summary of Qualifications
- Languages	- Functional Skills
- Activities and Interests	- Publications
- Volunteer Experience	- Academic Achievements

Jane / John Doe (EXAMPLE)
123 Main St # 1, Anytown Ontario A1A 1A1 (416) 555 - 1212
jdoe@x.com

Education

CITY COLLEGE, Toronto, Ontario   (1996 -2000)
Police Investigations Diploma
- Elected Class President and managed a budget of $5,000 and a team of 15 volunteers to deliver class social activities and educational assistance programs.

MAIN STREET COLLEGIATE, Toronto, Ontario   (1991-1996)
OSSD, OAC Certificate, Honour Roll, Senior English Award

Professional Experience

You Name It Security, Toronto, Ontario   (2000-present)
Security Guard
- Investigated and handled property disturbances arising from a variety of situations and resulting in reports, cautions or arrests.
- Organized and implemented a neighbourhood watch program for clients, taking a proactive role to reduce instances of break and enters in a residential complex.

Toronto Parks Department, Toronto, Ontario   (1995-1999)
Assistant Activity Implementer
- Scheduled and implemented a variety of after school activities for 50 – 60 children with fellow co-workers.
- Used a needs-based approach to assist children from diverse cultural backgrounds with a variety of problems, such as schoolwork, bullying and loneliness.

Volunteer
- Thanksgiving Food Drive - annually delivering food to needy people throughout the community
- Children's Aid Society – Special Buddy Program   (1995-1998)
- City College Orientation Leader   (1999)

Interests
- Shodan Black Belt in Jiu Jitsu, running, weight training, snowboarding, rock climbing, white water rafting, sport parachuting, water skiing and SCUBA diving.
- Piano – Royal Conservatory Grade 5. Guitar - Introductory lessons.

Computer Skills
- Excel, WordPerfect, PowerPoint
- Internet development, Outlook

The Interview

It is important to recognize that police services are looking for the best people for the job and will not try to consciously confuse you.

At this stage it is your interpersonal and communication skills that will help you land a job with the police service. The interviewer is looking for someone who is competent, likeable and who fits in with the organization's culture, goals, beliefs and values.

What Interviewers Tend to Look For

Friendly Personality

As a police officer, you spend a great deal of time with co-workers. Many days you are sitting beside them in the same car for more than ten hours. Every interviewer will ask themselves whether or not they could spend ten hours in a confined space with you. You must prove that you are likeable enough to do this.

Organizational Fit

Police services have a particular culture and it is important for interviewers to ensure that job applicants will fit into that culture. Suitability for the force includes a willingness to work shift work and overtime if required, give up your days off if you are needed for court, and an ability to function well as a member of a team. There is a list of other competencies outlined in the Resume Section.

It is important not to pretend to be something you're not. If you feel you wouldn't fit in with a police culture, then it is probably best for both you and the organization that you seek another career. It is important to ask these questions of yourself. Once in the interview stage, you should be confident that you would fit in with the culture.

Capable and Professional

Police services want competent personnel. A great deal of authority and responsibility comes with this job. You must demonstrate that you are capable of handling the responsibility and that you can perform under pressure. Again, it is important to review the core competencies outlined in the Resume Section.

Handling Pre-Interview Stress

Feeling nervous before an interview is perfectly normal. Politicians, entertainers and media personalities feel nervous prior to performances as well. The best way to handle the stress is to be well prepared. Once again, interviewers are not trying to trick you. They want you to succeed; it makes their job easier. Some things you should do before the interview include:

- Get a good night's sleep (this goes without saying, but bears repeating).
- Practice interviewing with friends, using the behavioural questions below.
- Wear professional clothing (suits or business dress).

You should bring all of the documents that the police service requests of you (transcripts, copy of your resume, portfolio) to the interview along with a pad of paper, a pen, a list of references and a list of questions you may have. Interviewers are often impressed if you have intelligent and researched questions about the job.

How to Influence the Hiring Decision

Understand the Police Service – Local Focus Interviews

It is important to have at least a rudimentary understanding of the police service to which you are applying. This information is available on most websites, or at the stations and employment office of the police service. Some information you should know would include:

- Rough size of the service (example: Toronto has about 5,000 uniformed officers.)
- Name of the commanding officer.
- Areas of service (example: Peel Region covers Mississauga, Brampton and Caledon.)
- Some major units within the department (mounted unit, traffic unit, ETF, etc.)
- Community specific issues that affect the police department. For example, Vancouver is a very ethnically diverse community where language barriers may exist. Hamilton is a region which includes both light and heavy industry. Calgary is a rapidly growing city with a great deal of on-going construction.
- The challenge that all municipal services are facing (asked to do more with less, biohazard training, threats of terrorism, etc.)

Before any interview, read the local newspaper of the community you are applying to for several weeks so that you are aware of the local issues and concerns.

Understand the Job

You have to understand that the job of a police officer is not just arresting criminals and tending to emergency situations. If asked a question about the daily duties of a police officer, you have to include as many of the roles as possible. Include:

- Ongoing training
- Maintaining and cleaning equipment
- Interacting with the public and developing community relations
- Filling out paper work and reports
- Solving community disputes
- Maintaining public order (which could include enforcing parking laws, illegal demonstrations, etc.)
- Enforcing the law (both traffic and criminal)
- Investigating occurrences and apprehending criminals
- Assisting victims
- Providing medical assistance where required

To prove that you understand the job, make sure that you include these less glamorous duties of a police officer.

First Impressions

First impressions are extremely important. Many judgements are made about a person within the first 30 seconds of an encounter (fairly or unfairly). It is your job to impress the interviewer(s). Three basic steps you can take to ensure that you make a great first impression are:

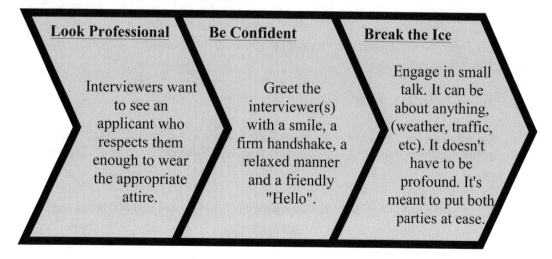

Look Professional

Interviewers want to see an applicant who respects them enough to wear the appropriate attire.

Be Confident

Greet the interviewer(s) with a smile, a firm handshake, a relaxed manner and a friendly "Hello".

Break the Ice

Engage in small talk. It can be about anything, (weather, traffic, etc). It doesn't have to be profound. It's meant to put both parties at ease.

Communication and Interpersonal Effectiveness

The interview process is a situation that tests your communication skills. You should be aware of the following:

Eye Contact	Maintain eye contact with the person you are addressing. This means looking at the person who is speaking to you. In interviews with more than one interviewer spend an equal amount of time on each person.
Body Language	Be aware of your position in your seat and your breathing pattern. Attempt to relax by taking steady breaths. Make sure you sit up straight in an interview. This will exhibit self-confidence and professionalism.
Gestures and Speech	Be aware of any gestures you use. Nod and maintain eye contact to indicate that you understand interview questions. Smile when appropriate, and be vocally expressive by alternating your tone where necessary. Be natural and avoid filler words such as "umm" and "like".

During the Interview

Make an effort to read the interviewers. Ask yourself whether they appear to be straining to follow you, if you are talking too fast (breathe more deeply), or too softly (speak louder). If they are writing frantically, that is usually a good sign, but make occasional pauses so that they can keep up. If you do not understand a question, ask them to repeat or clarify it. If you do not know the answer to one of their questions, admit it. Do not lie during the interview.

Prepare Stories Prior to the Interview

Interviewers may have some questions regarding your resume, or your past experiences. Make sure you are familiar with the content in your resume, and any tasks that you mention in it.

Many police services will use a behavioural-based interview method. This means that they will ask you questions about yourself and will ask you to describe events that have actually occurred in your past (usually in the last two years). Some examples of questions you should be prepared to answer include:

Give an example in your life when you:

- were involved in a stressful situation and how you dealt with it.
- were extremely angry and how you dealt with it.
- had to take the role of a leader, and how was the situation resolved.
- had to work as part of a team and explain what happened.
- had to resolve a conflict with other parties and how did you handled it.
- were up against an important deadline and how you handled the work.
- had a conflict with a supervisor and how you handled it.

There are many other behavioural questions, but these are some of the most common examples used by police services.

How to Answer Behavioural Based Questions

Each behavioural question is a story about your past. Make sure that the story you tell is relevant, clear, and even interesting (interviewers are only human). Each story should have:

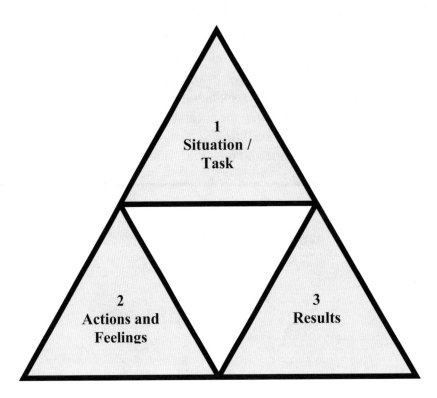

Step One - Understand the Question

This is vital. If you do not understand the question or what the interviewer is asking for, ask them to repeat it or explain it. There is no point giving a very effective answer to the wrong question. For example: one interviewee, asked about Ethnicity, spoke a great deal about Ethics during a police interview. The interviewers probably thought he was an idiot, but he was probably just nervous and didn't hear the question properly.

Step Two - Brief Synopsis

Let the interviewers know what you plan to talk about with a brief outline of the situation, with little detail. This will give you some time to organize your thoughts and the interviewers will understand where you are going. This should take no longer than a couple of sentences.

Example:

"I am going to tell you about a conflict I had with my boss while I was working as a personal trainer. It involved a situation where I was told to bill a client at a rate I didn't feel was justified. We dealt with it away from the customer and resolved it in a manner that satisfied myself, the manager, and the client."

Step Three - Full Story

A retelling of the story will demonstrate to the interviewers your competencies in dealing with the situation and your communication capabilities. Interviewers want a clear story, preferably in a chronological sequence. They are most concerned with your feelings during the situation, the actions you took, and the result of your actions. Always finish the story with the results of your actions. Keep these points in mind both while you are preparing for the interview, and when you are participating in it:

- Answer the question asked.
- Pause and think – don't rush in with an answer.
- Pay attention to the pronouns you are using. Interviewers want to know what "YOU" did. Use the pronoun "I" for your actions and "Us" for team actions. **DO NOT ALWAYS USE "WE".** You will fail the interview.

Bad Example:

"We formed a team to solve the problem. We brainstormed an idea to solve the problem. We then decided on a course of action and began to implement it. We handled task "A" while others handled task "B". We all had individual assignments."

Good Example:

"I formed a team to solve a problem. We brainstormed an idea to solve the problem. I then had to decide the course of action and we began to implement the solution. My friend John and I were responsible for task "A" while another group handled task "B". My particular assignment was to do "X".

- **Ensure you effectively explain the situation, your feelings, your actions and the result.**
- If necessary take pauses to collect your thoughts. There is no need to be constantly talking.

- Relax and enjoy telling the story. You should know it well, as you actually did it.
- Give focused and fluid answers.
- Avoid run-on answers.
- Give support for claims that are made, if possible.
- Show evidence of preparation work.

Other Interviewing Methods

While the majority of police services use behavioural interviews, you might also be asked technical or "what if" questions, or questions about your past. Some forces may ask:

- What would you do if you caught your father drinking and driving?
- Have you ever smoked marijuana?
- Could you arrest your brother?
- Have you ever committed an illegal act?

It is important to give these questions careful consideration and answer honestly. If you tried smoking marijuana when you were in high school, admit it and tell the interviewer why you didn't continue to use it. For example, you found it hurt the academic performance of your friends, or something along those lines.

"What if" questions are intended to challenge you, to see if you are the type of person who will immediately back down. This is not a trait the police service is looking for. Once you have made up your mind on an issue, stand by it. Interviewers may challenge you but this is part of the process. Just ensure that you give careful thought to the question to avoid defending a weak position. It is acceptable to credit the other opinion, but do not change your decision.

Completing the Interview

Just like the first impression, it is important to give a positive impression during the last few moments of an interview. If you have any questions for the interviewers, the end of the interview is when they should be asked. It is acceptable to have prepared questions written down. As you are leaving the room, smile at the interviewer(s) individually, walk up to each one, look into their eyes, shake their hands and personally thank them for their time.

Psychological Tests

Most police services in North America will have applicants undergo some form of psychological testing before offering them employment. If you get to this stage of an application process you are in very strong position. Some police services will have you speak to a psychiatrist or psychologist, while others will have you take a standardized psychological test, such as the Minnesota Multiphasic Personality Inventory-2™.

Psychological Interviews

This may be your first experience speaking to a professional in the psychology field. There isn't a great deal of advice to provide for you at this stage other than:

1) Relax

2) Be Honest

Professional psychologists or psychiatrists will not expect you to put on a show. They will be able to tell if you are trying to hide something, or answering questions in a dishonest manner in an attempt to impress them. DO NOT DO THIS. If you are asked how you are feeling, and there is something wrong, admit it. Everything you say will be kept in confidence.

Other strategies you can use to succeed at this stage are similar to the tactics you would employ during an interview: maintain eye contact, shake hands, and be respectful.

Standardized Psychological Tests

Standardized psychological tests such as the Minnesota Multiphasic Personality Inventory-2™ consist of hundreds of True-False questions. Two major reasons why psychologically healthy people can fail these tests are attempting to memorize patterns and reading meaning into the questions.

Memorizing Patterns

You have to look at each question individually. If you try to remember your previous answers or establish patterns, you may unintentionally demonstrate an undesirable trait, which could keep you from the job. Your score could also be invalid because you were not answering honestly. The test picks up discrepancies due to dishonesty. There are too many questions to remember previous answers and you will confuse yourself and risk failing the test if you attempt to memorize your answers.

Reading Meanings into Questions

A second fatal mistake is to read meaning into the questions. People often look at a simple question and ask, "What are they trying to figure out?" This type of thinking can cause problems. You may find a question like the one below on a psychological test.

Do you like little boys?   True   False

Some applicants would choose false believing that the test is attempting to uncover a sexual deviation. However, if an applicant answers false, what does that say? Why doesn't the applicant like little boys?

Whenever you encounter a question you are not sure how to answer, ask yourself the opposite question. This can clear up any problems you may have with the question. For example:

Do you not like little boys?   True   False

Once you have selected an answer, move on. Worrying about your answer is pointless, and no one answer will fail you or create a problem with your score. What these tests search for are patterns in your answers. Answering each question honestly and treating each question independently is the best strategy for standardized psychological tests.

Lie Detector Examinations and Integrity Questionnaires

There are several police services across North America that have begun to use Lie Detector Examinations on applicants. These are often performed along with Integrity Questionnaires. Applicants will be asked personal questions such as:

- How often do you drink alcohol?
- Have you ever driven a vehicle while intoxicated?
- Have you committed any crimes in the last three years?

All of these questions have to be answered honestly during both the questionnaire and during the lie detector examination. If there are discrepancies between the two examinations, if the lie detector indicates that you are lying, or if your answers aren't measurable, **your application may be permanently removed from the process and you may be prohibited from ever applying to the police service again.**

Strategies

1) Be Honest.

Police services understand that no one has a perfect past. No matter what your past transgressions have been, admit to them and be ready to explain what you learned from your mistakes.

- o Q. Have you committed any crimes in the last 5 years?
- o A. Yes. I worked at a grocery store, and on one or two occasion I took property without paying for it.

2) Demonstrate What You Learned.

If you are asked later about the situation, try to demonstrate what you learned.

- o I always felt bad about myself after I took the objects. They didn't belong to me and my actions were hurting the owners of the business after they gave me a job. I've learned that respect for property is important and I value people's possessions to a much greater degree.

3) Think About The Question Before Answering.

Give some thought to these questions before answering. Everyone has done something foolish in their past of which they aren't proud. Don't just write an answer down without giving it any thought. Answering "Yes" to a question such as "Have you ever driven while intoxicated?" will not get you disqualified from the application process, whereas lying about it and failing the lie detector test will.

4) Relax.

You are going to be nervous. The police service will understand this. Try to be well rested on the test date and have fun with the process. If you aren't hiding anything, you have nothing to worry about. Don't get nervous about admitting to past transgressions. However, if you have a serious criminal record, you might want to consider an alternative career choice.

5) Correcting Mistakes.

It is acceptable to provide a different answer on the lie detector examination than you did on the questionnaire if it was an honest mistake or if you remembered something during the test. Relax, answer the questions honestly and, at the end of the examination, mention to the examiner that you made a mistake and forgot to include something on the questionnaire. If you need to contact a recruiter at a later date and ask them to correct something, do so. Recruiters realize that you are nervous, but the best solution is still to read the questions carefully and answer them completely and honestly the first time.

6) Listen To Instructions.

Prior to beginning the examination or filling out the questionnaire, pay close attention to the instructors, read all instructions fully, and ask any questions you might have.

7) Clarifying Questions.

If a question is unclear, ask the recruiter to explain exactly what the question is looking for. Most of the questions should be straightforward and the recruiters should explain the process to you. But if something is unclear to you, ask for assistance.

General Suggestions

Preparation Prior to Testing

Check out the websites and contact the police service for which you are interviewing to ensure that you are familiar with the testing procedures and the content of the exams. Tests are often standardized but individual services may have variations. It is important to get as much information as possible from the department to which you are applying.

Practice on numerous tests to ensure that you are familiar with the content of the testing material.

Before Testing

Get enough sleep before the tests and enough food and water even if you are nervous. Try to remain relaxed and comfortable. Wear clothing that is professional but also comfortable to work in. If you are doing physical testing on the same day, you may want to wear athletic gear. Arrive early and ready to begin.

During the Test

Don't waste time on a question you are unable to answer; take a guess and move onto the next question. Make a note of answers you are not certain of, and review them if you have time after answering the remaining questions.

Pay attention to the answer sheet and the question number. Many applicants have failed as the result of an error on the scoring card. Every time you respond to a question, look at the answer card carefully and make sure that the number you are answering on the card matches the number of the question.

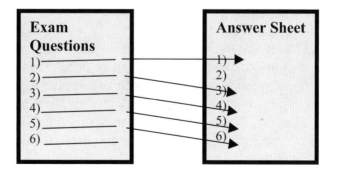

In the above example, even if the applicant answered the questions correctly, he or she would only get one out of the six questions right because of the errors on the scoring card. Keep this in mind when taking the test. Because they are computer scored, you will not be able to correct or explain yourself if you make a mistake on the answer sheet. This mistake is more common if you decide to skip a particular question. If you do, avoid making an order error by crossing off the question you skipped on the answer card.

Frequently Asked Questions

Q1. Should we attempt to conceal events in our past where we acted inappropriately?

We strongly advise against lying during the process at any time. We all have indiscretions in our past. If asked about them, the best solution is to accept responsibility. Explain that you were younger and less responsible at the time. Explain what you learned from the situation and how it made you a stronger person today. Police services will conduct an extensive background investigation and may have more information about you than you are aware. Lying will come back to haunt you.

Q2. I haven't completed my police foundations course yet. Should I still apply?

Currently there is no requirement for a college or university degree in order to be hired as a police officer in Canada. Many new recruits are actually hired after completing only their first year of a multi-year college or university degree. Police services are looking for dedicated, motivated people. Depending on your resume and past experience there is no need to finish diplomas or degrees before applying.

You should demonstrate throughout the hiring process that you will continue with your studies in the event that you aren't hired, or that you will finish relevant degrees even after being hired (such as a B.A.). If you left a program without finishing it, you should explain the reason for failing to complete a course in your resume or during an interview.

Reasons could include:
- an employment opportunity
- geographical move
- pursuing other studies, etc.

Q3. Do you recommend answering every question?

Yes, in each section of the exam you will be scored on how many questions you answer correctly. For the vast majorty of exams, you will not be penalized for wrong answers. If you are working through a question and can't figure it out, take a guess and move onto the next question. Test administrators will disqualify any tests if they feel an applicant is randomly guessing at answers. Work through the questions quickly, but concentrate on accuracy. If you find yourself guessing a lot in the course of your study, review the teaching material for that section.

If you are writing an exam with negative scoring (you get penalized for wrong answers) you should not take a guess unless you are reasonably confident you are correct. If you truly don't know the answer, and it is a completely random guess, leave it blank. Make sure you confirm negative marking with the test administrator on the test date.

Q4. Should I apply to multiple police services or only pick the one that I want?

Applying to forces you aren't interested in is an option. There are police services that attend police college graduation ceremonies and recruit from the graduating class. This saves the force the expense of training new officers. Police services are aware of this problem, so stress during any interview that you want to work for that force. DO NOT LIE AND SAY YOU AREN'T APPLYING ANYWHERE ELSE, but if the question comes up, answer that this city is your first choice for personal reasons (I lived in Regina my whole life, my wife just got a job down here in Halifax, my family is from the Ottawa area, I went to school and loved it here in Burnaby, etc.)

Teaching Material
Math

Addition

$$\begin{array}{r} 7 \\ + \quad 5 \\ \hline 12 \end{array}$$

$7 + 5 = 12$

The above two equations have the same value and are very straightforward. It is important to know that the order of numbers does not make a difference in addition (or multiplication). For example:

$$\begin{array}{r} 6 \\ + \quad 3 \\ \hline 9 \end{array}$$

same

$$\begin{array}{r} 3 \\ + \quad 6 \\ \hline 9 \end{array}$$

$243 + 716 = 959$
same
$716 + 243 = 959$

Some complications arise when larger numbers are used and you need to carry numbers.

Note: When you see a math problem laid out horizontally, as in the box immediately above, rearrange the numbers so that they are vertical (on top of each other) to make the addition easier to do.

Example:

$$\begin{array}{r} 3\ 5\ 1 \\ 6\ 9\ 9 \\ + 4\ 5\ 7 \\ \hline \end{array}$$

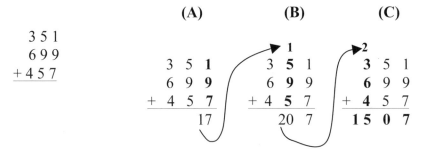

(A)
Start by adding up the numbers in the right most column. The result is 17. The seven remains but the one is carried over to be added to the next column of numbers.

(B)
The same rules apply to the sum 20 in the second column. The 0 remains in the second row, while the 2 is carried over to the column to the left to be added.

(C)
The final column is then added and the answer is recorded.

Subtraction

$$\begin{array}{r} 8 \\ - \quad 3 \\ \hline 5 \end{array}$$

$$8 - 3 = 5$$

The above two equations have the same value and are very straightforward. It is important to know that the order of numbers is significant in subtraction (and division). Different ordering will result in different answers. For example:

$$\begin{array}{r} 18 \\ - \quad 3 \\ \hline 15 \end{array} \qquad \text{different} \qquad \begin{array}{r} 3 \\ - 18 \\ \hline - 15 \end{array}$$

$$712 - 245 = 467$$
$$\text{different}$$
$$245 - 712 = - 467$$

Some complications arise when larger numbers are used and you need to carry numbers.

Example:

$$\begin{array}{r} 7\,4\,3 \\ - 5\,8\,9 \\ \hline \end{array}$$

(A)

The first task is to subtract the right most column. Because 9 is larger than 3, a unit has to be borrowed from the column to the left. The 4 in the middle column is reduced to 3, and the one is added to the right column, making the first row 13 - 9 = 4.

(B)

The second task is to subtract the second column. The same process is repeated. Borrow a 1 from the left column to allow the subtraction. The top number in the left column becomes 6, while the top number in the centre column becomes 13. 13 - 8 = 5. The left column would then be subtracted. 6 - 5 = 1.

Note: If subtracting more than 2 numbers, you cannot stack the numbers as you would in addition. Instead, work from the first subtraction to the last, two numbers at a time.

Multiplication

$$\begin{array}{r} 8 \\ \times \quad 6 \\ \hline 48 \end{array} \qquad 8 \times 6 = 48$$

The above two equations have the same value and are very straightforward. It is important to know that the order of numbers makes no difference in multiplication (or addition). For example:

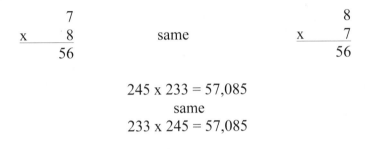

$$245 \times 233 = 57{,}085$$
$$\text{same}$$
$$233 \times 245 = 57{,}085$$

Multiplication, simply put, is adding groups of numbers. For instance, in the above example, the number 8 is being added six times.

8 x 6 = 48	7 x 7 = 49
8 + 8 + 8 + 8 + 8 + 8 = 48	7 + 7 + 7 + 7 + 7 + 7 + 7 = 49
9 x 5 = 45	6 x 3 = 18
9 + 9 + 9 + 9 + 9 = 45	6 + 6 + 6 = 18

It will be difficult to pass a police exam if you have to calculate all simple multiplication in this manner. You should memorize the basic multiplication tables for 1 through 12. Review the multiplication table in this book.

Some complications arise when larger numbers are used and you need to carry numbers.

Example:

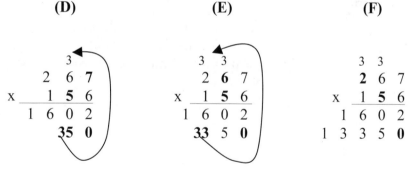

(A)
Begin by multiplying out the right row. The 2 is recorded in the right column and the 4 is transferred to the middle column and recorded as above.

(B)
The second step is to multiply the 6 in the middle column. 6 x 6 = 36. The 4 that was carried over from step A has to be added to the 36. The result is 40 and the 0 is recorded in the middle column. The four is then carried forward to left column as in step A.

(C)
The 6 then has to be multiplied to the left digit on the top number. 6 x 2 = 12. The four that was carried over from step B is added to the 12. The result is 16 and recorded as shown.

(D-F)
The next steps are to multiply the second digit in the bottom row (the 5) to each of the top digits. The 5 is multiplied to the 7, the 6 and the 2. The process is the same as steps A - C. If the number is 10 or larger the number is carried over, as above, and added to the next multiplication.

It is important to remember that the next multiplication set has to be recorded on the line below and lined up starting in the next column. Place a zero in the right column to ensure the digits line up properly

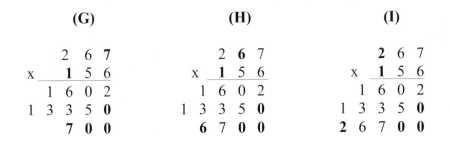

	(G)				(H)				(I)		
	2	6	7		2	6	7		**2**	6	7
x	**1**	**5**	**6**	x	**1**	**5**	**6**	x	**1**	**5**	**6**
1	6	0	2	1	6	0	2	1	6	0	2
1 3	3	5	**0**	1 3	3	5	**0**	1 3	3	5	**0**
	7	**0**	**0**	6	**7**	**0**	**0**	**2**	6	7	**0** **0**

The next steps are to multiply the left digit in the bottom number by each of the digits in the top number. The same process is used as outlined above if numbers have to be carried over.

Lining up of the digits is also necessary at this stage. Because you are multiplying from the hundreds column (the left most) you begin recording the answer in the hundreds column. Follow the same procedure as outlined above. Fill in the first two columns with zeros.

```
        2  6  7
   x    1  5  6
        1  6  0  2
     1  3  3  5  0
  +  2  6  7  0  0
     4  1  6  5  2
```

The final step is to add up the three numbers that were multiplied out. Treat the addition of these three numbers exactly as you would a regular addition problem. If you failed to line the numbers up properly, you will wind up with an incorrect answer. 41,652 is the final answer.

Note: Because complex multiplication questions (like the one above) involve addition, make sure you have a firm grasp of the addition section before trying to tackle multiplication.

Things to Watch For

Watch out for a multiplication question where the first digit in the bottom number is a zero, or where there are zeros in the equation. You still have to properly line up the digits. Note the highlighted zeros.

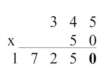

Remember that zero multiplied by any other number is zero. In this situation you begin multiplying with the 10's column (the 5). Because you are multiplying from the 10's column, you begin recording your answer there. Place a zero in the first column.

```
        3 4 5
  x         5 0
  1 7 2 5 0
```

When the four is multiplied to the 0, the result is 0. The number, which is carried over from multiplying 9 x 4 has to be added to 0, which results in the highlighted answer - 3.

```
          3
        6 0 9
  x           4
      2 4 3 6
```

In this situation there is no need to multiply the bottom ten's digit out, as the result will equal 0. You must, however, properly line up the numbers. Because the 3 is in the hundred's column, you must begin recording your answer in the hundred's column. That is why there are two highlighted zeros.

```
            4 5 2
    x       3 0 9
            4 0 6 8
+   1 3 5 6 0 0
    1 3 9 6 6 8
```

Multiplication Tables

	1	2	3	4	5	6	7	8	9	10	11	12
1	1	2	3	4	5	6	7	8	9	10	11	12
2	2	4	6	8	10	12	14	16	18	20	22	24
3	3	6	9	12	15	18	21	24	27	30	33	36
4	4	8	12	16	20	24	28	32	36	40	44	48
5	5	10	15	20	25	30	35	40	45	50	55	60
6	6	12	18	24	30	36	42	48	54	60	66	72
7	7	14	21	28	35	42	49	56	63	70	77	84
8	8	16	24	32	40	48	56	64	72	80	88	96
9	9	18	27	36	45	54	63	72	81	90	99	108
10	10	20	30	40	50	60	70	80	90	100	110	120
11	11	22	33	44	55	66	77	88	99	110	121	132
12	12	24	36	48	60	72	84	96	108	120	132	144

Use of the Table

To use this table, take a number along the top axis and multiply it by a number along the side axis. Where they intersect is the answer to the equation. An example of this is 7 x 3. If you find 7 on the side axis and follow the row until you reach the 3 column on the top axis, you will find the answer – 21.

Look for simple patterns to assist your memorization efforts. For example:

Whenever 10 is multiplied to another number, just add a zero.

    10 x 3 = 30   10 x 7 = 70
    10 x 10 = 100   10 x 12 = 120

Whenever 11 is multiplied by a number less than 9, just double the digit 11 is multiplied by.

    11 x 3 = 33   11 x 5 = 55
    11 x 7 = 77   11 x 9 = 99

One multiplied by any other number is always equal to that number.

    1 x 1 = 1   1 x 4 = 4
    1 x 8 = 8   1 x 12 = 12

Zero multiplied to any number is always zero.

    0 x 10 = 0   0 x 3 = 0

Nine multiplied by any number less than 11 adds up to 9.

    9 x 3 = 27   (2 + 7 = 9)
    9 x 9 = 81   (8 + 1 = 9)

Division

$$6 / 3 = 2 \qquad\qquad 6 \div 3 = 2$$

$$\frac{6}{3} = 2 \qquad\qquad 3\overline{)6}^{\,2}$$

The above equations have the same values and are very straightforward. It is important to know that the order of the numbers is significant in division (and subtraction). Different ordering of numbers will result in different answers. For example:

$$10 / 5 = 2 \qquad \text{different} \qquad 5 / 10 = 0.5$$

$$15 \div 5 = 3 \qquad \text{different} \qquad 5 \div 15 = 0.33$$

$$\frac{100}{10} = 10 \qquad \text{different} \qquad \frac{10}{100} = 0.1$$

$$10\overline{)50}^{\,5} \qquad \text{different} \qquad 50\overline{)10}^{\,0.2}$$

Simply put, division determines how many times a number will fit into another. Picture an auditorium with 100 chairs available. Several schools want to send 20 students to see a play in the auditorium. Now you need to determine how many schools can attend the play. This will require division.

By dividing 100 by 20 (100 ÷ 20) you come up with the number 5. Five schools can send 20 students to attend the play.

Long Division

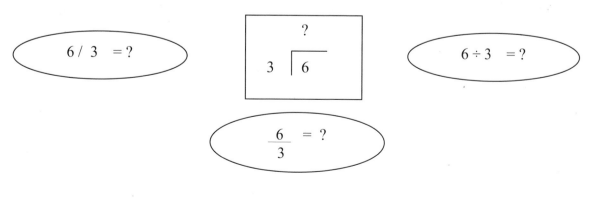

When performing long division, it is important to organize the information as is seen in the centre square. You have to understand how the different formats for division are transferred into the format seen above.

Example

$2653 \div 7 = ?$

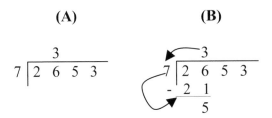

In order to answer a division question on paper, you must place the equation in the proper format. After this is accomplished you can begin to solve the problem.

(A)   **(B)**

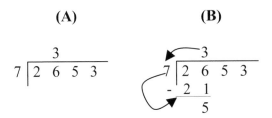

(A)
The first step is to focus on the highlighted area of the number under the bracket. You have to work with a number that is larger than the dividing number (7). Because 2 is smaller than 7, you have to work with 26. Ask yourself how many times you can multiply 7 without going over 26. If you count by 7's (7, 14, 21, 28) you'll realize that 3 is the most times that 7 will fit into 26.

(B)
With the information you have in section A, you now have to perform a simple multiplication. Take the top number (3) and multiply it by the dividing number (7). The answer is placed below 26 and then subtracted from the digits you were working with. (26 - 21 = 5) Make sure you keep the numbers in the proper columns. (If, after subtracting, the answer is greater than the dividing number, you need to start again using a larger top number.)

(C)   **(D)**

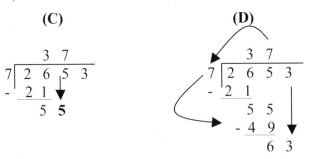

(C)

After subtraction, bring down the next digit to sit beside the solution. This becomes your new number to work with (55). Then repeat step A using this number. Determine how many times you can multiply 7 without exceeding 55. Place this digit above the next digit in the question on top of the bracket.

(D)

Next repeat step B. Multiply out the 7's and record your answer below the 55. Subtracting the numbers results in 6. Continue to work the same pattern, and bring down the next digit in the question to determine a new number to work with.

(E)

```
              3 7 9
        7  2 6 5 3
          - 2 1
              5 5
            - 4 9
                6 3
              - 6 3
                  0
```

(E)

The final steps in the process are to repeat the process. Determine how many times you can multiply 7 without going over 63. You can do this 9 times. When you multiply it out and subtract the result is 0. The answer to the question is shown above.

$$2653 \div 7 = 379$$

Decimals

There are times when you are dividing a number and, after the final subtraction, there is a value left over. This is a remainder. When this happens, you can choose whether or not to continue calculating the number. If you continue, 1 or more decimal points will be introduced.

Example:

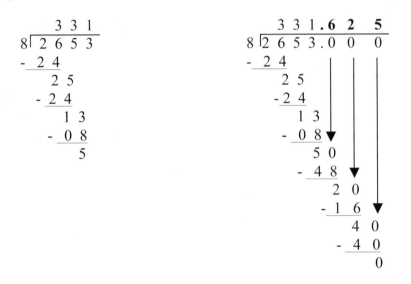

You must follow the same procedure with decimal places as you would with regular long division. Ensure that the digits are properly lined up, and continue adding 0's after the decimal places in the equation.

Decimals and Whole Numbers

You may be required to solve division problems with decimals already in place. Below are two examples of decimals occurring in division questions.

Example 1

$$5 \overline{)35.85} \qquad 5 \overline{)\overset{7.17}{35.85}}$$

To answer the question correctly, you have to place the decimal point in the answer directly above the decimal point in the question.

Example 2

$$27 \overline{)\overset{1060.0}{28620.0}}$$

When a decimal point is found in the denominator (the number of parts into which the whole is divided – bottom number of a fraction), then you must eliminate it before answering the question. This is achieved by shifting the decimal point however many spaces to the right it takes to create a whole number, in this example one space. This has to be matched by shifting the decimal place in the numerator (the number to be divided – top number of a fraction) by one space as well. If the numerator is a whole number, shift the decimal point right by adding a zero, as in the example above.

Example 3

$$3.5\overline{)46.55}$$

$$35\overline{)465.5} = 13.3$$

When a decimal point is found in both the numerator and the denominator you must combine both steps. First, you must eliminate the decimal place in the denominator, as in example 2. Then you have to ensure that the new decimal place lines up, as in example 1.

Hints

Long division becomes more complicated with higher numbers, especially higher denominators.

$$67\overline{)3015} = 0045$$
$$-268$$
$$335$$
$$-335$$
$$0$$

Using 0's to Line up Numbers

67 will not fit into 3, or 30. You will therefore have to work with 301. By placing 0's above the 3 and the 0, (highlighted), you will not make any errors with improperly aligned numbers.

Rounding Up

Determining how many times 67 will fit into 301 can be a difficult task. It may help to round 67 up to 70. By counting 70 four times, you will reach 280. Five times equals 350, which exceeds 301. Four is the best guess, and by multiplying it out, using 67 you are proven correct.

Disregarding Decimals

The majority of the answers on a police test will not require decimals. If your calculation of an equation gives you an answer with decimals, but none of the optional answers have decimals, stop calculating. Make a selection from the available options, or consider that you made a mistake. Quickly check your work, but don't spend too much time on one question that's causing you problems. Move onto the next question.

Zeros and Ones

Any time zero is divided by any other number the answer is 0.

$0 / 3 = 0$ $0 \div 25 = 0$ $\dfrac{0}{99} = 0$ $99 \overline{\smash{\big)}\ 0}^{\ 0}$

It is impossible for a number to be divided by 0. It is indefinable.

$9 / 0 =$ undefined $77 \div 0 =$ undefined $\dfrac{66}{0} =$ undefined

Any number divided by 1 is equal to itself.

$3 / 1 = 3$ $55 \div 1 = 55$ $\dfrac{1,297}{1} = 1,297$ $1 \overline{\smash{\big)}\ 38}^{\ 38}$

Place Value

It is important to maintain proper place value of digits when performing mathematical calculations. You must be able to convert written numbers into digits. For example:

Two million, forty thousand and two	2,040,002
One and a half million	1,500,000
Ten thousand and ten	10,010

You can practice place value questions by answering questions such as the ones below:

a) Write a number that is 100 more than 4, 904.
b) Write a number that is 1000 less than 478, 243.
c) What number is one more than 9,999?
d) What is the value of 5 in the number 241, 598?
e) What figure is in the ten thousands place in 4,365,243?
f) What number is 30,000 less than 423,599?

The answers are listed below.

Place value is important when lining up numbers for addition and subtraction questions. For example:

$$15 + 1043 + 603 + 20,602 =$$

$$\begin{array}{r} 20,602 \\ 1,043 \\ 603 \\ 15 \\ \hline 22,263 \end{array}$$

$$13.09 + 0.4 + 206 + 0.002 =$$

$$\begin{array}{r} 206.000 \\ 13.090 \\ 0.400 \\ 0.002 \\ \hline 219.492 \end{array}$$

One of the most common errors is failing to place digits correctly under one another, which often occurs when trying to calculate these problems in your head.

Answers to practice questions.

a) 5,004   b) 477,243

c) 10,000   d) 500

e) 6   f) 393,599

Make sure you are comfortable with the proper names for the location of digits in a number.

$$1, 234, 567.890$$

1 = millions column

2 = hundred thousands column

3 = ten thousands column

4 = thousands column

5 = hundreds column

6 = tens column

7 = ones column

8 = tenths column

9 = hundredths column

0 = thousandths column

Order of Operations

The following rules have to be obeyed while working with mathematical equations. There is an order to how numbers are manipulated and worked on.

B E D M A S

You should memorize this acronym, as it tells you how to proceed with an equation.

1)   **B** – Brackets

You must perform all mathematical calculations that occur within brackets before any other calculation in the equation.

2)   **E** – Exponents

After calculations within brackets are handled, you have to perform any calculations with exponents next.

3)   **D / M** – Division and Multiplication

Division and multiplication components are next. These are handled in the order they appear reading from left to right.

4)   **A / S** – Addition and Subtraction

The final calculations are individual addition and subtraction questions, which are performed in the order they appear reading from left to right.

The best way to understand this process is to work through several problems.

Example 1:		
6 + 5 x 3 – 7	Step 1: Multiplication	5 x 3 = 15
6 + 15 –7	Step 2: Addition	6 + 15 = 21
21 – 7	Step 3: Subtraction	21-7 = 14
Example 2:		
14 – 7 + 18 ÷3	Step 1: Division	18 ÷ 3 = 6
14 –7 + 6	Step 2: Subtraction	14 – 7 = 7
7 + 6	Step 3: Addition	7 + 6 = 13

Example 3:

$7 + (15 - 6 \times 2)$	Step 1: Brackets Remember to follow the order of operation within the brackets. (Multiply before subtracting.)	$6 \times 2 = 12$
$7 + (15 - 12)$		$15 - 12 = 3$
$7 + 3$	Step 2: Addition	$7 + 3 = 10$

Example 4:

$2(2 + 5)^2$	Step 1: Brackets	$2 + 5 = 7$
$2(7)^2$	Step 2: Exponents	$7^2 = 7 \times 7 = 49$
$2(49)$	Step 3: Multiplication	$2 \times 49 = 98$

Remember that two numbers separated only by brackets are multiplied together (a bracket = x.) $2(6) = 6 \times 2$

Practice Questions

Try these practice questions to see if you are comfortable with mathematical order of operation. The final answers are listed below.

a) $7 - 4 + 6 \times 8 \div 2$

b) $14 + 8(6 - 3)$

c) $30 - 3(5 - 2)^2$

d) $(5 - 1)(4 + 7)$

e) $75 - (6 \div (2+1))^2$

f) $10^2 - 10 + 3^2$

g) $(10 + 3) \times 2 + 6(5-2)$

h) $17 + 6^2(18 \div 9)$

i) $4(5+2-3+6)$

j) $10(6 + (15 - (10-5)))$

Answers

a) 27	b) 38	c) 3	d) 44
e) 71	f) 99	g) 44	h) 89
i) 40	j) 160		

Grouping Like Terms

You will come across mathematical problems where you have to group like terms together. Examples of this are very common with money. Whenever you are adding sums of money, there is no need to continually restate the same denominations. Below is an example of an equation adding up a suspect's money:

Denomination	# of Bills
$50	4
$20	3
$10	4

One means of calculating the total value of money seized is to individually add up all of the bills.

$$50 + 50 + 50 + 50 + 20 + 20 + 20 + 10 + 10 + 10 + 10$$

However, there is an easier and more orderly way of writing and working with this equation. Here is the statement rewritten separating the like terms.

$$(50 + 50 + 50 + 50) + (20 + 20 + 20) + (10 + 10 + 10 + 10)$$

Instead of adding all of the $50 bills together you can count the number of 50's and multiply that number by the value.

$50 + 50 + 50 + 50$	$=$	4×50 or $4(50)$
$20 + 20 + 20$	$=$	3×20 or $3(20)$
$10 + 10 + 10 + 10$	$=$	4×10 or $4(10)$

The statement can then be written more clearly as: $4(50) + 3(20) + 4(10)$

Remember that it doesn't matter what order the terms are in, so long as they remain together. The above equation could be restated any of the following ways:

$3(20) + 4(50) + 4(10)$ $20(3) + 50(4) + 10(4)$

$20(3) + 10(4) + 50(4)$ $4(10) + 3(20) + 4(50)$

Like terms can occur in any addition question. It doesn't have to be a monetary question. Any time you see two or more of the same number in an addition problem, they can be combined.

$5 + 6 + 3 + 5 + 2 + 6 + 5$	$=$	$3(5) + 2(6) + 3 + 2$
$75 + 63 + 75 + 63 + 75$	$=$	$3(75) + 2(63)$
$5 + 5 + 5 + 5 + 5 + 4$	$=$	$5(5) + 4$

Fractions

A fraction is simply a part of a whole thing. The example below is of a circle divided into four pieces. Each segment represents ¼ of the circle.

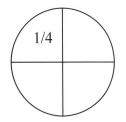

In each of the circles below, the same area is represented, but the area is divided into different numbers of equal parts.

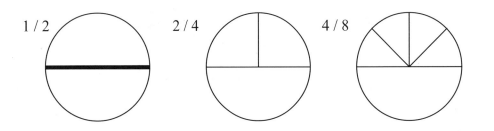

This diagram demonstrates that the fractions 1/2, 2/4 and 4/8 represent the same quantity.

The fractions 1/3, 2/6 and 3/9 are equivalent. You can determine fractions of equivalent value by multiplying both the numerator and the denominator of the fraction by the same number.

$$\frac{1 \times 7}{3 \times 7} = \frac{7}{21} \qquad thus \qquad \frac{7}{21} = \frac{1}{3}$$

A similar rule holds when dividing the numerators and denominators of fractions. This is necessary to reduce fractions to their lowest form.

$$\frac{5 \text{ divided by 5}}{15 \text{ divided by 5}} = \frac{1}{3}$$

Improper Fractions

When a fraction has a larger numerator than denominator then the fraction is larger than one. The diagram below illustrates an example of improper fractions.

$$3/2 = 1\ 1/2$$

Adding and Subtracting Fractions

Whenever you are adding or subtracting fractions, you have to ensure that the denominators of the fractions are the same. For example:

$$\frac{1}{2} + \frac{6}{8} \quad \text{does not equal} \quad \frac{7}{10}$$

By multiplying both the denominator and the numerator of 1/2 by 4, you will be able to add the fractions together. 1 / 2 becomes 4 / 8.

$$\frac{4}{8} + \frac{6}{8} = \frac{10}{8} = \frac{5}{4}$$

When you are adding and subtracting fractions, you also maintain the same denominator, and add or subtract the numerator.

$$\frac{3}{4} - \frac{1}{4} = \frac{2}{4} = \frac{1}{2} \qquad\qquad \frac{3}{18} + \frac{12}{18} = \frac{15}{18} = \frac{5}{6}$$

$$\frac{5}{10} - \frac{3}{10} = \frac{2}{10} = \frac{1}{5} \qquad\qquad \frac{7}{8} + \frac{5}{8} = \frac{12}{8} = 1\ \frac{1}{2}$$

Multiplying Fractions

When multiplying fractions, there is no need to find a common denominator. Simply multiply the two top numbers and then multiply the two bottom numbers. Multiplying two fractions together (other than improper) will result in a fraction that is smaller than the original numbers.

$$\frac{4}{5} \times \frac{3}{4} = \frac{12}{20} = \frac{3}{5} \qquad\qquad \frac{1}{2} \times \frac{1}{5} = \frac{1}{10}$$

$$\frac{3}{4} \times \frac{7}{18} = \frac{21}{72} = \frac{7}{24} \qquad\qquad \frac{3}{2} \times \frac{4}{5} = \frac{12}{10} = 1\ \frac{1}{5}$$

Dividing Fractions

Division with fractions is very similar to multiplying with fractions.

12 divided by 12 = 1	12 goes into 12 once
12 divided by 6 = 2	6 goes into 12 twice
12 divided by 4 = 3	4 goes into 12 three times
12 divided by 3 = 4	3 goes into 12 four times
12 divided by 2 = 6	2 goes into 12 six times
12 divided by 1 = 12	1 goes into 12 twelve times
12 divided by 1/2 = 24	1/2 goes into 12 twenty four times

This is logical when you think about the statement on the right. Whenever you are dividing by a fraction you have to multiply one fraction by the reciprocal of the other. That is, when you divide one fraction by another, you have to multiply one fraction by the inverse of the other. For example:

$$\frac{1}{2} \div \frac{6}{7} = \frac{1}{2} \times \frac{7}{6} = \frac{7}{12}$$

$$\frac{3}{4} \div \frac{4}{5} = \frac{3}{4} \times \frac{5}{4} = \frac{15}{16}$$

$$1\frac{3}{4} \div \frac{4}{5} = \frac{7}{4} \times \frac{5}{4} = \frac{35}{16} = 2\frac{3}{16}$$

Whenever dividing mixed fractions (1 1/2, 2 3/4 etc) you must use improper fractions (3/2, 11/4 etc).

Percentages

It is important to have a solid background in decimals and fractions before you try to handle percentage questions. Percentages are simply fractions. Per means "out of" and cent means "a hundred". Percentages are fractions with 100 as a denominator. They are often noted with this sign: %.

10 % means 10 out of 100 or $\dfrac{10}{100}$

13 % means 13 out of 100 or $\dfrac{13}{100}$

100 % means 100 out of 100 or $\dfrac{100}{100}$

100% means everything. 100% of your salary is your whole salary. You simply follow the same rules of conversion from fractions to decimals for calculating percentages. Simply move the decimal points two places to the left to convert percents to decimals. This is essentially dividing the percentage by 100.

Example: 75 %   = 0.75

8%   = 0.08

53.5 %   = 0.535

208 %   = 2.08

Any percent larger than 100% indicates more than the whole. For example:

A man's stock portfolio is worth 125% of what it was a year ago. This means that the stocks are now worth 25% more. If his stocks were worth $500 last year, they would be worth:

$500 x 125% =
$$\begin{array}{r} 500 \\ \times\ 1.25 \\ \hline \$\ 625 \end{array}$$

Percentages with Fractions

Some questions you encounter may incorporate percentages and fractions. Examples include 2 1/2 % or 33 1/3 %. In order to deal with these problems, you must first convert the percentages to improper fractions.

$$2\ 1/2\ =\ 5/2 \qquad\qquad 33\ 1/3\ =\ 100/3$$

After this step you simply carry out the division question.

$$\begin{array}{r} 2\,.\,5 \\ 2\overline{\smash{\big)}\,5\,.\,0} \\ \underline{4} \\ 1\,0 \\ \underline{1\,0} \\ 0 \end{array}\qquad\qquad\begin{array}{r} 3\,3\,.\,3\,3 \\ 3\overline{\smash{\big)}\,1\,0\,0\,.\,0\,0} \end{array}$$

Once you have the decimal equivalent of the percentage, you then follow the same rules that apply to a regular percentage. Divide the number by 100 or, more simply, move the decimal to the left twice. Thus:

$$2\ 1/2\% = 0.025 \qquad\qquad 33\ 1/3\% = 0.3333$$

Percentages You Should Memorize

25%	=	1 / 4	=	0.25
50%	=	1 / 2	=	0.5
75%	=	3 / 4	=	0.75
100%	=	4 / 4	=	1.00
33 1/3 %	=	1 / 3	=	0.333
66 2/3 %	=	2 / 3	=	0.666
10%	=	1 / 10	=	0.1
20%	=	1 / 5	=	0.2
40%	=	2 / 5	=	0.4
60%	=	3 / 5	=	0.6
80%	=	4 / 5	=	0.8

Decimal / Fraction Conversion Instruction

Fraction to Decimal

There are many situations where you will have to convert fractions to decimals. Decimals are often easier to work with. Changing fractions to decimals is simply a division problem. All you have to do is take the numerator and divide it by the denominator.

Examples:

$$1 / 2 = 2 \overline{\smash{\big)}\ 1.0} \quad \begin{array}{r} 0.5 \\ \hline 1.0 \\ - \ 1.0 \\ \hline 0 \end{array}$$

$$4 / 5 = 5 \overline{\smash{\big)}\ 4.0} \quad \begin{array}{r} 0.8 \end{array}$$

$$1 / 3 = 3 \overline{\smash{\big)}\ 1.000} \quad \begin{array}{r} 0.333 \\ - \ 0.9 \\ \hline 0.10 \\ - \ 09 \\ \hline 010 \\ - \ 09 \\ \hline 1 \end{array}$$

Mixed Fractions

Mixed fractions have to first be converted to improper fractions before they can be converted to decimals. Multiplying the whole number by the denominator and adding the numerator will achieve this. As soon as the improper fraction is found, you calculate the decimal in the same way as above.

Example 1

$$3 \frac{1}{2} = \frac{7}{2} \quad 2 \overline{\smash{\big)}\ 7.0} \quad \begin{array}{r} 3.5 \end{array}$$

Multiply 3 by 2, and then add 1. This is the new numerator, and the denominator remains the same.

Example 2

$$2 \frac{5}{6} = \frac{17}{6} \quad 6 \overline{\smash{\big)}\ 17.000} \quad \begin{array}{r} 2.833 \end{array}$$

Decimal to Fraction

When converting decimals to fractions, place value is extremely important. The first decimal point to the right of the decimal point is the tenths, followed by the hundredths, thousandths, etc. All you have to do is properly line up the place value with the proper denominator.

$$0.1 \quad \text{is a way of writing} \quad \frac{1}{10}$$

$$0.01 \quad \text{is a way of writing} \quad \frac{1}{100}$$

and

$$0.6 \quad \text{is a way of writing} \quad \frac{6}{10}$$

$$0.78 \quad \text{is a way of writing} \quad \frac{78}{100}$$

There is one zero in the denominator for every place to the right of the period in the original decimal.

Exponents

Exponents indicate how many times a number should be multiplied by itself. If a number is raised to the power of 2, the number should be multiplied by itself twice. If the number is raised to the power of 6, the number should be multiplied by itself 6 times.

$$2^2 = 2 \times 2 = 4$$

$$2^3 = 2 \times 2 \times 2 = 8$$

$$2^4 = 2 \times 2 \times 2 \times 2 = 16$$

$$2^5 = 2 \times 2 \times 2 \times 2 \times 2 = 32$$

$$7^2 = 7 \times 7 = 49$$

$$5^4 = 5 \times 5 \times 5 \times 5 = 625$$

Positive and Negative Integers

You must have an understanding of positive and negative integers and how they react when they are added, subtracted, multiplied and divided by each other. Look at the number line below. Positive integers exist to the right of the zero and negative integers exist to the left of the zero.

...-8 -7 -6 -5 -4 -3 -2 -1 0 1 2 3 4 5 6 7...

Adding Positive and Negative Integers
1) - 7 + 5 = -2   2) - 6 + 3 = -3
3) - 2 + 7 = 5   4) - 4 + 11 = 7

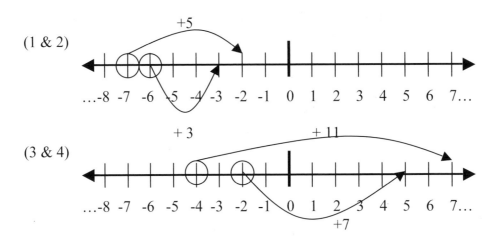

Subtracting Positive and Negative Integers
1) - 2 – 5 = -7   2) - 4 – 8 = -12
3) 4 – 7 = -3   4) 2 – 5 = -3

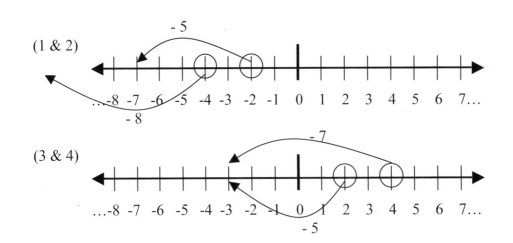

When adding and subtracting positive and negative integers you must know what to do when two signs are directly beside each other.

2 Positives	2 Negatives	Opposite Signs
+ + = +	- - = +	+ - = -

For instance:	6 + (+3)	6 + (-3)	6 - (-3)
	= 6 + 3	= 6 - 3	= 6 + 3
	= 9	= 3	= 9

Try these sample questions. The answers are below.

1) 5 – 9 =

2) – 4 + 6 =

3) – 5 – 2 =

4) 2 – 7 =

5) –2 + 5 =

6) 1 – 9 =

7) 4 – (+6) =

8) –2 –(-4) =

9) + 3 – (-6) =

10) 6 + (-4) =

11) 6 + (+2) =

12) -3 + (-2) =

Multiplying and Dividing Positive and Negative Integers

While multiplying and dividing positive and negative integers, remember the rules that apply to adding and subtracting integers with two signs directly beside each other.

2 Positives	2 Negatives	Opposite Signs
+ + = +	- - = +	+ - = -

You should break questions like this into two steps.

Step 1: Solve the equation ignoring the signs.

6 x (-3) = 18	- 5 x 4 = 20
5 x (-7) = 35	- 3 x (-4) = 12
-12 ÷ (-4) = 3	-21 ÷ 3 = 7
36 ÷ (-9) = 4	-64 ÷ (-8) = 8

If you ignored the + and – signs in front of the numbers you would end up with the answers above.

Step 2: Determine the + / - sign. The rules about + / - integers come into play. If there are two + signs, then the equation is positive. If there are two – signs, then the equation is also positive. If there is one + and one – sign, then the equation is negative.

$$6 \times (-3) = \mathbf{-18} \; (+ / -) \qquad\qquad - 5 \times 4 = \mathbf{-20} \; (- / +)$$
$$5 \times (-7) = \mathbf{-35} \; (- / +) \qquad\qquad - 3 \times (-4) = \mathbf{12} \; (- / -)$$
$$-12 \div (-4) = \mathbf{3} \; (- / -) \qquad\qquad -21 \div 3 = \mathbf{-7} \; (- / +)$$
$$36 \div (-9) = \mathbf{-4} \; (+ / -) \qquad\qquad -64 \div (-8) = \mathbf{8} \; (- / -)$$

The final answers are displayed in bold above.

Try these sample questions. The answers are posted below.

a) $3 \times (-6) =$ b) $-2 \times (-9) =$ c) $-18 \div (-9) =$

d) $7 \times 7 =$ e) $-72 \div 8 =$ f) $-12 \times (-9) =$

g) $7 \times (-6) =$ h) $-28 \div (-4) =$ i) $16 \div (-4) =$

j) $3 \times (-4) =$ k) $-45 \div (-15) =$ l) $-3 \times (2) =$

Answers to Sample Questions

1) $5 - 9 = \mathbf{-4}$ 2) $-4 + 6 = \mathbf{2}$ 3) $-5 - 2 = \mathbf{-7}$

4) $2 - 7 = \mathbf{-5}$ 5) $-2 + 5 = \mathbf{3}$ 6) $1 - 9 = \mathbf{-8}$

7) $4 - (+6) = \mathbf{-2}$ 8) $-2 - (-4) = \mathbf{2}$ 9) $+3 - (-6) = \mathbf{9}$

10) $6 + (-4) = \mathbf{2}$ 11) $6 + (+2) = \mathbf{8}$ 12) $-3 + (-2) = \mathbf{-5}$

---

a) $3 \times (-6) = \mathbf{-18}$ b) $-2 \times (-9) = \mathbf{18}$ c) $-18 \div (-9) = \mathbf{2}$

d) $7 \times 7 = \mathbf{49}$ e) $-72 \div 8 = \mathbf{-9}$ f) $-12 \times (-9) = \mathbf{108}$

g) $7 \times (-6) = \mathbf{-42}$ h) $-28 \div (-4) = \mathbf{7}$ i) $16 \div (-4) = \mathbf{-4}$

j) $3 \times (-4) = \mathbf{-12}$ k) $-45 \div (-15) = \mathbf{3}$ l) $-3 \times (2) = \mathbf{-6}$

Perimeters

Perimeter is defined as the border around an object, or the outside edge of an object.

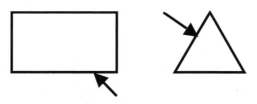

Perimeter is calculated by adding the sides of the object together.

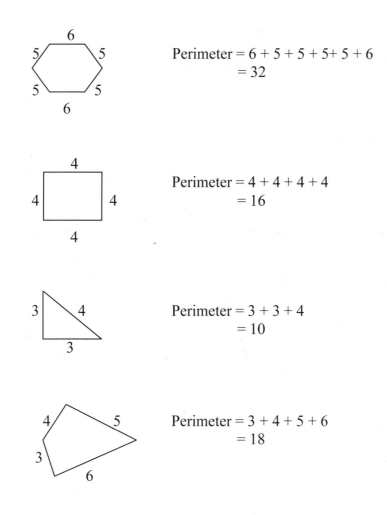

Perimeter = 6 + 5 + 5 + 5+ 5 + 6
= 32

Perimeter = 4 + 4 + 4 + 4
= 16

Perimeter = 3 + 3 + 4
= 10

Perimeter = 3 + 4 + 5 + 6
= 18

Circumferences

Circumference is also defined as the border around a shape, but is always associated with a circle.

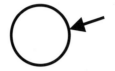

In order to determine the circumference of a circle, you must use a formula. You need to be familiar with some definitions.

$$\pi = 3.14 \text{ (pi)}$$

You are going to have to remember that pi is equal to 3.14.

Diameter (d)

Diameter is the distance from one edge of the circle, through the middle, to the opposite side of the circle.

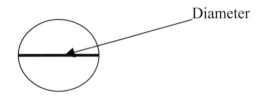

Radius (r)

Radius is defined as ½ of the diameter, or the distance from the mid-point of a circle to its outer edge.

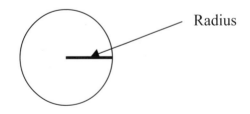

Formula for Calculating Circumference

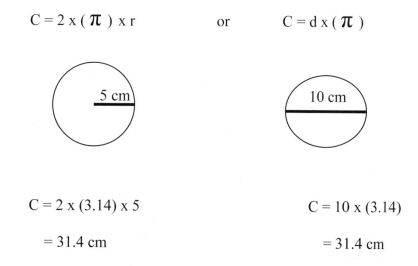

$$C = 2 \times (\pi) \times r \qquad \text{or} \qquad C = d \times (\pi)$$

$$C = 2 \times (3.14) \times 5 \qquad\qquad C = 10 \times (3.14)$$

$$= 31.4 \text{ cm} \qquad\qquad\qquad = 31.4 \text{ cm}$$

The information you are given in a question will dictate the formula you should use to calculate the circumference. If you are given the radius, calculate the diameter by multiplying by two. Dividing the diameter by two will give you the radius.

Areas

Area is space that is occupied within the borders of a shape. It is measured in units squared and is represented by the area shaded in the shapes below.

The three shapes you should know how to calculate area for are the triangle, rectangle and circle.

Area of a Rectangle or Square

To calculate the area of a square or rectangle, multiply the base of the object by its' height.

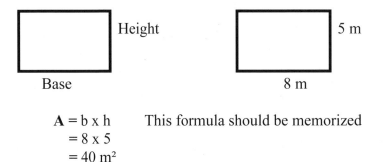

$$A = b \times h$$
$$= 8 \times 5$$
$$= 40 \text{ m}^2$$

This formula should be memorized

Area of a Triangle

To calculate the area of a triangle, follow the formula below.

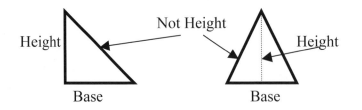

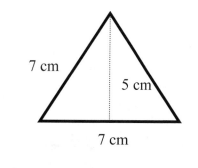

A = ½ x b x h   **This formula should be memorized.**
    = ½ x 7 x 5
    = 17.5 cm ^{2}

Remember that height is not necessarily an edge of the triangle, but the distance from the base to the top of the triangle.

Area of a Circle

To calculate the area of a circle, follow the formula below.

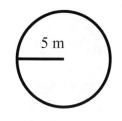

A = π (r) ^{2} **This formula should be memorized.**
    = (3.14) (5) ^{2}
    = (3.14) (25)
    = 78.5 m ^{2}

Other Shapes

You may have to calculate the area of shapes other than basic squares, triangles and circles. You can attempt to break shapes into smaller components and use the formulas above. For example:

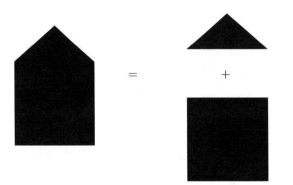

Calculate the area of the triangle and adding it to the area of the square results in the area of the whole shape.

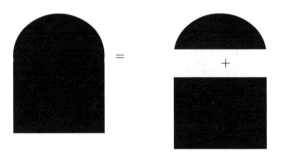

You can divide the shape on the left into a square and a half circle. Calculate the area of the square and the area of the circle. Divide the area of the circle in half and add the two together.

Volumes

Volume is defined as the area occupied by a three dimensional shape. If you pictured an empty cup, volume is the amount of liquid it contains. Calculating volume for different objects can be very difficult and involves complex formulas. We will discuss how to calculate the volume of three simple objects. Volume is always discussed in units cubed (example $3m^3$.)

Volume of a Cube

You should memorize the formula for calculating the volume of a cube.

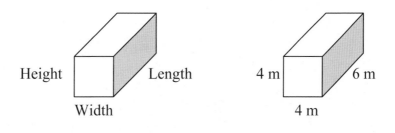

V = length x width x height
   = 6 x 4 x 4
   = 96 m ^{3}

Volume of a Cylinder

To calculate the volume of a cylinder, determine the area of the circle and multiply it by the height of the cylinder.

Radius = 5 m

Height = 10 m

$V = \pi$ (r) ^{2} x height
   = (3.14) (5)² (10)
   = 785 m ^{3}

Volume of a Triangular Shaped Object

To calculate the volume of an object like the one below, first calculate the area of the triangle and multiply it by the length of the object.

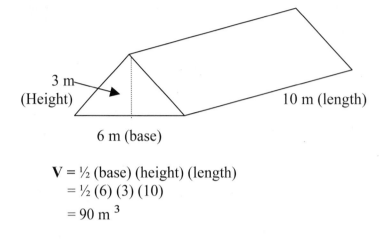

$$V = \tfrac{1}{2} \, (base) \, (height) \, (length)$$
$$= \tfrac{1}{2} \, (6) \, (3) \, (10)$$
$$= 90 \text{ m}^3$$

Metric Conversions

The key to understanding metric conversions is to memorize the prefixes and roots to each word. The root of each word indicates the basic measurement (litre, metre, gram), while the prefixes determine the relative size of the measurement (larger or smaller units – milli, centi, kilo, etc,).

Prefixes

All units in the metric system are easily converted because they are all based on units of 10. When converting between different measurements of the same base unit, it is as easy as shifting the decimal point.

For example:

432,000 millimetres
43,200 centimetres   ALL EQUAL EACH OTHER
432 metres
0.432 kilometres

Length

Length is used to measure the distance between points. The base unit for length is the metre. The most common units you'll encounter with length include:

Millimetres – small units (25 millimetres in 1 inch)
Centimetres – small units (2.5 centimetres in 1 inch)
Metres – larger units (1 metre = 3.2 feet or 1.1 yards)
Kilometres – large units (1.6 kilometres in 1 mile)

Prefix	Example	Sign	Conversion
Milli	Millimetres	mm	1 m = 1000 mm
Centi	Centimetre	cm	1 m = 100 cm
Deci	Decigram	dm	1 m = 10 dm
-	Metre	m	1 m = 1 m
Kilo	Kilometre	km	1 km = 1000 m

Volume

Volume is defined as the capacity of a given container. It usually measures the amount of liquid or gas that an object can hold. For example, the volume of a pop can is 355 millilitres, or the volume of a milk carton is 1 litre. The base unit for volume in the metric system is the litre. A litre is roughly the amount of milk that will fit into a milk carton or roughly three glasses of milk.

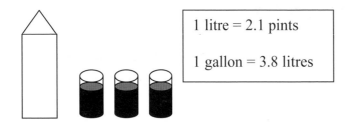

1 litre = 2.1 pints

1 gallon = 3.8 litres

The most common prefix used with volume is the millilitre (used to measure small amounts, such as tablespoons.) The majority of the time when measuring volume you will be using the litre measurement itself.

Prefix	Example	Sign	Conversion
Milli	Millilitres	mL	1 L = 1000 mL
Centi	Centilitres	cL	1 L = 100 cL
Deci	Decilitres	dL	1 L = 10 dL
-	Litres	L	1 L = 1 L
Kilo	Kilolitres	kL	1 kL = 1000 L

Mass or Weight

The base unit for weight in the metric system is the gram. The most common units you'll encounter with weight are:

Milligrams – very small (1000 milligrams in 1 gram)
Grams – small units (28.3 grams in 1 ounce)
Kilograms – large units (1 kilogram = 2.2 pounds)

Prefix	Example	Sign	Conversion
Milli	Milligrams	mg	1 g = 1000 mg
Centi	Centigram	cg	1 g = 100 cg
Deci	Decigram	dg	1 g = 10 dg
-	Gram	G	1 g = 1 g
Kilo	Kilogram	kg	1 kg = 1000 g

Algebraic Equations

Before beginning this section, make sure that you are comfortable with the rules of order of operation in mathematical equations. It is necessary to know in what order you add, subtract, divide and multiply in an equation.

Algebraic equations involve using letters and symbols to represent unknown numbers. In order to solve these equations you must isolate the unknown variable. We will begin with a couple of simple examples.

When solving algebraic equations, it is important to know the opposite mathematical operations. For example, subtraction is the opposite of addition and division is the opposite of multiplication. Square roots are the opposite of squaring. We will not cover square roots in this section.

$6 + y = 12$

$6 + y - 6 = 12 - 6$

$y = 6$

> In order to isolate the "y", eliminate a + 6 on the left hand side of the equation. In algebraic equations, whatever you do to one side of the equation you must also do to the other side. Subtract 6 from both sides.

$y - 3 = 15$

$y - 3 + 3 = 15 + 3$

$y = 18$

> In order to isolate the "y", eliminate a - 3 on the left hand side of the equation. Add 3 to both sides.

$7 y = 42$

$7 y / 7 = 42 / 7$

$y = 6$

> In this case, "y" is multiplied by 7. To eliminate a number that is being multiplied, divide by the same number. Divide both sides by 7.

$y / 12 = 5$

$y / 12 \times 12 = 5 \times 12$

$y = 60$

> In this case, "y" is divided by 12. To eliminate a number that is being divided, multiply by the same number. Multiply both sides by 12.

Practice solving some of these simple equations:

1) $y / 11 = 23$ 2) $15 + y = 63$ 3) $-5 + y = 10$

4) $13 (y) = 130$ 5) $5 y = 15$ 6) $6 + 3 + y = 56$

7) $2(y) = 56$ 8) $y / 8 = 4$ 9) $y (24) = 72$

Answers are below.

More Advanced Algebraic Equations

When solving equations, follow the order of operations which dictate that you perform equations within brackets, followed by exponents, then division and multiplication, and finally addition and subtraction. When isolating unknown variables, use the opposite order. We will not cover solving equations with exponents at this level.

$6 y + 12 = 84$

$6 y + 12 - \mathbf{12} = 84 - \mathbf{12}$

$6 y = 72$

$6 y / \mathbf{6} = 72 / \mathbf{6}$

$y = 12$

> In order to isolate the "y", first eliminate a + 12 on the left hand side of the equation. Subtract 12 from both sides. You are left with 6y = 12.
> To isolate "y", now simply divide both sides of the equation by 6.

$y / 3 + 12 - 2 = \mathbf{15 \ x \ 3} + 4$

$y / 3 + 12 - 2 = 45 + \mathbf{4}$

$y / 3 + 12 - 2 = 49$

$y / 3 + 12 - 2 + \mathbf{2} = 49 + \mathbf{2}$

$y / 3 + 12 = 51$

$y / 3 + 12 - \mathbf{12} = 51 - \mathbf{12}$

$y / 3 = 39$

$y / 3 \ x \ \mathbf{3} = 39 \ x \ \mathbf{3}$

$y = 117$

> You may encounter equations where one side has operations without an unknown variable. In cases like this, solve the side without an unknown variable FOLLOWING THE STANDARD ORDER OF OPERATION RULES.
>
> After you have accomplished this, solve the equation in the standard manner. People more advanced in math will be able to consolidate portions of the left side as well, but unless you are comfortable you should proceed the way outlined to the left.

$(6 - y) \times 3 = 24$

$(6 - y) \times 3 / \mathbf{3} = 24 / \mathbf{3}$

$(6 - y) = 8$

$6 - y - \mathbf{6} = 8 - \mathbf{6}$

$- y = 2$

$- y \times \mathbf{(-1)} = 2 \times \mathbf{(-1)}$

$y = - 2$

> Perform this equation following the standard rules. Leave the brackets until the end. When only the brackets remain, you can get rid of them as they no longer serve a purpose.
>
> When you are left with an equation where the unknown is isolated, but negative, simply multiply both sides of the equation by -1 to inverse the signs.
>
> The end result is that $y = -2$.

$18 / y = 2$

$18 / y \times \mathbf{(y)} = 2 \times \mathbf{(y)}$

$18 = 2 y$

$18 / \mathbf{2} = 2 y / \mathbf{2}$

$9 = y$

> One other tricky situation you may encounter is when "y" appears on the bottom of a division equation. In order to solve for "y", move it from the bottom of the division sign by multiplying both sides of the equation by "y". The result is $18 = 2 y$. Now solve the rest of the equation.

WHATEVER YOU DO TO ONE SIDE OF AN EQUATION YOU MUST ALSO DO TO THE OTHER SIDE.

More Practice Questions

a) $3 (y) + 6 - 10 = 89$

b) $(y) / 6 + 24 - 2 = 14$

c) $- y (3) + 55 = 105$

d) $5 y - 32 = 24 (3)$

e) $-32 + 6y/2 = 64$

f) $22 y + 16 (8) = 6 y$

Answers:

1) 253	2) 48	3) 15
4) 10	5) 3	6) 47
7) 28	8) 32	9) 3

a) 31	b) - 48	c) −16.7
d) 20.8	e) 32	f) − 8

Teaching Material
English

Common Grammar Errors

It is beyond the scope of this book to cover all grammar errors that can occur during a police examination. Below are merely some examples you may come across. If you feel your grammar is a significant barrier to landing the job, it would be prudent to review a grammar textbook, or perhaps take an English grammar course.

The Use of "Then" and "Than"

"**Then**" is used to indicate time. It has the same meaning as "afterwards", "subsequently" or "followed by".

> Ex: I went to the play, *and then* I went home.

"**Than**" is used in comparison. It can be used with the word "rather". It has the same meaning as "as opposed to", or "instead of".

> Ex: I would rather play baseball *than* hockey.

The Use of "Is When"

This is not correct. Use the term "occurs when."

> Ex: The best part of the movie *occurs when* the killer is revealed.

Subordinate Clauses

Be careful with subordinate clauses. If one clause has less emphasis (less importance) in a sentence, it is subordinate or dependent on the other clause. When these clauses occur at the beginning of the sentence, they can be tricky.

> Ex: *Since you began training,* you have been unable to work an entire shift.

If you rearrange the sentence you can understand how "since" acts as the conjunction.

> Ex: You have been able to work an entire shift **since you began training.**

Forming Plurals

It is difficult to determine the plural form of many words. Examples include:

Goose	Geese	Man	Men
Woman	Women	Mouse	Mice
Mother-in-Law	Mothers-in-Law		

Comparative Adjectives and Adverbs

Single Syllable Words:

To form the comparative adjective or adverb for most single syllable words, add "*-er*" to the end of the word. If there are three or more parties to compare, use the ending "*-est*."

Rafik was strong.
Bill was *stronger* than Rafik.
Pratik was the *strongest* of the three.

Sean is fast.
Sean is the faster of the two.
Sean is the fastest of the three.

Be careful. There are always exceptions to the rule in the English language. You should be able to tell by the sound of the words when you should use an alternative method of comparison.

I had a fun time at the party this year.
I had *more fun* this year than last year.
I had the *most fun* this year compared to all the other parties.

The words "funner" and "funnest" do not exist.

Multiple Syllable Words:

As with the example "fun", multiple syllable words use linking words while making comparisons. When comparing two parties, use the word "*more*"; and while comparing three or more parties, use the word "*most*".

He was *more eager* than her to finish the project.
He was the *most eager* of the three to finish the project.

Shelley was *more intelligent* than Michael.
Lucy was the *most intelligent* of the group.

Subject / Verb Agreement

It is important to make sure that the verb agrees with the noun it relates to. There are six types of persons in the English language:

I
You (singular)
He / She / It

We
You (plural)
They

In English, there are several ways that subjects and verbs relate to each other. Here are a couple:

I	*run / do / was*	We	*run / do / were*
You	*run / do / were*	You	*run / do / were*
He / She / It	*runs / does / was*	They	*run / do / were*

Be careful of confusing the subject and verb agreement.

Example:	I run fast.	I do well.	I **don't** understand.
	He run**s** fast.	He do**es** well.	He **doesn't** understand.

This can be difficult if there is a clause between the subject and the verb. When analyzing a sentence, try to read the sentence without the clause to determine if there is subject / verb agreement.

> Example: ***Dheena***, along with the rest of us, ***does*** well.
> Read aloud: ***Dheena does well.*** "Dheena do well" doesn't sound right.

The Use of "It's" and "Its"

This is often wrongly expressed.
"It's" is a contraction that translates into "it is".

> ***It's*** getting late. = ***It is*** getting late.
> I'm tired and ***it's*** time to go. = I'm tired and ***it is*** time to go.

"Its" refers to possession. It is the equivalent to an apostrophe "s".

The train and all ***its*** passengers were safe.
The train and all **the train's** passengers were safe.

The Use of "There", "Their" and "They're"

These are also often confused. Here are the definitions:

> There: a location, nearby, in attendance, present
> The book is over **there,** on the table.

> Their: a possessive pronoun implying ownership, belonging to them,
> I took **their** advice and followed through with the job.

> They're: a contraction, meaning "they are"
> **They're** going to arrive late because of the snow.

The Use of "Two", "To", and "Too"

Make sure you follow these definitions. Use the correct "to/too/two" in the proper place.

> <u>To</u>: in the direction, toward, near, in order to.
> I went **to** the store **to** buy some bread.

> <u>Too</u>: also, as well, in addition, besides, and excessively.
> The teacher handed out an "A" to Bill and to Cindy, **too.**
> Shayna and Jeff just left **too**.
> The pizza deliverer took **too** long, so the pizza was free.

> <u>Two</u>: the number
> There were **two** beavers sitting on the log.

Verb Tenses

When reading a passage, ensure that the verbs in a sentence agree and that verbs discussing the same idea are in the same tense. For example, if you are speaking in the past in one sentence, you must remain consistent in the sentence following.

> Incorrect
> Bill **ran** to the store very quickly. He **is taking** Sally with him.
> Sean **reads** at a fourth grade level and **studied** very hard.

> Correct:
> Bill **ran** to the store very quickly. He **took** Sally with him.
> Sean **reads** at a fourth grade level and **studies** very hard.

Adverbs and Adjectives

Adverbs are used to modify or compliment verbs, adjectives or other adverbs. They generally explain how (gently), when (soon), or where (fully). A common trait of adverbs is to end in "*-ly*". However, this is not a reliable way to tell adverbs and adjectives apart.

Adjectives are used with nouns to describe a quality or modify a meaning. (old, tall, curly, Canadian, my, this...)

If the word you are describing or modifying is a noun, make sure you use the adjective form of the word. If the word is a verb, adjective, or adverb, use the adverb format.

He ran **quickly** down the street.	- Adverb quickly (how he runs)
He was a very **quick** thinker.	- Adjective quick (describing the thinker)
It was a **very large** house.	- Adverb very (describing large)
	- Adjective large (describing house)

It was a **loud** song.	- Adjective loud (describing song)
She sang **loudly**.	- Adverb loudly (modifying sang)

Uses of Commas in Lists

When a list is presented in a sentence, use commas between list items and a conjunction to separate the last two items on the list. It is not wrong to add an additional comma before the conjunction, but it is unnecessary.

He was going to bring his **toys, clothes, books and cookies** to class.

Angela was going to the Maritimes by **plane, train or boat**.

Uses of the Apostrophe

Apostrophes are used to indicate ownership.

Bill's school was one of the best in the country. (the school to which Bill went)
Martha's mirror was cracked. (the mirror belonging to Martha)

Meanings of "Fair" and "Fare"

People often confuse these two words. Definitions are listed below.

Fair: just, reasonable, light, fair haired, pale

He was a **fair** judge and handed down reasonable sentences.
The boy was very **fair**, and would burn easily in the sun.

Fare: charge, price, ticket, tariff, passenger

The **fare** for the plane was rather steep.

Subject / Object Noun Agreements

Depending on its role in the sentence, pronouns take on different forms. Below is a list.

Subject		**Object**	
I	We	Me	Us
You	You	You	You
He / She / It	They	Him / Her / It	Them

If the pronoun is acting as a subject, use a subject pronoun.

Subject	**Object**
Tim and I went to the baseball game.	Tim threw the ball to me.
He was the last one to leave.	Shayna surprised her at the party.
They will come later.	Alex passes the gravy to them.

The major distinction between a subject and an object is the manner in which the verb relates to the pronouns. A subject tends to perform the verb, while an object tends to have the verb performed on it. Read the examples above and see if you understand the difference. If not, you will have to check with a grammar textbook.

Double Negatives

Avoid using double negatives when both speaking and writing. Examples include:

I do **not** want **no** gum.	I do **not** want **any** gum.
You ca**n't** go to **no** store.	You ca**n't** go to **any** store.
The sergeant has**n't no** time.	The sergeant has**n't any** time.

The uses of "From" and "Off"

When receiving objects, goods or information, remember that the word "from" is correct even though in common spoken language we often use the word "off".

The doctor received the X-rays **from** the technician.
She pulled the book **from** the cupboard.

The Uses of "Stayed" and "Stood"

This is similar to the "From" and "Off" problem mentioned above. You often hear the word "stood" used in spoken language, but "stayed" is the correct word to use.

Stood is the past tense of stand (position, place, locate). Stayed is the past tense of stay (remain, wait, reside.)

I should have stayed with my fellow officers in the tough times.
The nurse stayed by the patient all night long.

The Use of Amount and Number

Generally speaking, we use "**amount**" with something that is measured or can't be counted, such as weights or volumes. We use "**number**" to describe quantities that are countable.

She had a large **amount** of liquid in the test tube.
There was a large **amount** of chocolate used in the recipe.
There were a large **number** of soldiers in the army.
The **number** of signs on the highway is enormous.

Run-On Sentences

Watch out for run-on sentences when writing. When two or more separate independent clauses are incorrectly joined, this is a run-on sentence. An independent clause is the part of a sentence that could stand alone. If you put a period at the end of an independent clause, it could serve as a sentence.

Here is an example of a run-on sentence:

Jamie was extremely angry when he missed his final chemistry exam, he went back to his dormitory and yelled at his roommate for failing to wake him up.

There are several ways to deal with a run-on sentence.

1) Make two Separate Sentences.

This is the easiest way to correct the problem. Simply add a period and start the second sentence with a capital letter.

> Correct:
> Jamie was extremely angry when he missed his final chemistry exam. He went back to his dormitory and yelled at his roommate for failing to wake him up.

2) Use a semicolon to separate the independent clauses.

Semicolons can often replace periods, but a comma can't. Do not capitalize the word immediately after a semicolon.

> Correct:
> Jamie was extremely angry when he missed his final chemistry exam; he went back to his dormitory and yelled at his roommate for failing to wake him up.

3) Use a subordinating conjunction with one of the clauses.

A subordinating conjunction is used to turn one of the clauses from an independent clause to a dependent clause. Examples of subordinating conjunctions include "because" and "since".

> Correct:
> Since Jamie was extremely angry when he missed his final chemistry exam, he went back to his dormitory and yelled at his roommate for failing to wake him up.

4) Use a comma and a coordinating conjunction between the two clauses.

Coordinating conjunctions can connect two clauses. The most common coordinating conjunctions include "and", "or", "but", and "so".

> Correct:
> Jamie was extremely angry when he missed his final chemistry exam, so he went back to his dormitory and yelled at his roommate for failing to wake him up.

5) Use a semicolon, conjunctive adverb and comma to separate the clauses.

Conjunctive adverbs can connect clauses. Examples of these adverbs include: "therefore", "moreover", "however", and "nonetheless". In order to properly use these adverbs, place a semicolon before the adverb and a comma after the adverb.

> Incorrect:
> Jamie was extremely angry when he missed his final chemistry exam, therefore he went back to his dormitory and yelled at his roommate for failing to wake him up.

> Correct:
> Jamie was extremely angry when he missed his final chemistry exam; therefore, he went back to his dormitory and yelled at his roommate for failing to wake him up.

Sentence Fragments

A sentence fragment is an incomplete sentence. There are two ways to change a sentence fragment to a complete sentence.

1) Add Words

Incorrect:
> Justin, running across the front lawn and enjoying his childhood days.
> (incomplete sentence)

Correct:
> Justin was running across the front lawn and enjoying his childhood days.
> (complete sentence)

2) Take Away Words

Creating a complete sentence from a sentence fragment can also be achieved by removing words from the sentence fragment.

Incorrect:
> While Trevor was completing the exam but having difficulty coming up with the answer to question #51.

Correct:

Trevor was completing the exam but having difficulty coming up with the answer to question #51.

Other Common Grammar Errors

Attend -	go to, be present at, concentrate
Tend -	be inclined, be likely, to have a tendency
Lose -	misplace, unable to find, to be defeated
Loose -	unfastened, wobbly, slack, movable
Threw -	hurled, tossed, past tense of "to throw"
Through -	from first to last, during, in the course of
Weather -	the seasons, elements, temperatures
Whether -	question of if, introducing an alternative possibility
Bear -	an animal in the woods, or to tolerate, stand, put up with
Bare -	to expose, naked, uncovered

Syllogisms

Everything that burns is combustible.
Wood burns.
Wood is combustible.

A syllogism is a form of logical reasoning where two premises lead to a conclusion. The first premise can be either positive or negative, and is usually a universal statement. The second statement can be universal or particular. From these two premises a logical and valid conclusion can be reached.

Either he will be convicted or acquitted.
He was not acquitted.
He was convicted.

In the above example, we are told that there are only two alternatives. In the second premise, we are told that one alternative didn't occur, so we can deduce that the other alternative is true.

Rules & Hints

1) You must assume that the statements are true.
You must take the statements at face value. You can't bring outside knowledge into the logical reasoning. For example:

Rocks are smarter than frogs. - (Premise 1)
Frogs are smarter than men. – (Premise 2)
Men are not as smart as rocks. – (Logical conclusion)

The above syllogism makes logical sense, even though logic tells you that men are more intelligent than both rocks and frogs. Be careful with syllogisms where there are no absolute statements. For example:

2) Be careful with syllogisms where there are no absolute statements.
For example:
Some living things are animals.
Some animals are mammals.

Based on these two sentences, you might want to conclude that some mammals are living things. Based on logical reasoning, this would be incorrect. To illustrate this, replace the word "mammals" with the word "dead".

Some living things are animals.
Some animals are dead.

It would be incorrect to assume that some dead are living things.

3) Be careful of qualifying words such as "only".

There is a big difference between the following two statements.

If he wins, he will celebrate (he may celebrate even if he doesn't win).

and

Only if he wins, he will celebrate (he will not celebrate unless he wins).

4) Applying the forms.

It is a good idea if you have difficulty solving a syllogism, attempt to apply the formulas below. Write the formulas out on a piece of paper if you have to.

6) Reordering sentences.

If you are organizing your syllogisms into forms, and you are still confused, attempt to reverse the order of the statements and apply the form again. This may clear up some confusion. There are some examples of this in the forms below.

For additional information and help with syllogisms review some of the posts in the PolicePrep Forum as there are some very good ones. In addition you can review some material found on Wikipedia through the link below.

http://en.wikipedia.org/wiki/Syllogism

Forms

Syllogisms can take many forms. Below are several forms that you may come across. You can replace the letters with any words or groups of words and the logic will hold. You may have to memorize some of the forms, but do your best to try and understand why the forms make sense and are logical. If you think through them, they should start to make sense, and the more practice questions you do, the better you will get at it.

1)

Either A or B. - (Premise 1)	John decided he would either run or take the bus.
B. - (Premise 2)	John decided to take the bus.
Not A. - (Logical Conclusion)	Therefore John did not run.

2)

Either A or B.	Susan was planning on studying or taking a break with friends.
Not B.	None of her friends were available to go out.
A.	Therefore Susan decided to study.

3)

If A then B.	If the solution makes sense, then we will have to adopt it.
A.	The solution made sense.
B.	Therefore we adopted it.

4)

If A, then B.	If it is cold then everyone outside will wear coats.
Not B.	No one outside is wearing coats.
Not A.	Therefore it is not cold outside.

5)

If A then B.	If we take the bus then we will arrive in time.
If B then C.	If we arrive in time then we will win the game.
If A then C.	Therefore if we take the bus then we will win the game.

Same as:	Note: You cannot assume that if C happens then A must have
If A then B.	occurred. The team could win even if they do not take the bus.
If C then A.	
If C then B.	

6)

No A are B.	None of the animals that were kept in the zoo were wild.
Some C are B.	Some of the tigers were extremely wild and aggressive.
Some C are not A.	Some of the tigers were not animals kept in the zoo.

Same as:	Note: You cannot assume that all of the tigers were not kept in
No A are B.	the zoo.
Some C are A.	
Some C are not B.	

7)

No A is B.	No team members are blonde.
All B are C.	All blondes have blue eyes.
Some C are not A.	Therefore some people with blue eyes are not team members.

Note: You cannot assume that all people with blue eyes are not team members, as there is no mention whether or not brunettes or some other group have blue eyes and are members of the group. You also cannot know for certain whether or not some team members have blue eyes or not. It is not known.

8)

No A are B.	No factories are emission compliant bodies.
No B are C. (or No C are B).	No emission compliant bodies are in N.A.
No definite conclusion	A conclusion cannot be reached between the
between A and C.	factories and N.A.

9)

Some A are B.	Some people at the meeting were visitors from France.
All B are C.	All visitors from France had come from the south by Nice.
Some C are A.	Therefore some people visiting from the south of France were
	at the meeting.

10)

Some A are B.	Some of the children in the city have cholera.
Some B are C.	Some people who have cholera are female.
No definite conclusion.	

Note: From the statements you cannot draw any conclusions. The statements do not indicate that any of the children in the city are female, nor do they state that the females with cholera live in the city. You can only draw conclusions from within the sentences such as: Some of the people in the city have cholera (sentence one) and at least some females have cholera (uncertain whether all of them do or not).

11)

Some A are B.   Some buildings have copper plumbing.
All A are C.   All buildings are made of brick.
Some C are B.   Therefore some things made of brick have copper plumbing.

Note: This is different than the format Some A are B and All B are C.

12)

All A are B.   All guitar players are women.
Some B are C.   Some women are athletes.
No definite conclusion between A and C.

Note: You cannot conclude that some guitar players are athletes in this case. The women who are athletes might be a completely different group and might include guitar players, but might not.

13)

All A are B.   All Grass is green.
All C are B.   All the candies are green.

The only conclusion you can reach is that A and C share the property of B. Very few logical conclusions will be reached with this form.

14)

All A are B.   No one willing to sacrifice comfort is a traveler.
No B are C.   All ecological people are willing to sacrifice comfort.
No C are A.   Therefore no travelers are ecological people.

Same as: Note: This example is the same format of argument. The only
No A are B.   difference is the lines have been reversed (No B are C, followed
All C are B.   by All A are B.) The logic and reasoning are the same.
No C are A.

15)

All A are B.   All of the men in the room are baseball players in the room.
All B are C.   All of the baseball players in the room are athletic people in the room
All A are C.   All of the men in the room are athletic people in the room.
Or
Some C are A.

Note: This is similar to the if A then B, if B then C, where logical conclusions about A can be reached from C (all of the men are athletic), but the only logical conclusion that can be reached about C from A is that some C are A.(you can't assume that all athletic people are men, there may be women or children in the room as well). Nor can you reach an absolute conclusion about B from A, only some B are A (you can't assume that all of the baseball players in the room are men. Some could be women or children as well.)

16)

All A are B.	All packages are fragile.
Some C are not A.	Some boxes are not packages.
Some C are B.	Some boxes are fragile.

Same as:
Some A are not B.
All B are C.
Some C are B.

Written Communication Test

Police services in English-speaking jurisdictions across North America will require that you have a good understanding of the English language. As a police officer, it is imperative that you are able to express yourself succinctly and be able to filter, analyze and organize information into a comprehensive and legible report.

Before taking any practice written exams, review the material below.

Report Intro

Many police services will ask you to write a report based on a sequence of data. They are assessing your ability to sort through the data, reach a logical conclusion and present the information in a clear coherent manner. There are several things you must keep in mind while performing this exercise.

- **There will be irrelevant information included in the question.**
  - Ensure that you discard information that doesn't add to the report.
  - Examples of this include: descriptions of districts a distance from the scope the report is to focus on. (In a traffic collision scene, is it really relevant that there is a bridge a kilometre down the road?)

- **The information will be presented in a random order.**
  - When describing the event in your report, organize it into chronological order.
  - Include the times where appropriate.

- **You will have to analyze and recreate the event <u>concisely and clearly</u>.**
  - Follow the KISS principle - Keep It Simple Stupid
  - Keep the language simple and the sentences clear. You are not being graded on the size of the words you use.
  - Be sure of your spelling and grammar.
  - Write the report in a legible format. If the marker can't read it, you will fail.

- **You will be under time pressure.**
  - Pay close attention to the time while writing the report.
  - Set an adequate amount of time to read the question, sort out the information and write the report.

Information Gathering

As you are going through the information, you should be pulling out relevant information and sorting it. There are six basic questions that you should be addressing while writing your report.

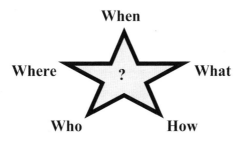

- If possible, "why" should be included, but be careful not to invent details in the report

While reading through the report, pull out information that seems relevant. Sort it into categories and make rough notes. Some categories you should group the information into include:

- time	- date
- location	- involved parties
- evidence at scene	- property description
- other	

There are other categories that may be more relevant, depending on the scenario.

Report Writing

It cannot be stressed enough that, as a test applicant, you should follow the KISS rule. Police reports are factual, relevant, and clear. Below is a list of suggestions on how to write the report.

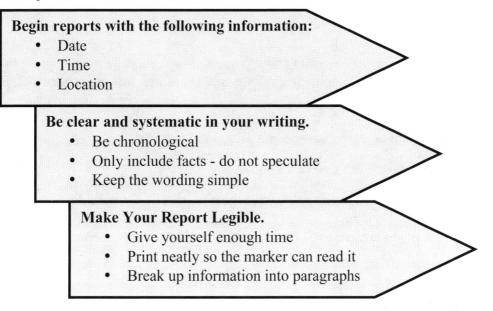

Begin reports with the following information:
- Date
- Time
- Location

Be clear and systematic in your writing.
- Be chronological
- Only include facts - do not speculate
- Keep the wording simple

Make Your Report Legible.
- Give yourself enough time
- Print neatly so the marker can read it
- Break up information into paragraphs

Practice writing as many reports as you can. Observe the formats used in this book and on the PolicePrep website.

Essay Writing

There are several police services across North America that will require you to submit an essay on a topic of their choice. You will be given a time limit (some are as little as 10 minutes) to organize and compose your thoughts and write an essay or paragraph. If you are asked to do this, you will be marked on:

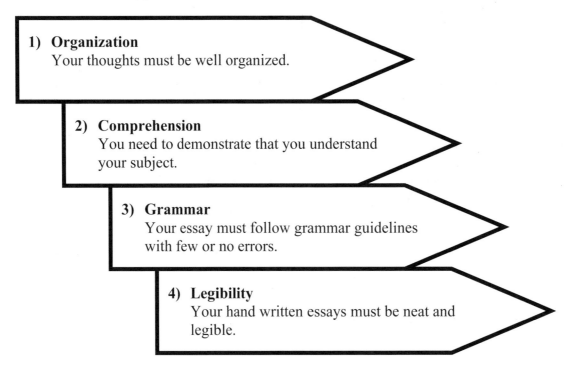

1) **Organization**
   Your thoughts must be well organized.

2) **Comprehension**
   You need to demonstrate that you understand your subject.

3) **Grammar**
   Your essay must follow grammar guidelines with few or no errors.

4) **Legibility**
   Your hand written essays must be neat and legible.

Possible Topics

Police services may ask you to write about anything, so there is very little you can do in terms of preparing for the content of the essay. There are, however, general topics which tend to come up often.

- What challenges are police services facing in the future?

- Is diversity in the work force a good thing?

- What is the most important characteristic a police officer should have?

You could be asked to answer one of these, or any another question, in essay form.

Prior to Writing

Organize your thoughts in point form on a scrap of paper before you begin writing.

Example: What challenges are Police services facing in the future?

- Budget Cuts   - Terrorist Threats

- Racial Profiling and Race Relations   - Youth Violence

- Aging Police Personnel

No matter how long your list of points, you should focus on three at most.

Structuring Your Essay

Write an essay that is appropriate for the time limit you are given. If the limit is 10 minutes, you will only have time to write a paragraph. If you are given thirty minutes or longer, structure your essay into multiple paragraphs. Break your paragraphs down in the following manner:

Single Paragraph

- Introductory Sentence

- Supporting Point # 1

- Supporting Point # 2

- Supporting Point # 3

- Concluding Sentence

Example of Single Paragraph Essay:

There are many challenges facing police services in the new millennium that will require a great deal of personal commitment and dedication from all members of the service. The threat of terrorism in a post-9/11 world will require greater vigilance on the part of police officers and stronger ties with community members to gain information about terrorist threats. Dealing with terrorist threats is made more difficult with cutbacks to policing budgets, which will force members of the services to find creative solutions to these problems. A third problem police services across Canada face is the increase in youth violence and civil disobedience. Police services will be required to work closely with youth groups, school staff and social workers to help reduce violence. These are some of the problems that police services will have to deal with in the future, which will require hard work, personal sacrifice and partnerships within the police services and with other important organizations.

Multiple Paragraphs (Keep it to fewer than five paragraphs).

- Introductory Paragraph

  - State the position you are taking. This can be to agree or disagree with a statement, or to support both sides.

  - Briefly state arguments you will make (in one or two sentences).

- Paragraphs # 2, 3 and 4

  - State your point.

  - Provide your evidence.

  - Comment on the point.

- Concluding Paragraph

  - Restate the position you made in one or two sentences.

Example of Multi-Paragraph Essay:

Police services across Canada face several challenges in the coming years that will require a great deal of personal sacrifice and commitment on the part of members of the organization. These challenges range from the increasing threat of terrorism, cuts to law enforcement budgets and increases in the level and intensity of youth violence. In order to solve these problems, police officers will need to work more cooperatively with each other and with other relevant organizations in society.

Since September 11, 2001, police forces across North America have had to elevate their awareness of potential threats and create plans to handle emergency situations that may result from a terrorist attack. Preparing for possible attacks requires resources to train officers, and additional resources are needed to be ready for deployment in the event of an attack. Events that may, in the past, have been dismissed, need to be taken seriously. Recently, for example, Toronto's subway system had to be shut down when passengers detected a strange odour. This situation required officers to coordinate with transit, media and fire personnel to resolve the problem.

Paragraph #3– Budget Cuts

Paragraph #4 – Youth Violence

Terrorist threats, budget cuts and youth violence do pose challenges that police services will have to overcome. By having dedicated officers, and by working with outside agencies, police services will succeed in meeting these challenges.

Summary Tips

- Time yourself appropriately. Spend a couple of minutes writing your main ideas out in point form before beginning.

- Don't write too much. You are under a time limit. Make your points simple and give yourself enough time to print legibly.

- Keep your words simple. Don't use words if you don't know how to spell them.

- If you are writing multiple paragraphs, each paragraph should contain one idea. If you are only writing one paragraph, separate your ideas by sentence.

- Don't attempt to include too much information. Keep your points clear and simple.

- BE ORGANIZED! Follow the formats shown above for your essays and paragraphs.

Inductive Reasoning

Inductive reasoning is the process of reaching general conclusions based on observing a number of specific instances. Using these observations you conclude that something or a group of things is generally true. For example:

Observances:

"I've noticed that every time I eat crab, shrimp or squid, I get a stomach ache.

Conclusion:

Therefore whenever I eat seafood, I will get a stomach ache."

The argument above starts with specific observances (eating crab, shrimp and squid) and comes to a very general conclusion about what can or can't be eaten (all seafood). The conclusion is supported by the previous observations.

Common Errors

When answering questions like this, it is a mistake to include information that is not in the question to reach a conclusion. The answer may be correct in life but, if not drawn from the information in the question, do not include the evidence in your decision making process. Below are examples of conclusions that may be true in life, but are incorrect because they are not based on the information above.

Incorrect conclusion #1
    I will get a stomachache from the seasoning I use.

Incorrect conclusion #2
    I will get a stomachache from eating in a hurry.

Base your answers strictly on the information that is given to you in the question.

Deductive Reasoning

Deductive reasoning is the process of reaching specific conclusions based on a general observation, rule or belief. A general rule, observation, or belief is stated and you are able to determine whether specific actions or results will occur. For example:

General Rule:

"I have an allergic reaction to all nuts, which causes my throat to close."

Conclusion:

"If I eat cashews my throat will close. If I eat walnuts my throat will close."

Instead of reaching broad generalizations or conclusions, determine if a specific example fits the data.

Common Errors

As mentioned above, it is incorrect to include information that is not in the question to reach your conclusion. The answer may be correct in life, but if the information is not drawn from the question, you should not include it in your decision making process. Below are examples of conclusions that may be true in life, but would be incorrect because they are not based on the information above.

Incorrect conclusion #1
    If a bee stings me, my throat will close up.

Incorrect conclusion #2
    I am not the only person in the world who has this allergy.

Base your answers only on the information that is available to you in the question.

Teaching Material
General

Observation and Memory

Memory

Developing your memory is a skill like any other, and will improve the more you practice. There are several methods to go about doing this.

1) Practice as many of the RCMP practice tests as possible to become familiar with the methods used during the real exam.
2) Practice reading passages and pictures in newspapers and magazines. Focus on names, and test yourself 30 minutes later to see how you did.
3) Have a friend note the makes, colours, and license plates of a few cars in an area and test yourself 30 minutes later.
4) Form pictures or links in your mind to assist your memory. For example, if you see a mug shot of a person that reminds you of your friend, link that friend to the mug shot in order to memorize it. Here is an example using license plates.

954 PNY	- remember 954 **P**eople in **N**ew **Y**ork
651 ZTZ	- remember 651 **Z**ee **T**ea**Z**e (the tease)
421 PLM	- remember 421 **PL**u**M**ber

Do whatever works for you. (Psychologists have found that by making expressions graphic, people remember them more easily.)

Observation

The goal of this exercise is to test your observation capabilities. When comparing the faces, focus on features that will not change (assume there is no plastic surgery involved). Focus on the shapes of the eyes, the size and appearance of the nose and the shape of the face. Ignore features that can be altered easily such as hairstyle, facial hair, clothing, glasses, etc.

Tips to improve your observation skills include:

1) Take the RCMP practice exams in this book (or on the website) to become familiar with the testing process.

2) Purchase "spot the difference" puzzles.

3) Do word find puzzles in local papers.

Facial Visualization Questions

Facial visualization questions are common in entrance exams. They test your powers of observation and ability to spot similarities and differences between suspects that look alike. This is a necessary skill for a police officer, as you will be asked to locate suspects with vague descriptions, or you may be dealing with an old photo or need to visualize what a suspect would look like with glasses, facial hair, etc.

Assume that the suspect's facial appearance has not changed in any permanent way. For example, a suspect might comb his or her hair differently, put on glasses, wear a different hat or grow facial hair. Any changes to bone structure, weight or facial features that would require plastic surgery should be excluded.

Which of the following four suspects matches the man shown above?

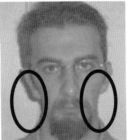
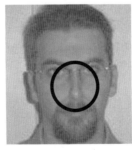

You should focus on areas of the face that are difficult to change. As the circles demonstrate in the first and third photos, there seems to be an inconsistency with the cheek structure and general shape of the jaw. The jaw is too wide in the first photo and too narrow in the third. The fourth photo is a close match but the nose is not the right shape.

Some of the tests will use actual photographs of suspects, while others will use cartoon drawings of suspects. The same principles apply. Focus on:

- Shape of the head
- Shape and placement of the eyes
- Shape of the nose
- Shape of the chin
- Shape of the cheeks

Try to overlook or disregard any easy changes that a suspect can make to his/her appearance, such as:

Change in hairstyle   Glasses   Jewellery
Change in facial hair   Hats

Eliminate as Many Choices as Possible, then Guess

You will not be penalized if you guess incorrectly in these tests. Because there is a time limit, you must be efficient and use your time optimally. Don't waste too much time on one question. Look at your four options, eliminate as many as possible, and then guess which of the remaining ones is best. Remember, the questions will get more difficult throughout the test, so expect to spend more time on later questions than on the earlier ones.

Judgement Section

Framework for Analysis

It is important to have a framework for how you will approach judgement questions during an examination process. You must know how to establish hierarchies in order to prioritize activities and handle conflicting job requirements. Below is a possible value hierarchy that can be used to resolve difficult decisions.

1) Protection of Life and Limb.
This is a police officer's first priority and supersedes all other decisions. This includes the lives of officers as well.

2) Obeying Orders in Emergency Situations
Officers have to be able to follow instructions even though they may not fully understand the justification for them.

3) Protection of Property
This is a primary duty of police officers.

4) Performing other Required Duties
Officers then must act as required to keep the peace, enforce the law, and maintain order.

Remember that while you are performing your duties, your priorities include:

1) Assisting Endangered People (including victims of crime, injured people, etc.)

2) Keeping the Peace (calming disorder, preventing destruction)

3) Enforcing the Law (fairly and impartially)

4) Maintaining Order (investigating suspicious events, working with community members, correcting traffic problems)

5) Assisting Others Who Need Help (disabled, children, elderly, etc.)

Core Competencies

Review the list of core competencies found in the resume section. Remember that officer safety is paramount.

Mapping

The mapping questions that you will encounter on the PATI exam involve determining how quickly you can travel between intersections. In the map below, each box is an intersection. The lines in between each intersection represent one city block.

You will be asked questions such as: how long would it take you to drive from A to B if it takes 3 minutes to drive each block? A to B represents one block of travel time, so the trip would take three minutes.

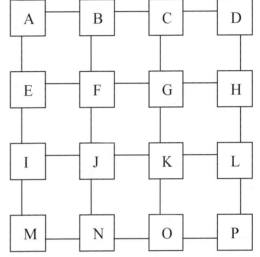

When you are calculating time for mapping questions, the most efficient way to do this is to add up the total number of blocks and then multiply the number of blocks by the time it takes to navigate each block.

For example, if it takes 3 minutes to drive a block, and you must drive from A to K, your best course of action would be to count the number of blocks from A to K. The fastest route would be 4 blocks.

Now multiply 4 x 3 = 12 minutes.

Be prepared for questions that involve changes in times for turning corners, routes that are obstructed and combining modes of transportation at different speeds. For example, if you are told that every turn requires an additional 30 seconds of travel time, choose a route with as few turns as possible. Example B below requires fewer turns, so it would be the faster route in this scenario.

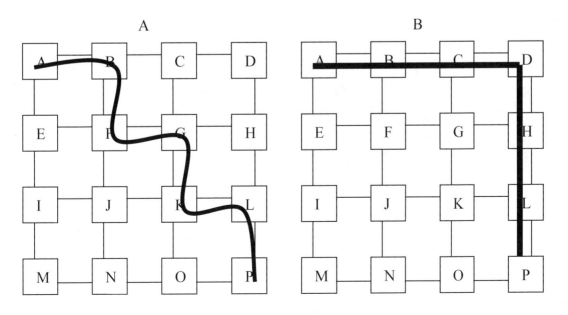

Pattern Solving

When attempting to solve patterns look for consistent changes and developments. These changes can include, but are not exclusive to:

1) Number of objects
2) Size of objects
3) Colour of objects
4) Shape of objects
5) Rotation / Flip of objects
6) Number of unique identifying marks

There are a number of different clues you must look for. The only way to improve your skills for this stage of the exam is to practice the puzzles in this book, on the website or puzzle books you may find in bookstores.

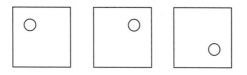 The object is rotating clockwise by ¼ turns. The next logical shape would be:

 The object is steadily increasing by one larger circle each time. The next logical shape would be:

Sometimes you have to ignore information to detect the pattern.

 You must ignore the shapes in this case. The image is increasing the number of highlighted objects one at a time (0, 1, 2, 3). The next logical shape would be:

Matching

Matching questions are intended to challenge your observation skills. You will be given four images and be asked to select the image that does not belong. There are a variety of differences that you will have to watch out for including, but not exclusive to:

1) Different lines / shapes on an object (for example, longer hair).

2) Different shapes (round versus square).

3) Odd versus even numbers.

4) Different component shapes (curved lines versus straight).

5) Different meanings the images represent (men or women).

Example 1:

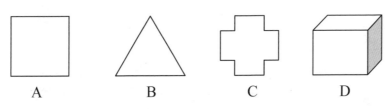

D is the only image that is three dimensional in nature and therefore does not belong.

Example 2:

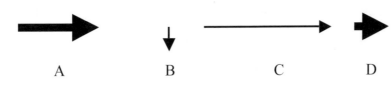

B is the only image not pointing right and therefore does not belong.

RCMP Answer Sheet

Book 1

	A	B	C	D	
1	○	○	○	○	___
2	○	○	○	○	___
3	○	○	○	○	___
4	○	○	○	○	___
5	○	○	○	○	___
6	○	○	○	○	___
7	○	○	○	○	___
8	○	○	○	○	___
9	○	○	○	○	___
10	○	○	○	○	___

Total ___

Book 2

	A	B	C	D	
1	○	○	○	○	___
2	○	○	○	○	___
3	○	○	○	○	___
4	○	○	○	○	___
5	○	○	○	○	___
6	○	○	○	○	___
7	○	○	○	○	___
8	○	○	○	○	___
9	○	○	○	○	___
10	○	○	○	○	___

Total ___

Book 3

	A	B	C	D	
1	○	○	○	○	___
2	○	○	○	○	___
3	○	○	○	○	___
4	○	○	○	○	___
5	○	○	○	○	___
6	○	○	○	○	___
7	○	○	○	○	___
8	○	○	○	○	___
9	○	○	○	○	___
10	○	○	○	○	___

Total ___

Book 4

	A	B	C	D	
1	○	○	○	○	___
2	○	○	○	○	___
3	○	○	○	○	___
4	○	○	○	○	___
5	○	○	○	○	___
6	○	○	○	○	___
7	○	○	○	○	___
8	○	○	○	○	___
9	○	○	○	○	___
10	○	○	○	○	___

Total ___

Book 5

	A	B	C	D	
1	○	○	○	○	___
2	○	○	○	○	___
3	○	○	○	○	___
4	○	○	○	○	___
5	○	○	○	○	___
6	○	○	○	○	___
7	○	○	○	○	___
8	○	○	○	○	___
9	○	○	○	○	___
10	○	○	○	○	___

Total ___

Total _____ / 50

RCMP Practice Exam

The RCMP test is divided into five books. You will be required to answer all five books at once during the actual testing, so it is recommended that you practise all books in one sitting. The tests are timed and have the following format:

Format: 5 books, 10 questions per book
Time: 15 minutes per book
Content: Composition (spelling, grammar, vocabulary), Comprehension, Judgment, Observation, Logic and Problem Solving.

Do each test in order as this is how you will be tested by the RCMP. The only materials allowed are pencils and scrap paper. No calculators, books, or counting devices are allowed. Use a clock or stopwatch to keep track of the time.
Detach the answer key to take the test.

Detach the answer key to take the test.

Goals

The e-RPAB is marked out of 5 and you must receive at least 3.2 / 5 to pass the exam. This works out to 64%, so your goal on these tests is a mark of 32 / 50 or higher.

In order to be a more competitive candidate, you should be aiming for a mark in the mid 80% range (or higher than 4.0 / 5 on the actual exam). The following marks convert to the opposite percentages.

Practice RPAT Score (out of 50)	%
32	64%
40	80%
45	90%
50	100%

Question 1

Which of the following is the best definition of the word "reduction"?

a) The process of converting smaller quantities into larger quantities.

b) A process of thinking synthesizing events into logical conclusions.

c) The amount by which something is reduced.

d) Calculating the difference when one quantity is taken away from another

Question 2

The weather is _____ today than it _____ yesterday.   Which of the following words will correctly complete the sentence above?

a) more warm, was   b) more warm, were

c) warmer, were   d) warmer, was

Question 3

Which of the following people matches this suspect?

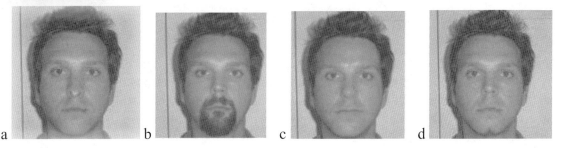

a   b   c   d

Question 4

You are working as a solo unit and you receive a call from a dispatcher to attend a noise complaint from Mrs. Smith for an unruly group of teenagers in the local park. A neighbour called in the complaint stating she believed that they were smoking drugs. You pull up to the park in your cruiser and view a group of 7 individuals in their late teens / early 20's sitting on at a picnic table approximately 50 meters away.   What is the first action you should take?

a) Ask dispatcher if there is any available back up.

b) Approach the group on your own.

c) Walk around the park and see if there are any other groups.

d) Call the members of the group to come over to your vehicle.

Question 5

Upon approaching the group you observe several males playing cards and smoking cigarettes. How should you approach the males?

a) What are you guys doing in this neighbourhood?

b) Are any of you smoking drugs?

c) Afternoon gentlemen, we are here because of a noise complaint, have there been any problems here?

d) Mrs. Smith called in to complain about the noise you guys are making, you'll have to leave.

Question 6

Arrange the following sentences into the most logical sequence of events.

1) Constable Garreth approached the driver to ask about the accident.

2) Constable Jones took a statement from Janice Grogan and advised that the male driver was charged.

3) Police received a radio call of a woman struck by a vehicle while crossing on a red light.

4) The driver had the strong odor of alcohol on his breath and he was arrested for Impaired Driving.

5) The woman was rushed to the hospital by ambulance with life threatening injuries and in an unconscious state. Her name was Janice Grogan.

a) 5, 3, 1, 4, 2   b) 3, 5, 1, 4, 2   c) 3, 5, 4, 2, 1   d) 1, 4, 3, 5, 2

Question 7

You are required to walk a victim through a local neighbourhood where she was followed by a stalker and physically assaulted. You need to note the directions of travel for court purposes. She advises that she was heading home from work and got off the bus at Steeles Avenue. She walked 2 blocks along Steeles before making a right onto Columbia Drive. She made a left onto Carling Crescent, walked about 10 meters and noticed the accused following her. She picked up her pace and made a right onto Rideau Street. As she was walking along Rideau the accused attempted to grab the victim. The victim fought back and escaped. She ran down Rideau before making a left onto Park Street heading north and making it home safely. The accused ran the opposite way down Park Street and was last seen by the victim making a left onto Rideau Street.   What direction was the victim walking as she made her way along Steeles Avenue?

a) North   b) South   c) East   d) West

Question 8

Rita is able to read 30 pages an hour. For an assignment she has two books to read. The first book has 1,350 pages, second book has 2,010 pages. How many hours will it take Rita to finish both books?

a) 75   b) 110   c) 112   d) 121

Question 9

John travels 75 KM to work each way. If he averages 120 KM/Hr, how long (Minutes) does he spend driving to and from work each day?

a) 1.25   b) 75   c) 50   d) 60

Question 10

Constable Smith issued 16 speeding tickets and 5 drinking under influence charges last month. The Police department had a total 64 speeding tickets and 20 DUI charges last month. What percentage of speeding tickets issued last month was made by Constable Smith?

a) 12%   b) 29%   c) 10%   d) 25%

Question 1

Which of the following words can be defined as: the belief that you are superior, and all other forms of culture are inferior?

a) Bigotry   b) Sustenance   c) Simple-mindedness   d) Maintenance

Question 2

Because police officers are forced to work both day and night shifts, it is important that they maintain a healthy diet and exercise regime. If they do not receive enough nurishment, physical activity and rest, they will have difficulty performing their jobs. Officers sometimes complain that they have become nocturnal creatures like bats.

   Which of the following words is misspelled in the sentence above?

a) Regime   b) Nurishment   c) Receive   d) Nocturnal

Question 3

The next two questions are based on the following paragraph. Canada's police may need special new powers in the wake of the September 11 attacks to deal with the threat of global terrorism. But those powers must not put innocent Canadians at risk by permanently eroding civil rights to counter what could be a passing threat. Striking the right balance between freedom and security is the goal that Justice Minister Anne McLellan is attempting to do with revisions to the Criminal Code and other laws. There is pressure to deliver security today, and worry about freedom tomorrow. Nowhere is that attitude more obvious than in Prime Minister Jean Chrétien's coolness to incorporating a "sunset clause" into McLellan's proposed changes, known as Bill C-36. Instead of implementing the "sunset clause" he promises Parliament will review the law three years from now. But he balks at letting the new police powers to expire by introducing a sunset clause that would force the government to introduce fresh legislation to keep the powers alive. Inconvenient though such a clause might be to Chrétien or his successor, it is a mechanism that can be used to protect civil freedoms and rights. That's the view of the Senate committee studying the bill, which wants a five-year clause for many of the provisions. The bill is no minor fit of bureaucratic tinkering. It is sweeping, tough and untested. As currently drafted, the bill lets police hold people in "preventive detention" for up to 72 hours without being charged, if they are suspected of having terrorist links.   According to the above passage, which one of the following statements is true?

a) A sunset clause will force a future government to revoke Bill C-36 in the future if they want it removed.

b) A sunset clause will automatically make Bill C-36 obsolete after a period of time

c) A sunset clause will increase the powers of the police for a longer period of time.

d) Bill C-36 violates personal freedoms and is unnecessary.

Question 4

According to the above passage, which one of the following statements is true?

a) Jean Chretien will include a sunset clause in the legislation of Bill C-36.

b) Jean Chretien has promised to have parliament revoke the law in three years.

c) The Senate committee will not pass Bill C-36.

d) Bill C-36 is untested and makes sweeping tough changes to the Criminal Code.

Question 5

Which one of the following statements is supported by the above passage?

a) There is always a need for government to balance freedom and security.

b) The balance of security and freedom is only important in times of war.

c) The police will have the right to arbitrarily arrest people for 72 hours.

d) Police are pushing for this new law to fight terrorism.

Question 6

Which of the following people matches this suspect?

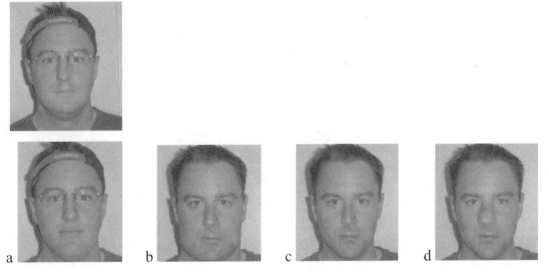

Question 7

There is a group of 17-year-old boys standing on a street corner talking loudly, and causing a disturbance in a residential area. It is very early in the morning. Your best option would be to:

a) Summon assistance from another unit in the area.

b) Disperse the group by letting them see your vehicle.

c) Arrest everyone present.

d) Arrest whoever appears to be the leader of the group.

Question 8

You are working at 10:00 pm and you happen to see two males loitering by a video store that you have never seen before. The video store is directly beside a grocery store that does a bank deposit every night between 10 and 10:30. What action should you take?

a) Monitor the situation until after the deposit is made.

b) Order the loiterers to be on their way.

c) Investigate the males and search them for weapons.

d) Sneak into the grocery store and inform the owner about a potential robbery.

Question 9

Tim needs to fill three 20L barrels with oil. If his oil dispenser flows at 100 mL/s, how long will it take him to fill the 3 containers? (Minutes)

a) 100   b) 75   c) 50   d)10

Question 10

Which Platoon is working the most hours during a given week in September?

Cell Block Data

Cell Blocks	Capacity	Other Information
Cell Block A	220	Maximum Security
Cell Block B	200	Medium Security
Cell Block C	250	Medium Security
Cell Block D	125	Maximum Security / Solitary
Cell Block E	25	Transfer Holding Cells

Shift	Hours
Days	0600-1600
Afternoons	1500-0100
Nights	2300-0700

Note: shift start times occur on the day of the rotation calendar.

Shift Rotation September

	Mon	Tues	Wed	Thurs	Fri	Sat	Sun
Platoon A	Off	Off	Nights	Nights	Nights	After	Days
Platoon B	After	Days	Off	After	Off	After	After
Platoon C	Days	After	After	Off	Off	Nights	Nights
Platoon D	Nights	Nights	Off	Off	Days	Days	After
Platoon E	Off	Off	Days	Days	After	Nights	Nights

Cell Inspection Dates (cells must be emptied)

Date	Cell Block	Time Booked
Thurs Sept 4	A	0700 – 0900
Mon Sept 8	D	1500 – 1700
Wed 17 Sept	C	0600 – 0800
Tues Sept 23	A	2230 – 0030
Thurs Sept 25	D	1200 – 1400
Fri Oct 3	B	0500 – 0700

Cell Repair Dates (cells must be emptied)

Date	Cell Block	Time
6 – 7 Sept	Block A	All Day
13 – 14 Sept	Block C	All Day
20 – 21 Sept	Block D	All Day
4 – 5 Oct	Block E	All Day

a) Platoon A   b) Platoon B

c) Platoon C   d) Platoon D

Question 1

I should have _____ at your bedside, but I had to pick up the report _____ your doctor.   Which of the following words will correctly complete the sentence above?

a) stood, from   b) stayed, from   c) stayed, off   d) stood, off

Question 2

Which of the following words can be defined as: to drive out, to eject from position of office or employment?

a) Oust   b) Downsize   c) Compensate   d) Rationalize

Question 3

Which of the following people matches this suspect?

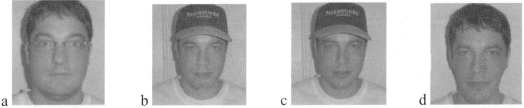

a   b   c   d

Question 4

You are investigating a 16-year-old homeless female located at Spadina Avenue and Queen Street. After talking to the young woman and performing a computer check you discover that she is a run away and there is a missing person report on file for her logged by her parents one week ago in a town approximately 200 km away. You have no authority to arrest the female, or detain her in any way.   Your options:

a) Detain the woman and make arrangements for her parents to pick her up. Despite the laws, you know it is too dangerous for her in that area.

b) Talk to the female and get as much information about her as possible.

c) Continue on with other matters. There are hundreds of missing people out there anyway.

d) Advise the woman to attend a female shelter for lodgings and food.

Question 5

After talking to the female for some time she tells you her parents do not care about her, and are too busy with the careers. She states that she has never been abused, but feels neglected. You tell her:

a) Grow up, and stop being such a baby.

b) Inform the female that her parents are actively searching for her and have a missing person report in the system.

c) Tell her she is probably right. Who would care about a child who runs away on their parents?

d) Advise her, you are sorry she feels that way, but the police are not social workers.

Question 6

Four friends were competing in a University Case Competition. The judges unfortunately lost the results of the competition. Only the following information was available. Kavi, who didn't wear green, beat Brendon. Laurie beat the person who wore yellow. The person, who wore number 3, wore green. The person who wore number 2 finished first whereas Alan came last. The person who finished second wore green, Brendon wore yellow and the person wearing red beat the person wearing blue. Only one person wore the same number as the position they finished.   What number did the winner wear?

a) 1   b) 2   c) 3   d) 4

Question 7

Who came in 3rd place?

a) Brendon   b) Kavi   c) Alan   d) Laurie

Question 8

What colour was Laurie wearing?

a) Yellow   b)Red   c) Blue   d) Green

Question 9

Greg began his 500KM road trip to Montreal at 2am. His averaged speed for the first hour of the trip was 110km/hr. What average speed does Greg need to maintain if he is to reach Montreal by 6am?

a) 110   b) 125   c) 130   d) 150

Question 10

Nina is trying to print her thesis paper on an inkjet printer that prints 4 pages/minute. How long will it taker her to print 2 copies, if her thesis is 1400 pages long? (Minutes)

a) 350   b) 700   c) 900   d)1400

Question 1

Which of the following words can be defined as: a geometric figure with seven sides?

a) Hexagon   b) Octagon   c) Heptagon   d) Decagon

Question 2

If they are unsuccessful and _____ pass the interview stage, _____ going to have to reapply after waiting six months.   Which of the following words will correctly complete the sentence above?

a) doesn't, their   b) don't, their   c) don't, they're   d) don't, there

Question 3

Beset by a troubled administration and serious money woes that could mean tax hikes or service cuts, Vancouver needs a top bureaucrat who can provide a steady hand on the tiller. A city search committee has unanimously picked Jill Huang to be the new chief administrative officer. Council should enthusiastically endorse this choice when it debates the issue in council this week. Huang's former work in the City of Victoria, her term as commissioner of community and neighbourhood services with the Vancouver and her most recent job as interim chief administrative officer give her strong qualifications to take on this big job. She has the mettle and the smarts to manage a city with a $6 billion operating budget and 22,000 employees. She has the backbone to make hard decisions and the sensitivity to ensure that the vulnerable are not victimized. Huang has earned the respect of staff and councilors alike and has a good rapport with Mayor Davis; something that her predecessor, Gene Barron, never enjoyed, which ultimately led to his departure in December. Unlike someone hired from outside the city, Huang is already well acquainted with the personalities and issues at City Hall. If selected, Huang would take on the job with a "to do" list already filled with tasks.   Which of the statements below is supported by the above article?

a) Gene Barron had good rapport with Mayor Davis and city staff.

b) Jill Huang will be a better Chief Administrative Officer then Gene Barron.

c) Jill Huang was unanimously picked by a city search committee to be the new Chief Administrative Officer.

d) Mayor Davis has ultimate say over who is the new Chief Administrative Officer.

Question 4

What general theory is the writer trying to put forth?

a) Jill Huang lacks the experience of Gene Barron.

b) Jill Huang will be a better fit with the general environment in Vancouver than Gene Barron.

c) Handling the city's budget is too large of a task for one person.

d) City council should be cautious about endorsing Jill Huang for the position.

Question 5

Which of the following people matches this suspect?

a   b   c   d

Question 6

Scenario: Dispute   You are working as a police officer and are attending a call at a local grocery store for a potential theft in progress. The call taker had trouble understanding the complainant due to a language barrier and there is no specific information. You have been assigned to the call as it is in your area. Upon arriving on the scene you discover the storeowner arguing with a male at the cash register. What is your first course of action?

a) Arrest the male before he flees the scene.

b) Separate the parties and ask the male what happened first.

c) Separate the parties and get the storeowner's account first.

d) Talk to both parties together.

Question 7

When taking a statement from an assault victim what is the least important piece of information out of the list below?

a) The name, address, and age of the victim.

b) The location of the assault, the suspect's description, why the assault occurred.

c) The names of the victim's relatives and family members.

d) When the assault occurred, the nature of the injuries to the victim.

Question 8

Place the following sentences in the most logical sequence of events.   1) The argument began to lose control and the police were called.   2) James Kaylan consumed nine beers over a four hour period prior to attending a local tavern.   3) James was arrested for being intoxicated in a public place.   4) James began arguing with Todd over Julie, who Todd had just met.   5) As James walked into the Tavern he saw Todd talking to his ex wife, Julie.

a) 5, 2, 4, 1, 3   b) 2, 5, 4, 1, 3   c) 2, 5, 4, 3, 1   d) 5, 2, 4, 3, 1

Question 9

In 1997, Kingston had a population of 99,873 people. Since nobody in the city has more than 99,871 hairs on their heads, what is the probability that at least two of these heads have exactly the same number of hairs?

a) 0%   b) 25%   c) 75%   d) 100%

Question 10

The average rainfall in Waterloo has increased at an annual rate of 2%. If the total rain fall was 856mm in 2002. What is the expected rainfall in 2005? (mm)

a) 907.4   b) 908.4   c) 873.12   d) 900

Question 1

Police have been experimenting with alternative forms of transportation in recent years. The bicycle unit is one unique example of these experimentations and is responsible for increased police visibility. Officers are less confined in congested areas and can often respond quicker then police cruisers.　Which of the following words is misspelled in the sentence above?

a) Experimenting　　b) Unique　　　　c) Alternative　　　d) Increassed

Question 2

Wind and the Willows is a favourite _____ book. Shelley who received a copy from her mother couldn't _____ to throw it away.　Which of the following words will correctly complete the sentence above?

a) childrens, bear　　b) children's, bear　　c) childrens, bare　　d) children's, bare

Question 3

Which of the following people matches this suspect?

a

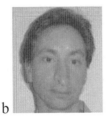
b

c

d

Question 4

While off-duty you attend a party with several friends. At the party you detect a strong odor of marijuana. You become aware that there are several people smoking marijuana and possibly doing heavier drugs on the second floor. What is the most appropriate response from the list of options below?

a) Avoid the area of the party where the drugs are located.

b) Leave the party for the night.

c) Disregard the drugs and continue socializing at all levels of the house.

d) Work the door in case other police arrive, so you can tell them everything is under control and that they should not come in.

Question 5

You are off duty and are attempting to get your vehicle fixed. The mechanic advises you that the bill will be $500. You feel this is pretty high and is unreasonable, but you order the repairs anyway. What is the most appropriate response?

a) Show up to the garage on duty, in uniform to pressure the mechanic for a cheaper price.

b) Show the mechanic your badge and ask for a discount.

c) Pay the mechanic the agreed upon price.

d) Watch the mechanic and pull him over for speeding. Offer to ignore the fine if he gives you a discount on the service.

Question 6

The police force has had five different police dogs over the past 10 years. They were named Sniffy, Dopey, Butch, Princess and Puff. Princess was not the first. Puff was the last dog used. Butch was on the force before Sniffy and after Princess. Who was the first dog the force used?

a) Dopey　　　　　　b) Princess　　　　　　c) Butch　　　　　　d) Sniffy

Question 7

If you were in Paris and had to be in Los Angeles as early as possible what route would you take?

Departing City: Paris

Destination	Departure Time (local time)	Arrival Time (local time)	Cost (US$) (1st Class)	Cost (US$) (Coach)	Airline
London	1100 hrs	1100 hrs	$ 200	$ 120	Air France
Toronto	1000 hrs	1100 hrs	$ 1000	$ 500	Air Canada
New York	0900 hrs	0900 hrs	$ 1000	$ 650	Air France
Los Angeles	0800 hrs	1500 hrs	$ 2000	$ 1200	US Airways

Departing City: London

Destination	Departure Time (local time)	Arrival Time (local time)	Cost (US$) (1st Class)	Cost (US$) (Coach)	Airline
Paris	0700 hrs	0900 hrs	$ 250	$ 150	B.A.
Toronto	1000 hrs	1200 hrs	$1200	$ 800	B.A.
New York	0900 hrs	1100 hrs	$ 900	$ 500	US Airways
Los Angeles	1000 hrs	1500 hrs	$ 2200	$ 1500	B.A.

Departing City: New York

Destination	Departure Time (local time)	Arrival Time (local time)	Cost (US$) (1st Class)	Cost (US$) (Coach)	Airline
London	2200 hrs	0900 hrs	$ 950	$ 800	B.A.
Toronto	1500 hrs	1600 hrs	$ 200	$ 120	Air Canada
Paris	1900 hrs	0900 hrs	$ 1000	$ 600	Air France
Los Angeles	0800 hrs	1000 hrs	$ 500	$ 200	US Airways

Departing City: Toronto

Destination	Departure Time (local time)	Arrival Time (local time)	Cost (US$) (1st Class)	Cost (US$) (Coach)	Airline
London	1700 hrs	0600 hrs	$800	$400	Air Canada
Paris	1700 hrs	0700 hrs	$1100	$650	Air France
New York	1100 hrs	1200 hrs	$200	$120	US Airways
Los Angeles	1200 hrs	1400 hrs	$450	$225	Air Canada

Time Differences Between Regions

	Paris	London	New York	Toronto	Los Angeles
Local Time	0000 hrs	2300 hrs	1700 hrs	1700hrs	1400 hrs

a) Paris – New York – Los Angeles

b) Paris – London – Los Angeles

c) Paris – Toronto – Los Angeles

d) None of the above

Question 8

Which are the next three numbers in the pattern below?

2 , 4 , 8 , 16 , 32 ...

a) 34, 38, 46   b) 2, 4, 8   c) 64, 128, 256   d) 64, 124, 252

Question 9

The following questions refer to the following scenario:

	Murders	Thefts	Robberies
1998	4	359	64
1999	3	376	66
2000	6	412	72

Above are important crime statistics for the town of Surrey. Below are the estimated costs to investigate each crime.

Murder $3000
Theft $ 200
Robbery $ 600

What was the total budget in 1999 for these three crimes?

a) $115,600   b) $123,800   c) $109,400   d) $140,500

Question 10

By what percent did the number of robberies increase from 1998 to 2000?

a) 12.5%   b) 11.1%   c) 6.6%   d) 88.9%

RCMP 1 Answer Key

Book 1	Book 2	Book 3	Book 4	Book 5
1) C	1) A	1) B	1) C	1) D
2) D	2) B	2) A	2) C	2) B
3) B	3) B	3) C	3) C	3) A
4) A	4) D	4) B	4) B	4) B
5) C	5) A	5) B	5) B	5) C
6) B	6) C	6) B	6) C	6) A
7) A	7) B	7) A	7) C	7) C
8) C	8) A	8) D	8) B	8) C
9) B	9) D	9) C	9) D	9) B
10) D	10) B	10) B	10) B	10) A

Book 1

Question 1

Reduction is the amount by which something is reduced.

Question 2

"Warmer" is required in the first blank as it is a comparative adjective between two objects. "Was" is required in the second blank to agree with the singular subject "it".

Question 3 – NA

Question 4

Concern for safety is one of the key competencies for being a police officer. Approaching a large group with very little information alone can be dangerous. Groups would be more cooperative with two officers and if something should happen, an additional officer would be available.

Question 5

Answer 3 is the least confrontational. It tells the individuals why you are there, white at the same time asking for any further information that they can share. It would be unwise to bring up the complainants name in this situation. It may cause repercussions against her.

Question 6

B is the answer. First the radio call was received, followed by transporting the victim to the hospital, the officer approaching the other driver, making an arrest and finally informing the victim.

Question 7

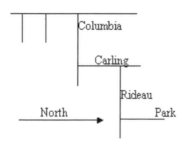

Question 8

C - First calculate the total number of pages Rita must read [1,350 + 2,010 = 3,360]. Then divide the total number pages by her reading speed [3,360/30 = 112 minutes]

Question 9

B - We need to calculate John's total return trip driving distance [75 + 75 = 150KM]. Then divide total distance by his average driving speed [150/120=1.25hr]. Then convert 1.25 hours to minutes by multiplying by 60, to arrive at 75 minutes.

Question 10

D - Total speeding tickets issued = 64; speeding tickets issued by Constable = 16. Thus percentage = 16/64 x 100% or 25%

Book 2

Question 1

Bigotry is the belief that you are superior, and all other forms of culture are inferior.

Question 2

The correct spelling is nourishment.

Questions 3 – 6   **NA**

Question 7

By making the teenagers aware of your presence, they will most likely leave without any further action. If they remain, or you are required to approach the group, back up would be necessary.

Question 8

Standing outside a video store is a common occurrence and doesn't warrant immediate action. It would be prudent to keep your eye on the situation to ensure that nothing happens.

Question 9

D - First determine volume of three containers [3 x 20L = 60L]. Then convert fill rate from mL/s to L/min. Recall 1L = 1000mL and 60s = 1 minute; 100 / 1000 x 60 = 6L/min];   Then divide total volume by fill rate [60 / 6 = 10 minutes]

Question 10

B Platoon works 50 hours (4 afternoons + 1 day at 10 hours each equals 50 hours). The next closes platoon works 2 nights and 3 days/afternoons for a total of 46 hours.

Book 3

Question 1

"Stayed" and "from" are required in the blanks to make grammatical sense.

Question 2

Oust can be defined as to drive out, to eject from position of office or employment.

Question 3 NA

Question 4

Information seeking is one of the core competencies of being a police officer. Gathering as much information as possible about the female is extremely important. This information will have to be relayed to the parents. By taking the time to investigate the matter, you are demonstrating initiative, which is another of the core competencies of being a police officer. It is said in the question that you have no right to detain the female, and it would be a mistake to do so in real life and as part of an employment exam. Police services are not looking for officers who break the rules or abuse authority. Option B is the best answer.

Question 5

Community - service orientation is a core competency of being a police officer. It is important to know that your role as a police officer is to help people. Police should not be judgmental and should take an active interest in assisting the female. Option B is the best choice.

Question 6 - 8

1st - Kavi - # 2 - Red

2nd - Laurie - # 3 - Green

3rd - Brendon - # 1 - Yellow

4th - Alan - # 4 - Blue   The following graph should help you start organizing your information.

	Green	Yellow	Red	Blue
Kavi	No			
Brendon				
Laurie		No		
Alan				

	Green	Yellow	Red	Blue
No. 1	No			
No. 2	No			
No. 3	Yes	No	No	No
No. 4	No			

Order of Winners

Kavi	Laurie
Brendon	Yellow

Question 9

C - First step is to realize Greg has traveled 110km in the first hour. Then subtract total distance from the traveled distance to determine the distance remaining [500-110 = 390km]. Then divide by the total number of hour remaining [390km/3hrs = 130km/hr]

Question 10

B - Step one is to calculate total pages required to be printed. [1,400 x 2 = 2,800]. Then divide by printing speed [2,800 / 4 = 700 minutes]

Book 4

Question 1

A heptagon is a geometric figure with seven sides.

Question 2

"Don't" is required to agree with the subject "they". In the second blank "they're" is required meaning "they are".

Question 3 – 5   NA

Question 6

Information seeking is one of the key competencies for being a police officer. You received very little information from the call and you do not know what happened before you arrived. The male has not fled up until this point and it's safe to assume that he would have known police had been called. You should speak to the parties first. The best option as a police officer is to talk to one person at a time. The parties should be separated. Because the storeowner was the one to call police, you should address her first. Answer C is the best choice.

Question 7

All other options are vital pieces of information that would be required in an assault report.

Question 8

James first drank the beer, then walked into the tavern. The argument occured, lost control, and finally James was arrested.

Question 9

Since there are more people then there are total hairs on anyone's head, at the very least two people <u>must</u> share the same number of hairs.

Question 10

B -

The annual increase in rain fall from one year to the next is 2%.
Starting at 856mm (2002), begin to calculate the rain fall for the following years: 856 x 1.02 = 873.12mm (2003);
Then 873.12 x 1.02 = 890.58mm (2004);
Finally, 890.58 x 1.02 = 908.4 mm (2005).

Book 5

Question 1

The correct spelling is increased.

Question 2

The first blank requires "children's" indicating possession. The second blank requires "bear" meaning to stand.

Question 3   NA

Question 4

Obstructing police is obviously the wrong answer. So is ignoring the drugs completely as you are required by law to enforce laws. Once you are aware of the drugs it would be inappropriate to remain. You do not know how much are present, or what other drugs may be in use.

Question 5

It would be inappropriate to use your position as a police officer to exploit other members in society for personal gain. People often feel intimidated by police officers and may unwillingly offer favors they wish they hadn't.

Question 6

1 - Dopey

2 - Princess

3 - Butch

4 - Sniffy

5 - Puff

Question 7

The quickest root would be to take a flight from Paris - Toronto - Los Angeles. You would arrive at 1400 hrs.

Question 8

The numbers are doubling.   2, 4, 8, 16, 32, 64, 128, 256, 512 etc.

Question 9

Step 1: Determine the individual costs by multiplying the number of investigations by the costs associated with them.

Murder:	3 x $3,000 = $9,000
Theft:	376 x $200 = $75,200
Robbery:	66 x $600 = $39,600

Step 2: Simpy sum the total costs up to arrive at the budget for 1999.

$9,000 + $75,200 + $39,600 = $123,800

Question 10

Robberies increased from 64 to 72 which is a change of 8 (72 – 64 = 8). Next, determine what the change represents as compared ot the original number. This is accomplished by dividing the change in robberies by the number of robberies in 1998.

```
        0 . 1  2  5      which equals 12.5%
   64 | 8 . 0  0  0
    -   6  4
        1  6  0
    -   1  2  8
           3  2  0
       -   3  2  0
                  0
```

Ontario Practice Exam

The PATI exam is divided into 6 different components with 15 questions in each section. You will be able to go back and forth between each section during the test. You will have 90 minutes to answer all 90 questions. In addition, you will have 1 hour to complete a Written Communication Test.

Mapping
Measures ability to calculate times while following travelling directions.
Math
Basic math operations: addition, subtraction, division and multiplication, algebraic equations, fractions and decimals.
Matching
Measures your observation skills.
Problem Solving
Measures ability to apply basic math operations.
Syllogisms
Measures ability to understand logical inferences.
Pattern Solving
Measures ability to observe and detect consistencies and patterns.
Written Communication Test
Measures ability to use the English language.

The only materials allowed are a pencil and the attached scrap paper. No calculators, books or counting devices are allowed. Use a clock or stopwatch to keep track of time.

Detach the answer key to take the test.

PATI Answer Sheet

Mapping	A	B	C	D
1	○	○	○	○
2	○	○	○	○
3	○	○	○	○
4	○	○	○	○
5	○	○	○	○
6	○	○	○	○
7	○	○	○	○
8	○	○	○	○
9	○	○	○	○
10	○	○	○	○
11	○	○	○	○
12	○	○	○	○
13	○	○	○	○
14	○	○	○	○
15	○	○	○	○

_____ / 15

Mathematics	A	B	C	D
1	○	○	○	○
2	○	○	○	○
3	○	○	○	○
4	○	○	○	○
5	○	○	○	○
6	○	○	○	○
7	○	○	○	○
8	○	○	○	○
9	○	○	○	○
10	○	○	○	○
11	○	○	○	○
12	○	○	○	○
13	○	○	○	○
14	○	○	○	○
15	○	○	○	○

_____ / 15

Matching	A	B	C	D
1	○	○	○	○
2	○	○	○	○
3	○	○	○	○
4	○	○	○	○
5	○	○	○	○
6	○	○	○	○
7	○	○	○	○
8	○	○	○	○
9	○	○	○	○
10	○	○	○	○
11	○	○	○	○
12	○	○	○	○
13	○	○	○	○
14	○	○	○	○
15	○	○	○	○

_____ / 15

PATI Answer Sheet

Problem Solving				
	A	B	C	D
1	O	O	O	O
2	O	O	O	O
3	O	O	O	O
4	O	O	O	O
5	O	O	O	O
6	O	O	O	O
7	O	O	O	O
8	O	O	O	O
9	O	O	O	O
10	O	O	O	O
11	O	O	O	O
12	O	O	O	O
13	O	O	O	O
14	O	O	O	O
15	O	O	O	O

_____ / 15

Syllogisms				
	A	B	C	D
1	O	O	O	O
2	O	O	O	O
3	O	O	O	O
4	O	O	O	O
5	O	O	O	O
6	O	O	O	O
7	O	O	O	O
8	O	O	O	O
9	O	O	O	O
10	O	O	O	O
11	O	O	O	O
12	O	O	O	O
13	O	O	O	O
14	O	O	O	O
15	O	O	O	O

_____ / 15

Patterns				
	A	B	C	D
1	O	O	O	O
2	O	O	O	O
3	O	O	O	O
4	O	O	O	O
5	O	O	O	O
6	O	O	O	O
7	O	O	O	O
8	O	O	O	O
9	O	O	O	O
10	O	O	O	O
11	O	O	O	O
12	O	O	O	O
13	O	O	O	O
14	O	O	O	O
15	O	O	O	O

_____ / 15

Total Score _____ + _____ + _____ + _____ + _____ + _____ = _____ / 90

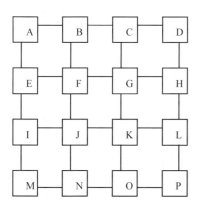

Each square labelled A – P represents the corner of an intersection. The lines in between the squares represent a city block. The time it takes to travel one city block is:

In a car: 1 minute
On a bike: 2 minutes
On foot: 3 minutes

Answer the following questions based on the map and information above.

Question 1

What is the shortest amount of time it would take to travel from F to P using any means you wanted?

A – 3 minutes   B – 4 minutes
C – 5 minutes   D – 6 minutes

Question 2

There is a parade in town and vehicles are not permitted to travel on or cross blocks E - H or C - O. If you drive to one of those blocks, you will have to walk the rest of the way. A bike can get through the intersections. How quickly could you travel from M to D?

A – 6 minutes   B – 9 minutes
C – 12 minutes   D – 15 minutes

Question 3

While on bike patrol, you experience a problem with the bike that will take 2 minutes and 30 seconds to fix. You are at corner J when a call comes for a woman in distress at corner O. How quickly could you could be there without a car?

A – 6 minutes   B – 6 minutes, 30 seconds
C – 7 minutes   D – 7 minutes, 30 seconds

Question 4

There is construction on the roads B - N that prevents any cars from crossing. Using any combination you wish, without using the same means twice, how quickly could you travel from H - A?

A – 5 minutes   B – 6 minutes
C – 7 minutes   D – None of the above

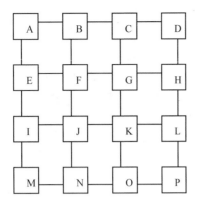

Each square labelled A – P represents the corner of an intersection. The lines in between the squares represent a city block. The time it takes to travel one city block is:

In a car: 1 minute
On a bike: 2 minutes
On foot: 3 minutes

Answer the following questions based on the map and information above.

Question 5

Due to traffic congestion, you now have to add 30 seconds every time you make a turn while driving. How quickly could you travel from P to F?

A – 5 minutes, 30 seconds   B – 6 minutes
C – 4 minutes   D – None of the above

Question 6

Which of the following would be the shortest trip?

A – Driving from H to M   B – Biking from P to J
C – Walking from A to E and driving from E to F
D – Biking from P to L and walking from L to K

Question 7

What is the shortest amount of time it would take to travel from A to L if you have to go through both intersections G and J?

A – 6 minutes   B – 7 minutes
C – 10 minutes   D – 14 minutes

Question 8

John got lost walking home from school. He visited intersections K, J, and A before arriving home at D. What is the shortest amount of time that he was walking?

A – 7 minutes   B – 21 minutes
C – 24 minutes   D – None of the above

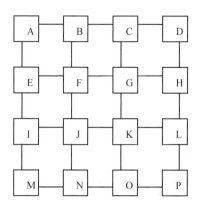

Each square labelled A – P represents the corner of an intersection. The lines in between the squares represent a city block. The time it takes to travel one city block is:

In a car: 1 minute
On a bike: 2 minutes
On foot: 3 minutes

Answer the following questions based on the map and information above.

Question 9

A bike race travelled through town. It started at intersection A, travelled through intersections G, J and twice through F before finishing at K. What is the shortest amount of time the bike race could have been?

A – 16 minutes   B – 12 minutes
C – 9 minutes   D – None of the above

Question 10

John lives at intersection M. Including intersection M, John walked to 5 different intersections before returning home. What is shortest amount of time John's walk took?

A – 18 minutes   B – 21 minutes
C – 15 minutes   D – None of the above

Question 11

Jennifer walked from A to D and then biked back to A without using any of the same streets. What is the shortest possible length of the trip?

A – 17 minutes   B – 20 minutes
C – 22 minutes   D – None of the above

Question 12

A police officer started at intersection B and looked for a lost child at the following intersections: F, G and I before returning to intersection B to report. How quickly could this task be accomplished if he had to add 30 seconds every time the car made a right or left-hand turn at an intersection?

A – 9 minutes   B – 9 minutes, 30 seconds
C – 10 minutes   D – 10 minutes, 30 seconds

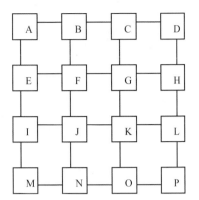

Each square labelled A – P represents the corner of an intersection. The lines in between the squares represent a city block. The time it takes to travel one city block is:

In a car: 2 minute
On a bike: 4 minutes
On foot: 6 minutes

Answer the following questions based on the map and information above.

Question 13

There is a parade in town and vehicles are not permitted to travel on or cross roads E - H or C - O. If you drive to one of those blocks, you will have to walk the rest of the way. A bike can get through the intersections. What is the quickest time you could travel from M to D?

A – 24 minutes   B – 34 minutes
C – 28 minutes   D – None of the above

Question 14

There is construction on the roads B - N, which prevent any cars from crossing. Using any combination you wish, without using the same means twice, what is the fastest time it would take you to travel from H - A?

A – 15 minutes   B – 14 minutes
C – 13 minutes   D – None of the above

Question 15
Which of the following would be the shortest trip?

A – Walking from P to K.   B – Biking from E to H.
C – Driving from J to D.   D – They will all take the same time.

Mathematics

Question 1

Solve for "y":

$3y - 2(18) = 3$

A   10
C   15

B   13
D   None of the above

Question 2

$17.895 \times 0.4 =$

A 7.158
C 0.7158

B 7.368
D   None of the above

Question 3

$-21.4 - 2.3 =$

A - 19.1
C - 15.9

B -20.1
D   None of the above

Question 4

Solve for "y":

$(24 - y) / 4 = 4$

A   8
C - 8

B - 6
D None of the above

Question 5

$15.21 - (-22.91) =$

A - 7.7
C   38.12

B 36.12
D None of the above

Question 6

$25.12 - 12.48 \times 2 + 10.65 =$

A   10.81
C   20.77

B 35.93
D   None of the above

Question 7

$1/2 + 3/4 - 1/3 =$

A $1 / 6$ B $13 / 12$
C $2 / 3$ D None of the above

Question 8

Solve for "y":

$y + y - 14 = 28$

A 21   B 14 and 7
C 19   D None of the above

Question 9

$- 12.621 + 4.698 =$

A $- 17.319$ B $- 7.923$
C $- 8.823$ D None of the above

Question 10

$- 13.67 (- 12.15) =$

A $- 25.82$ B $- 1.52$
C 166.0905   D None of the above

Question 11

Solve for "y":

$- (2y) / 6 + 18 (6) = 15 (2)$

A 432   B 243
C 324   D None of the above

Question 12

$54.82 \times 2.15 =$

A 117.863   B 116.001
C 115.999   D None of the above

Question 13

Solve for "y":

$3y - 2(21) = 3$

A   13   B   15
C   18   D   None of the above

Question 14

$25.72 \times 3.17 =$

A   83.51   B   82.98
C   79.35   D   None of the above

Question 15

$- 21.4 - 2.3 =$

A   -19.7   B   -24.3
C   -23.7   D   None of the above

Matching

For each of the following twelve questions, select the image that does not belong.

Questions 1

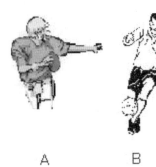

A   B   C   D

Question 2

A   B   C   D

Question 3

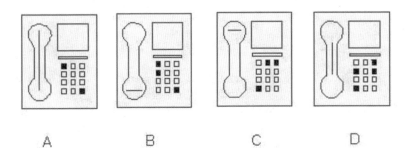

A   B   C   D

Question 4

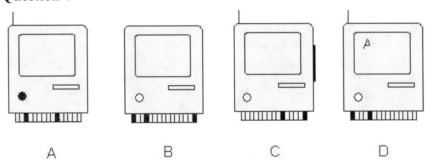

A   B   C   D

Question 5

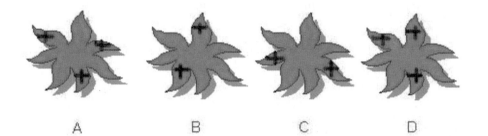

A   B   C   D

Question 6

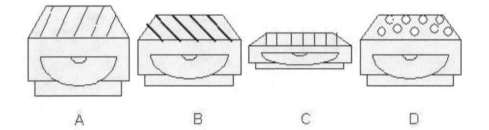

A   B   C   D

Question 7

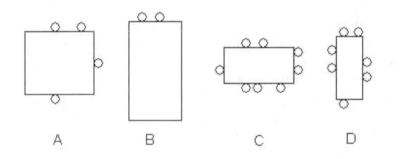

A   B   C   D

Question 8

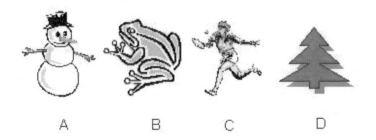

A   B   C   D

Question 9

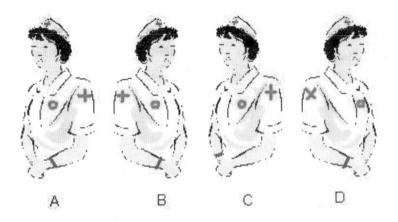

A   B   C   D

Question 10

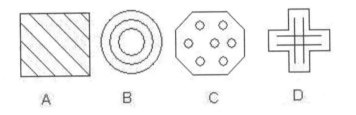

A   B   C   D

Question 11

C H K Z

A   B   C   D

Question 12

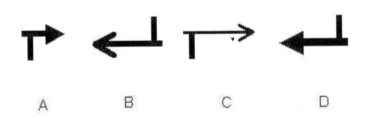

A   B   C   D

Question 13

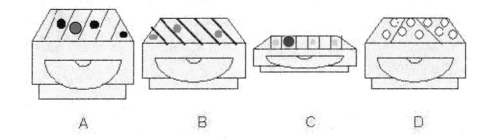

Question 14

Question 15

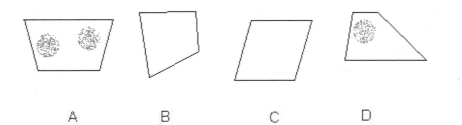

Problem Solving

Question 1

Arrested Person	Amount of Cocaine	# of $100 bills	# of $50 bills	# of $20 bills
Yong	2.9 kg	137	115	31
Sharma	1.7 kg	132	39	30
Hatch	0.8 kg	43	116	79

After a drug investigation, police officers seized the above items from three involved parties. 1 gm of cocaine is worth: $80.

How much cash did the officers take from suspect Sharma?

A) $15,750   B) $201

C) $151,750   D) $14,750

Question 2

What is the total value of the total goods seized from all involved parties?

A) $480,500   B) $479,600

C) $479,500   D) $479,400

Question 3

What percentage of the total cash belonged to Hatch?

A) 29.6%   B) 24.6%

C) 19.6%   D) 34.6%

Question 4

There are 4 children in the Smith family. Each child is married and has 3 babies. We must give 4 stuffed animals to each baby. How many stuffed animals do we need to buy?

A) 48   B) 52

C) 50   D) 54

Question 5

A man drove for 5 hours. In that time he completed 2/8 of his journey. How many more hours is he going to drive for?

A) 14   B) 15

C) 16   D) 17

Question 6

There are 18 slices in a pizza. Mike ate ½ of the pizza. Jim ate 2/6 of the pizza. Daren ate the remaining slices. How many slices did Daren eat?

A) 5   B) 4

C) 3   D) 2

Question 7

Illio put change in a bottle. He put in 2 pennies, 5 quarters, 3 dimes and 1 nickel. What is the probability of picking out a penny?

A) 18%   B) 42%

C) 35%   D) 8%

Question 8

Natasha Kaya worked 5 hours a day, 35 hours a week. She earns $6 an hour. How much will she earn in 3 weeks?

A) $590   B) $606

C) $620   D) $630

Question 9

If you get 4 eggs a day, how many weeks will it take to get 364 eggs?

A) 13   B) 6

C) 18   D) 8

Question 10

Jane Green bought 4 tapes at $6 each. She then found $9 on the street corner. She now has $59. How much money did Jane have before she bought the tapes?

A) $74   B) $89

C) $90   D) $56

Question 11

Billy was making a pen for his puppies. He had four pieces of wood. Two of the pieces of wood were 9 meters long. The other two pieces of wood were 3 meters long. After Billy has built the pen, what will its perimeter be in meters?

A) 19   B) 17

C) 24   D) 28

Question 12

A woman and her daughters went shopping. Each woman spent $13 on goods. At the end of the day they discovered that a total of $91 was spent. How many daughters are there?

A) 5   B) 7

C) 6   D) 4

Question 13

The following questions refer to this table:

GRADUATE	RUNNING	STRENGTH	FLEXIBILITY
Nam Le	33/45	45/50	62/70
Steve Laramy	40/45	42/50	63/70
Phil Bevilaqua	38/45	40/50	???/70

* All three scores are combined to come up with the overall fitness mark.

What percentage of the total mark does the strength component comprise?

A) 43.5% B) 50.0%

C) 30.3% D) 23.8%

Question 14
What was Steve Laramy's overall test percentage?

A) 87.9% B) 90.2%

C) 85.3% D) 89.2%

Question 15
What would Phil need to achieve in flexibility to achieve an overall score of 88.5%?

A) 65 B) 67

C) 68 D) 70

Syllogisms

For the following twelve questions select the logical conclusion.

Question 1

Baseball players or cricket players will use the field.
Sean is a baseball player and will be using the field.

A – Sean may play cricket as well.
B – Cricket players will use the field as well.
C – Cricket players will not be using the field.
D – None of the above.

Question 2

If found guilty, Kevin will be sent to jail.
No one is going to jail.

A – Kevin may be found guilty tomorrow.
B – Kevin was found guilty.
C – Kevin may go to jail.
D – None of the above.

Question 3
No convicts are innocent.
Some men are innocent.

A – Some men are not convicts.
B – Only women are convicts.
C – All convicts are men.
D – None of the above.

Question 4
Some cops are athletic.
All cops are human.

A – All humans are athletic.
B – Some humans are athletic.
C – All cops are athletic.
D – None of the above.

Question 5

No priests are women.
All students are priests.

A – Some students are women.
B – No women are students.
C – Different students are women.
D – None of the above.

Question 6

If there are weapons then there is fighting.
If there is fighting then there is bloodshed.

A – If there is bloodshed then there are weapons.
B – There may be weapons without fighting.
C – Fighting can occur without bloodshed.
D – None of the above.

Question 7

None of the victims were women.
All statements were from women.

A – Some statements were from victims.
B – Some men were victims.
C – No victims gave statements.
D – None of the above.

Question 8

No trout are mammals.
Some water animals are trout.

A – Water animals are not mammals.
B – Some water animals are not mammals.
C – Some water animals are mammals.
D – None of the above.

Question 9

Everything that lives, breathes.
No rocks breathe.

A – Some rocks live.
B – Everything that breathes, lives.
C – Some things that are alive, are rocks.
D – None of the above.

Question 10
Either the Blue Jays win or the Yankees win.
The Yankees do not win.

A – The Blue Jays may win.
B – The Blue Jays win.
C – The teams play again later on.
D – Both B and C.

Question 11
Genocide is never justifiable.
War is sometimes justifiable.

A – Some wars are not genocide.
B – All wars are not genocide.
C – Genocide can be justified if it takes place in a war.
D – None of the above.

Question 12
Some men are courageous.
Some soldiers are courageous.

A – Some men are soldiers.
B – All men are soldiers.
C – Some soldiers are not men.
D – None of the above.

Question 13
True love never dies.
Sean stopped loving Chantelle.

A – True love does not exist.
B – Nothing lasts forever.
C – Sean and Chantelle did not experience true love.
D – None of the above.

Question 14
No frogs are reptiles.
Some amphibians are frogs.

A – Some amphibians are not reptiles.
B – No amphibians are reptiles.
C – Some frogs are not amphibians.
D – None of the above.

Question 15

Either *NYPD Blue* or *Law and Order* is on.

NYPD Blue is not on.

A – *Law and Order* cannot be on at the same time as *NYPD Blue*.

B – *Law and Order* may be on.

C – *NYPD Blue* is on later.

D – None of the above.

Pattern Solving

For the following 12 questions, select the image that completes the pattern.

Question 1

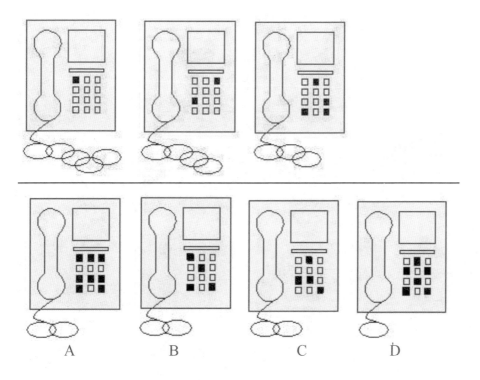

Question 2

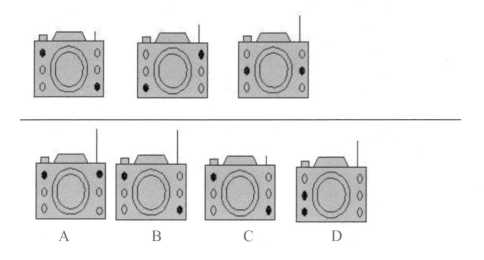

Question 3

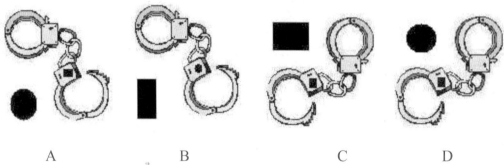

| A | B | C | D |

Question 4

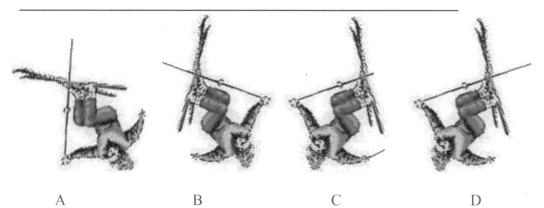

| A | B | C | D |

Question 5

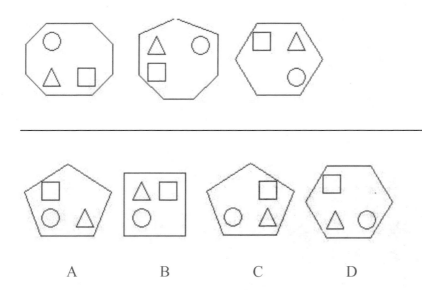

A   B   C   D

Question 6

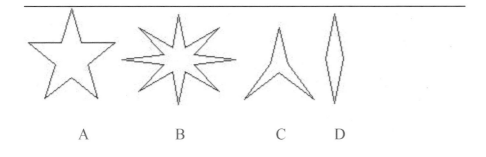

A   B   C   D

Question 7

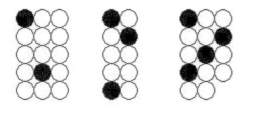

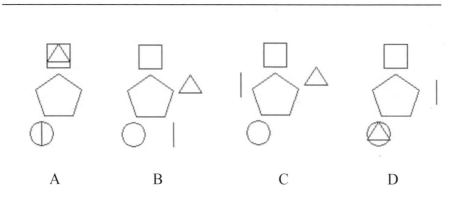

A   B   C   D

Question 8

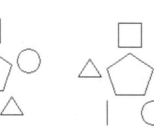

A   B   C   D

Question 9

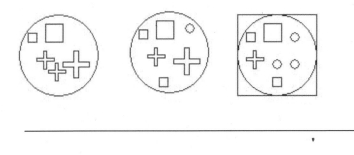

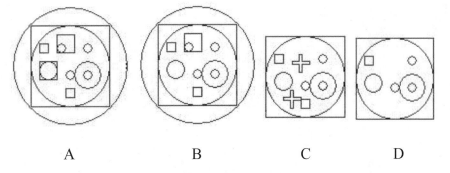

Question 10

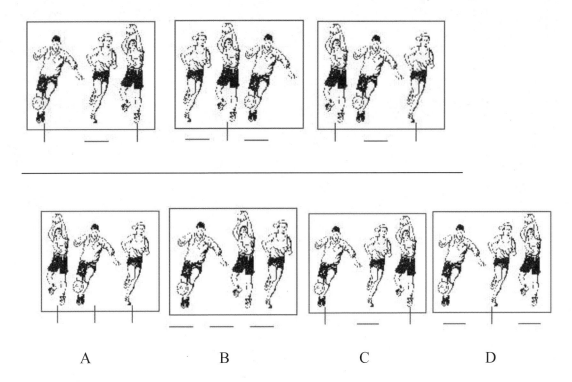

Question 11

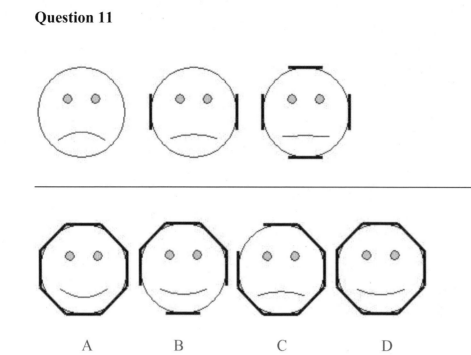

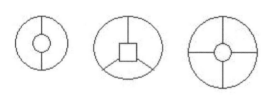

| A | B | C | D |

Question 12

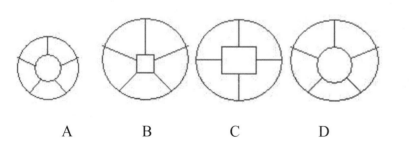

| A | B | C | D |

Question 13

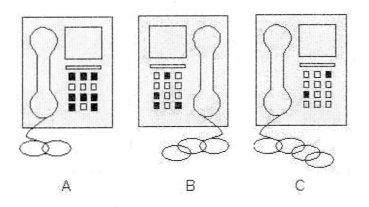

A   B   C

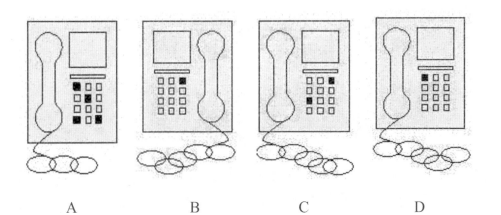

A   B   C   D

Question 14

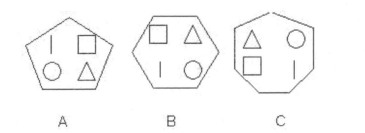

A   B   C

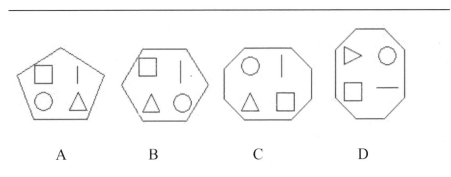

A   B   C   D

Question 15

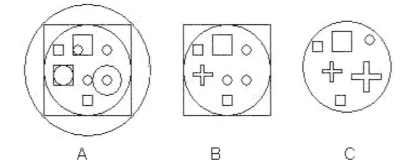

A   B   C

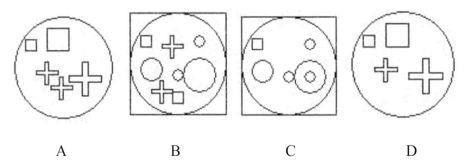

A   B   C   D

Written Communication Test_

Write a summary of important details and a report based on the information below. Give yourself one hour to complete the report.

Scenario 1: Traffic Collision

A red Honda was parked on the right shoulder of the expressway with light damage to the rear bumper. Police responding to the call got on the expressway at the nearest on – ramp, Jameson Avenue. There were skid marks in the far right lane approximately 10 meters long. It had rained the day before in the early afternoon. A large cube van was parked in the lane with severe damage to the front of the truck. The vehicles were all in the eastbound lanes of the Gardiner Expressway. Motorists were slowing down to take a look at the damage to the vehicles involved. There were billboards advertising watches that could be seen from the accident scene. That stretch of highway was flat and straight. Police arrived on scene about 8:38 am. Traffic was heavy, stop and go, heading eastbound from where the accident occurred. A blue Cavalier was parked in front of all the other cars with moderate damage to the rear bumper and light damage to the front. Police received a cell phone call at 8:32 am from a victim involved in the accident. It was a clear day and the sun was extremely bright. There was an abandoned car parked in the westbound lanes on the right shoulder 100 meters away. A black Ford Escort was parked on the shoulder of the expressway with moderate damage to the front and severe damage to the rear. The road was dry. It was Monday, April 12. The skid marks ended at the tires of the cube van. There were no injuries.

Answers

Mapping	
1)	B
2)	C
3)	A
4)	A
5)	D
6)	C
7)	B
8)	B
9)	B
10)	A
11)	D
12)	B
13)	A
14)	D
15)	C

Mathematics	
1)	B
2)	A
3)	D
4)	A
5)	C
6)	A
7)	D
8)	A
9)	B
10)	C
11)	D
12)	A
13)	B
14)	D
15)	C

Matching	
1)	C
2)	A
3)	C
4)	B
5)	D
6)	D
7)	D
8)	A
9)	C
10)	B
11)	A
12)	A
13)	C
14)	B
15)	C

Problem Solving	
1)	A
2)	C
3)	B
4)	A
5)	B
6)	C
7)	A
8)	D
9)	A
10)	A
11)	C
12)	C
13)	C
14)	A
15)	C

Syllogisms	
1)	C
2)	D
3)	A
4)	B
5)	B
6)	D
7)	C
8)	B
9)	D
10)	B
11)	A
12)	D
13)	C
14)	A
15)	A

Patterns	
1)	A
2)	B
3)	A
4)	A
5)	C
6)	D
7)	C
8)	B
9)	A
10)	D
11)	B
12)	B
13)	B
14)	C
15)	A

Detailed Solutions to Problems

Mapping

1) By the fastest route, there are 4 blocks between F and P. The most efficient means of travel is by car at 1 minute per block. The answer is 4 minutes **(B)**.

2) You can drive from M – I – J – F in 3 minutes and walk from F – B – C – D in 9 minutes for a total of 12 minutes. The fastest bike route would also be 12 minutes. **(C)**

3) If you fix the bike, the trip takes 6 minutes and 30 seconds (4 minutes travel time + 2 minutes 30 seconds to fix the bike). If you walk, it takes 6 minutes **(A)**.

4) The fastest route using any means available would be to drive from H – D – C – B in 3 minutes, then bike from B – A in 2 minutes, for a total trip of 5 minutes **(A)**.

5) You can travel with only one turn if you take route P – O – N – J – F. The number of blocks travelled is 4 at 1 minute each plus 30 seconds for making a turn at intersection N. Total travel time is 4 minutes, 30 seconds **(D)**.

6) The most direct route from H – M is to drive in 5 minutes. Biking from P to J would take 9 minutes. Walking from A to E and driving from E to F would take 4 minutes. Biking from P – L and walking from L – K would take 5 minutes. **(C)**

7) You have to backtrack to complete this journey and drive from A – B – F – J – F – G – J – L for a total of 7 minutes **(B)**.

8) You will walk a minimum 7 blocks to pass through all of the intersections, for a total of 21 minutes **(B)**.

9) The best route for the bike race is to travel A – B – F – G – F – J – K for a total time of 12 minutes **(B)**.

10) In order to walk through 5 intersections, you will have to backtrack over one intersection. The shortest route is M – I – J – N – O – N – M and would take 18 minutes **(A)**.

11) The shortest route would take you from A – B – C – D – H – G – F – E – A, for a total of 19 minutes (9 minutes walking, 10 minutes biking) **(D)**.

12) The route from B – F – G – F – E – I – E – A – B has 8 blocks travelled for a total of 8 minutes, add 3 turns (at F, E, A) for a total of 1 minute 30 seconds. Therefore, the fastest trip would be 9 minutes 30 seconds **(B)**.

13) In this situation you would have to walk a minimum of 3 blocks (18 minutes) plus drive 3 blocks (6 minutes). It would be equally fast to bike the whole route (6 blocks) for a total of 24 minutes. **(A)**.

14) The fastest combination would be to drive from H - B (3 blocks) and bike from B - A (1 block) for a total of 10 minutes. **(D).**

15) The shortest route is to drive 4 blocks, J-D, for a total time of 8 minutes. **(C).**

Math

1) $3y - 2(18) = 3$
$3y - 36 = 3$
$3y = 39$
$y = 13$

2) $17.895 \times 0.4 = 7.158$

3) $-21.4 - 2.3 = -23.7$

4) $(24 - y) / 4 = 4$
$24 - y = 16$
$24 = 16 + y$
$y = 8$

5) $15.21 - (-22.91) =$
$15.21 + 22.91 = 38.12$

6) $25.12 - 12.48 \times 2 + 10.65 =$
$25.12 - 24.96 + 10.65 = 10.81$

7) $1/2 + 3/4 - 1/3 =$
$6/12 + 9/12 - 4/12 = 11/12$

8) $y + y - 14 = 28$
$2y - 14 = 28$
$2y = 42$
$y = 21$

9) $-12.621 + 4.698 = -7.923$

10) $-13.67 (-12.15) =$
$-13.67 \times -12.15 = 166.0905$

11) $-(2y) / 6 + 18 (6) = 15 (2)$
$-(2y) / 6 + 108 = 30$
$-(2y) / 6 = -78$
$-(2y) = -468$
$y = 234$

12) $54.82 \times 2.15 = 117.863$

13) $3y - 2(21) = 3$
$3y - 42 = 3$
$3y = 45$
$y = 15$

14) $25.72 \times 3.17 = 81.5324$

15) $-21.4 - 2.3 = -23.7$

Matching

1) Only winter sport, no ball. **(C)**

2) Only non-land vehicle. **(A)**

3) Only phone with button used in middle row. **(C)**

4) Only object with two unique features (3 stripes at bottom and no antenna). **(B)**

5) Only plant with mark on two leaves beside one another. **(D)**

6) Object with circular marks on top. **(D)**

7) Object with an odd number of circles attached (7). **(D)**

8) Only non-living object. **(A)**

9) Only woman with no unique features. **(C)**

10) Only shape without any sides. **(B)**

11) Only letter without any straight lines. **(A)**

12) Only object with a short top arrow. **(A)**

13) Only image without diagonal lines across the top. **(C)**

14) This one you may find tricky. As you say each of the letters, only one of them doesn't have a long "e" sound. **(B)**

15) All of the other images have sides and angles that are unequal. In image C, all sides and angles are equal (it's a rhombus). **(C)**

Problem Solving

Question 1
This question involves straight multiplication and addition.

Step 1: Multiply out all of the cash flows for each dollar denomination.

$$\$100 \times 132 = \$13,200$$

Step 2: Add the total cash together from the separate denominations.

$$\$13,200 + \$1,950 + \$600 = \$15,750 \ \textbf{(A)}$$

Question 2
This involves straight addition and multiplication. Multiply the values of the bills by the number of bills. Remember to include the value of the drugs as well. If you run into any difficulties solving this problem, review the addition and multiplication sections of the teaching material.

The answer is $479,500 **(C).**

Question 3
This question requires division, addition and multiplication. First, find a total for all the cash that was confiscated. Then divide the amount of cash that Hatch has by the total value of the money seized.

Total Value of Cash Seized = $47,500

Value of Hatch's Cash = $11,680

$$47,500 \overline{)11680.0000} \quad 0.2458 \quad \text{or } 24.6 \% \ \textbf{(B)}$$

Question 4
This question is a two-stage multiplication problem. The first step is to determine how many babies there are. This is accomplished by multiplying the number of babies by the number of children. After this is determined, you multiply the number of babies by the number of toys needed for each baby.

4 children with 3 babies each
$$4 \times 3 = 12$$

4 toys for each baby
$$12 \times 4 = 48 \ \textbf{(A)}$$

Question 5

This question is a multi-step problem. The first step is to determine how long the ultimate journey will be. You will have to understand how fractions work for this problem.

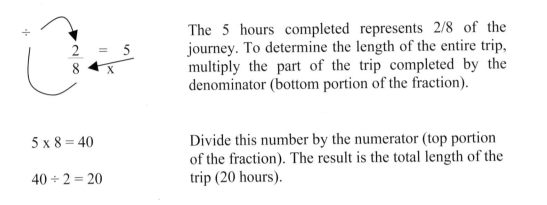

The 5 hours completed represents 2/8 of the journey. To determine the length of the entire trip, multiply the part of the trip completed by the denominator (bottom portion of the fraction).

5 x 8 = 40

40 ÷ 2 = 20

Divide this number by the numerator (top portion of the fraction). The result is the total length of the trip (20 hours).

The second step is to determine how much time is left. He has already driven for 5 hours. This becomes a simple subtraction problem.

20 hours total trip with 5 hours already driven:

20 – 5 = 15 **(B)**

Question 6

This question involves multiplication, division, addition and subtraction. The first step is to determine how many slices Mike and Jim ate.

18 total slices

1 / 2 - Mike

2 / 6 - Jim

To determine the number of slices each had, multiply the fraction by the total number. This is a two-stage process.

$$18 \times \frac{1}{2} = \frac{18}{2} \qquad\qquad 18 \times \frac{2}{6} = \frac{36}{6}$$

Multiply the numerator in both questions by 18. The denominator remains the same. After this, divide the numerator by the denominator.

$$\frac{18}{2} = 9 \qquad\qquad \frac{36}{6} = 6$$

Mike had 9 slices and Jim had 6 slices. Adding them together reveals that 15 slices have been eaten. This is now a subtraction problem.

18 total slices with 15 already eaten.
18 – 15 = 3 **(C)**

Question 7

For this problem, determine the total number of coins and divide that number by the total number of pennies.

The total coins are:
2 pennies
5 quarters
3 dimes $2 + 5 + 3 + 1 = 11$
1 nickel   (Remember to include the pennies)

As soon as this is accomplished, divide the number of pennies by the total number of coins. This involves decimal long division.

```
     0. 1 8 1
11 | 2. 0 0 0
```

To express this number as a %, multiply the number by 100.
(0.18 x 100 = 18%) **(A)**

Question 8

Many word problems attempt to fool you with irrelevant information. You must determine what information is useful to solve the problem.

5 hours per day   Here the number of hours per day is not
35 hours per week   necessary to solve the problem. It is a distraction.
$6 an hour
3 weeks total

This problem is a multi-step multiplication problem. Determine how much money is made in one week and then multiply that number by the number of weeks.

1) 35 x $ 6 = $ 210
2) $ 210 x 3 = $ 630 **(D)**

Question 9

To solve this problem, determine how many eggs can be produced a week by multiplying 4 x 7 = 28.

Next divide 364 by 28 for the answer.

```
        13 (A)
28 | 364
```

Question 10

To solve this problem, work backwards using subtraction and multiplication.

$ 59 now
$ 9 found on corner
$24 spent on tapes ($6 x 4 = $24)

Starting with the $59, subtract the $9 that Jane found because she did not have that before she bought the tapes.

$59 - $9 = $50

Then add back the money she spent on the tapes. This will give you the answer.

$50 + $24 = $74 **(A)**

Question 11

To answer this question, you will need to calculate the perimeter. Perimeter is the border around an area. To calculate the perimeter, add up all the sides of the rectangle. The perimeter is represented by the dotted lines below.

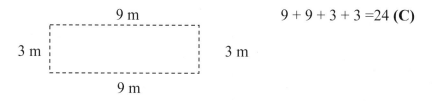

9 + 9 + 3 + 3 = 24 **(C)**

Question 12

This is a two-step problem with a little trick involved. The first step is to determine how many people there are in total. This is a simple division problem.

$91 total spent
$13 spent each

$$13 \overline{)91}$$
$$\begin{array}{r} 7 \\ 13 \overline{)91} \\ -\underline{91} \\ 0 \end{array}$$

Remember that the question asks how many daughters there are. Because the mother is included in the above calculation, subtract 1 to reach the answer.

7 – 1 = 6 **(C)**

Question 13

This is a simple division problem. If you have difficulties with this question, review the section on decimals and division in the teaching material. You have to divide the strength component (50) by the total test score (165, the sum of the three tests).

$$165\overline{)50.000} \quad 0.303 \text{ which equals } 30.3\%$$

$$
\begin{array}{r}
0.\,3\,0\,3 \text{ which equals } 30.3\% \\
165\,\overline{\smash{)}\,5\,0.\,0\,0\,0} \\
-\,4\,9\,5 \\
\hline
5\,0\,0 \\
-\,4\,9\,5 \\
\hline
5
\end{array}
$$

Question 14

The solution is reached by dividing the sum of the Steve's test scores by the total sum of the test score.

Steve's Mark: 40 + 42 +62 = 145
Test Score: 45 + 50 +70 = 165

$$
\begin{array}{r}
0.\,8\,7\,8\,7 \text{ which rounds to } 87.9\% \\
165\,\overline{\smash{)}\,1\,4\,5.\,0\,0\,0\,0}
\end{array}
$$

Question 15

To solve this problem you should first discover what score would be required to achieve an 88.5% on the test. An algebraic equation should be set up. If you set "Y" as the mark required to achieve an 88.5%, the equation will look like this:

Y / 165 = 0.885

To isolate "Y", multiply both sides by 165

Therefore: Y = 146

If Phil requires 146 / 165 on the test to pass, subtract what he has received on the other two tests (78) from 146.

Therefore: 146 – 78 = 68

Syllogisms

The logic for the following questions is:

1) Either A or B.
   A.
   Not B.

2) If A then B.
   Not B.
   Not A.

3) No A are B.
   Some C are B.
   Some C are not A.

4) Some A are B.
   All B are C.
   Some C are A.

5) No B are C.
   All A are B.
   No C are A.

6) If A then B.
   If B then C.
   If A then C (not if C then A)

7) No A are B.
   All C are B.
   No C are A.

8) No A are B.
   Some C are A.
   Some C are not B.

9) All A are B.
   No C are B.
   No C are A.

10) Either A or B.
    Not B.
    A.

11) No A is B.
    Some C are B.
    Some C are not A.

12) Some A are B.
    Some B are C.
    No definite conclusions.

13) All A is B.
    No C is B.
    No C is A.

14) No A is B.
    Some C is A.
    Some C is not B.

15) Either A or B.
    Not A.
    B.

1)   Declining number of rings on cord, doubling the number of highlighted buttons **(A)**.

2)   Expanding antenna, black circles traveling clockwise by one circle each image **(B)**.

3)   Image rotating clockwise by 90 degrees. Alternating circles and squares on the handcuffs and in the corner **(A)**.

4)   Object rotating clockwise 90 degrees, 45 degrees, 22.5 degrees (50% less per turn). One pole decreasing in size, one expanding **(A)**.

5)   Image losing one side with each image (8,7,6,5). Internal images rotating 90 degrees **(C)**.

6)   Number of points on each image cut in half (16, 8, 4, 2) **(D)**.

7)   Number of rows alternating 3,2,3,2. Number of black circles increasing by 1 each image (2,3,4,5) **(C)**.

8)   Square is stationary. Circle moves one space clockwise, triangle moves two spaces clockwise and line moves one space counterclockwise each image **(B)**.

9)   Crosses decreasing by one (3,2,1,0), squares increasing by one (2,3,4,5), circles doubling each image (1, 2, 4, 8) **(A)**.

10) Players moving from left to right. Lines on bottom alternating between horizontal and vertical **(D)**.

11) Face changing from frown to smile. Number of lines surrounding face increasing by two's each image (0,2,4,6) **(B)**.

12) Object divided in 1/2's, 1/3's, 1/4's, 1/5's. Size of shape steadily increasing. Object in middle alternating between a circle and a square **(B)**.

13) Number of buttons blackened is being cut in half (8,4,2,1). Receiver is alternating between left and right side. **(B)**.

14) Large image has steadily increasing number of sides (5,6,7,8). Images inside shape are rotating to nearest corner, counter-clockwise, with each image. **(C)**.

15) The number of crosses is growing by one (0,1,2,3). The total number of circles is being cut in half (8,4,2,1) and the number of squares is decreasing one per image (5,4,3,2). **(A)**.

Written Communication Test Sample Answer

Time: Shortly before 8:32 am.
Monday, April 12.

Location:
Eastbound Gardiner Expressway, east of Jameson Avenue. Right lane.

Evidence at Scene:
Red Honda - damage rear bumper (light).
Blue Cavalier - damage front (light), rear (moderate)
Black Ford Escort - damage front (moderate), rear (severe)
Cube Van - damage front end (major).
Skid Marks - 10 meters in length, right lane, ending at the cube van.

Other: Bright sunny morning.
Driving into the sun.
Rush hour traffic, heavy (stop and go).
Dry Road
Straight, flat section of the highway.

Report

On Monday, April 12, around 8:32 am, there was a 4-vehicle accident eastbound on the Gardiner Expressway east of Jameson Avenue. The accident occurred in the right lane during morning rush hour traffic, driving into the morning sun. The traffic was heavy, and in a state of stop-and-go. That stretch of the road was flat and straight. The road was dry.

The most likely explanation for the accident is that the cube van was approaching slower moving, or stopped, traffic. The driver of the cube van applied his brakes heavily and began to skid, striking a black Ford Escort and causing severe damage to the front of the cube van and the rear of the Escort. The Escort was pushed into a blue Cavalier, causing moderate damage to the front of the Escort and to the rear of the Cavalier. The Cavalier then struck a red Honda, causing light damage to the front of the Cavalier, and to the rear of the Honda.

There were no injuries involved in the accident.

Saskatchewan Practice Exam

The SIGMA test consists of 72 questions covering areas such as spelling, problem solving, logic, reading comprehension and mapping questions. You will have 35 minutes to answer all 72 questions. During the actual exam, if you are penalized for incorrect answers, do not randomly guess at questions. If you are reasonably confident you have the correct answer, then make an answer choice, but if it is a complete random guess, leave the choice blank, as you may be penalized for incorrect answers. Make sure you confirm this with the test administrator on the exam date.

You will also be required to write an essay based on an unknown topic. We strongly recommend you review the essay component we have in this book. The only materials allowed pencils and scrap paper. No calculators, books, or counting devices are allowed. Use a clock or stopwatch to keep track of the time.

Detach the answer key to take the test.

Sigma Answer Key

A B C D E
1) ○○○○○ _____
2) ○○○○○ _____
3) ○○○○○ _____
4) ○○○○○ _____
5) ○○○○○ _____
6) ○○○○○ _____
7) ○○○○○ _____
8) ○○○○○ _____
9) ○○○○○ _____
10) ○○○○○ _____

A B C D E
11) ○○○○○ _____
12) ○○○○○ _____
13) ○○○○○ _____
14) ○○○○○ _____
15) ○○○○○ _____
16) ○○○○○ _____
17) ○○○○○ _____
18) ○○○○○ _____
19) ○○○○○ _____
20) ○○○○○ _____

A B C D E
21) ○○○○○ _____
22) ○○○○○ _____
23) ○○○○○ _____
24) ○○○○○ _____
25) ○○○○○ _____
26) ○○○○○ _____
27) ○○○○○ _____
28) ○○○○○ _____
29) ○○○○○ _____
30) ○○○○○ _____

A B C D E
31) ○○○○○ _____
32) ○○○○○ _____
33) ○○○○○ _____
34) ○○○○○ _____
35) ○○○○○ _____
36) ○○○○○ _____
37) ○○○○○ _____
38) ○○○○○ _____
39) ○○○○○ _____
40) ○○○○○ _____

                 A B C D E   A B C D E
41) ◯ ◯ ◯ ◯ ◯ _____   51) ◯ ◯ ◯ ◯ ◯ _____
42) ◯ ◯ ◯ ◯ ◯ _____   52) ◯ ◯ ◯ ◯ ◯ _____
43) ◯ ◯ ◯ ◯ ◯ _____   53) ◯ ◯ ◯ ◯ ◯ _____
44) ◯ ◯ ◯ ◯ ◯ _____   54) ◯ ◯ ◯ ◯ ◯ _____
45) ◯ ◯ ◯ ◯ ◯ _____   55) ◯ ◯ ◯ ◯ ◯ _____
46) ◯ ◯ ◯ ◯ ◯ _____   56) ◯ ◯ ◯ ◯ ◯ _____
47) ◯ ◯ ◯ ◯ ◯ _____   57) ◯ ◯ ◯ ◯ ◯ _____
48) ◯ ◯ ◯ ◯ ◯ _____   58) ◯ ◯ ◯ ◯ ◯ _____
49) ◯ ◯ ◯ ◯ ◯ _____   59) ◯ ◯ ◯ ◯ ◯ _____
50) ◯ ◯ ◯ ◯ ◯ _____   60) ◯ ◯ ◯ ◯ ◯ _____

                 A B C D E
61) ◯ ◯ ◯ ◯ ◯ _____
62) ◯ ◯ ◯ ◯ ◯ _____
63) ◯ ◯ ◯ ◯ ◯ _____
64) ◯ ◯ ◯ ◯ ◯ _____
65) ◯ ◯ ◯ ◯ ◯ _____
66) ◯ ◯ ◯ ◯ ◯ _____
67) ◯ ◯ ◯ ◯ ◯ _____
68) ◯ ◯ ◯ ◯ ◯ _____
69) ◯ ◯ ◯ ◯ ◯ _____
70) ◯ ◯ ◯ ◯ ◯ _____
71) ◯ ◯ ◯ ◯ ◯ _____
72) ◯ ◯ ◯ ◯ ◯ _____

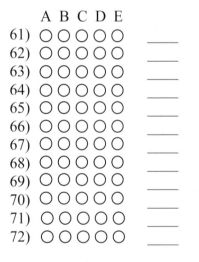

Total: _____ / 72

Sigma Exam
Identify the misspelled words in the following questions.

Question 1

Despite many complaints and concerns <u>from citizens</u>, the instances of <u>retaliation for</u> testifying in court are very rare. Despite this <u>rarety</u>, officers should be vigilant of suspects <u>who</u> attempt to intimidate witnesses.

a) rarety   b) retaliation for

c) from citizens   d) who

Question 2

The rookie officers <u>undertook</u> extensive training and development programs in order to prepare them for the <u>daunting</u> tasks that would lie <u>ahead</u> of them as they <u>commensed</u> their police duties.

a) undertook   b) daunting

c) lie ahead   d) commensed

Question 3

The <u>viscious</u> canine attacked the young woman and her <u>sibling</u>. When animal control arrived they managed to <u>subdue</u> the animal through <u>tranquilizers</u> and harnesses.

a) viscious   b) sibling

c) subdue   d) tranquilizers

Question 4

There were thousands of <u>demonstrators</u> at Parliament Hill protesting the <u>atrocities</u> of <u>foriegn</u> governments with <u>horrible</u> human rights records.

a) demonstrators   b) atrocities

c) foriegn   d) horrible

Question 5

<u>Psychology</u>, <u>sociology</u> and <u>criminalogy</u> are several examples of courses that can be taken at university which help prepare students for a <u>potential</u> career in policing.

a) psychology   b) sociology

c) criminalogy   d) potential

Question 6

Police unions are becoming <u>increasingly</u> involved in local politics. They have started supporting particular political <u>campaigns</u>. This has caused some <u>contraversy</u>, as there are several groups who feel the police should remain <u>apolitical</u>.

a) increasingly   b) campaigns

c) contraversy   d) apolitical

Question 7

Because police officers are forced to work both day and night shifts, it is important that they maintain a healthy diet and exercise <u>regime</u>. If they do not <u>receive</u> enough <u>nurishment</u>, physical activity and rest, they will have difficulty performing their jobs. Officers sometimes complain that they have become <u>nocturnal</u> creatures, like bats.

a) regime
b) nurishment
c) receive
d) nocturnal

Question 8

Officers enjoy many social activities and <u>celebrations</u>. The degree of <u>friendship</u> prevalent among officers is probably the result of the intense pressure and <u>dependence</u> that officers have on <u>eachother</u> during the course of their duties.

a) celebrations
b) dependence
c) friendship
d) eachother

Question 9

Once <u>transferred</u> to the marine unit, officers <u>undergo</u> intense training, including SCUBA, and <u>naudical</u> lessons. The marine unit is a highly desirable division, in which, officers are selected based on <u>competencies</u> they acquired through their policing experience.

a) transferred
b) undergo
c) naudical
d) competencies

Question 10

Stress is <u>inherent</u> to the job of police officers. In order to deal with it, police associations across Canada have arranged <u>counselling</u> with <u>psychiatrists</u> and mandatory leave after <u>incountering</u> life threatening situations.

a) inherent
b) counselling
c) psychiatrists
d) incountering

Question 11

Identify which of the following words is misspelled in the following questions.

a) ability
b) staple
c) compatible
d) specifically
e) none of the above

Question 12

Identify which of the following words is misspelled.

a) corruption
b) withdrawal
c) unecessary
d) disappearance
e) none of the above

Question 13

Identify which of the following words is misspelled.

a) disability

b) fradulent

c) gradually

d) university

e) none of the above

Question 14

Identify which of the following words is misspelled.

a) rehabilitation

b) grasping

c) progresion

d) negotiable

e) none of the above

Question 15

Identify which of the following words is misspelled.

a) front

b) government

c) implication

d) inspector

e) none of the above

Question 16

Expendable means:

a) able to Grow

b) disposable

c) careful

d) watchful

Question 17

Abominable means:

a) Hateful

b) snowman

c) violent

d) a bomb

Question 18

Mystique means:

a) foggy

b) air of mystery

c) failed

d) began

Question 19

Affluent means:

a) strapped

b) fluid

c) considerate

d) wealthy

Question 20
Daunting means:

a) extensive

c) charming

b) developed

d) discouraging

In the following questions, fill in the blank with the most appropriate word.
Question 21
Due to the size of the _____, Billy had to put on his glasses to read the letter.

a) paper

c) pencil

b) print

d) sun

Question 22
In science class, James learned that rapid cell growth is called _____.

a) proliferation

c) proteination

b) progression

d) protection

Question 23
If while driving you see a ball bounce into the road, you should look for a _____ to come next.

a) bat

c) child

b) car

d) cat

Question 24
When dealing with a suspect, it is important to _____ the questions you plan on asking to make sure there are no pauses while reading notes.

a) ask

c) drill

b) memorize

d) categorize

Question 25
Wreckers were called in to assist in the _____ of the old buildings downtown.

a) construction

c) printing

b) planning

d) demolition

Question 26
Identify the statement that is grammatically correct.

a) Due to the impending court date, been placed in hiding, Ms. Jones has.

b) Ms. Jones due to the impending court date has to be placed in hiding.

c) Due to the impending court date, Ms. Jones has to be placed in hiding.

d) Due to the impending court date; Ms. Jones has to be placed in hiding.

Question 27

Identify the statement that is grammatically correct.

a) Most people are forced to testify in open court. This is not true for young children.

b) Children are not forced to testify in open court. But most are.

c) Children is not forced to testify in open court. They are not like most people.

d) Most people forced to talk in open court. This is not true for young children.

Question 28

Identify the statement that is grammatically correct.

a) Timmy, John, and Bill all gone to the store together to buy food for the party.

b) Timmy, John, and Bill all went to the store together to buy food for the party.

c) Timmy, John, Bill all went to the stores together to buy food for the party.

d) Timmy, John, and Bill all having gone to the store together to buy food for the party.

Question 29

Identify the statement that is grammatically correct.

a) The convention came to town and bringed all of the traffic with it.

b) The convention come to town and brought all of the traffic with it.

c) The traffic come to town when the convention brought it in.

d) The convention came to town and brought all of the traffic with it.

Question 30

Identify the statement that is grammatically correct.

a) Each student has to show identification before been allowed to enter the examination room.

b) Before being allowed to enter the examination room, each student had to show identification.

c) Each student had to show before being allowed to enter the examination room identification.

d) Before being allowed to enter the examination room, each students had to show identification.

In the following questions, fill in the blank with the most appropriate word.
Question 31

The movie had already started _____ the film projector broke down.

a) when   b) while

c) since   d) although

Question 32

She couldn't attend the opera, _____ she had tickets.

a) or

b) although

c) besides

d) therefore

Question 33

He wasn't certain, _____ he could make an educated guess.

a) therefore

b) but

c) indeed

d) while

Question 34

Indicate any punctuation errors in the sentence below.

Before <u>taking</u> the tickets the teenager must clock <u>in,</u> Then she <u>can</u> begin <u>work.</u>

a) taking

b) in,

c) can

d) work.

e) No correction required

Question 35

Indicate any punctuation errors in the sentence below.

When <u>planning</u> an outing with <u>children,</u> many things need to be <u>considered:</u> Safety <u>is</u> first and foremost.

a) planning

b) children,

c) considered:

d) is

e) no correction required

Question 36

A man drove for 6 hours. In that time he completed 2/6 of his journey. What is the total length of his journey?

a) 18 hours

b) 12 hours

c) 24 hours

d) 30 hours

Question 37

Doug was responsible for filling out insurance requisitions at his office. In May, he was able to process 1,322 requests. In June his number of requests completed fell by 15%. In July he was able to improve on his June numbers by 17%. How many requisitions did Doug complete in July?

a) 1,300

b) 1,315

c) 1,348

d) 1,412

Question 38

There are 4 offspring in the Yang family. They live in 6 different houses. Each offspring is married and has 3 babies. We must give 4 stuffed animals to each baby. How many stuffed animals do we need to buy?

a) 48   b) 50

c) 52   d) 54

Question 39

A computer software package costs $24.07 at the store. A customer gives 2 twenty-dollar bills. How much change does the customer receive?

a) $15.73   b) $15.83

c) $15.93   d) $16.13

Question 40

Carlene needs to save $1,440 to take a trip. She works 45 hours a week and earns $8 an hour. How many weeks will she have to work in order to save for the trip?

a) 2   b) 3

c) 4   d) 5

Question 41

Tim needs to fill three 20L barrels with oil. If his oil dispenser flows at 100 mL/s, how long will it take him to fill the 3 containers? (Minutes)

a) 100   b) 75

c) 50   d) 10

Question 42

James ran 2 miles in 12 minutes. He has to run another 5 miles and wants to average a 7-minute mile over the entire run. What will James have to run the remaining 5 miles in, on average, to accomplish this?

a) 6.3 min / mile   b) 7.4 min / mile

c) 8.6 min / mile   d) 10.2 min / mile

Question 43

Which of the following witness statements is the most likely description of the suspect? Each of the statements is from a different witness.

a) 6'2, 150 lbs, dreadlocks, pierced nose, baggy blue jeans, male Hispanic, red sweater with a hood

b) Crew cut hair, male black, 6'1, 210 lbs, baggy blue jeans, red sweater with a hood, pierced nose.

c) Male black, 6'2, dreadlocks, pierced nose, 210 lbs, baggy blue jeans, red sweater with a hood.

d) Dreadlocks, male black, 6'2, tattoo left forearm, 210 lbs, baggy blue tracksuit, green sweater.

Question 44

Which of the following witness statements is the most likely description of the theft? Each of the statements is from a different witness.

a) There were two young children in the mall. The young white boy walked up to the clerk and began speaking with her. The young black boy went to the back of the store and took a large pop. When they left the store the boys shared the pop.

b) There were two young children in the mall. The young black child walked up to the clerk and began speaking with her. The other young white boy went to the back of the store and took a large milk. When they left the store the boys shared the pop.

c) There were two young children in the mall. One child was hanging out near the front of the store, acting as a look out. The other young white boy went to the back of the store and took a large pop. When they left the store the boys shared the pop.

d) There were two young children in the mall. The young black child walked up to the clerk and began speaking with her. The other young white boy went to the back of the store and took a large pop. When they left the store the boys shared the pop.

Question 45

Which of the following witness statements is the most likely description of the suspect? Each of the statements is from a different witness.

a) 5'5, 120 lbs, male Hispanic, brown hair with grey strands, wearing beige pants, a brown jacket, and black shoes.

b) tanned complexion, red hair with grey strands, wearing a brown jacket, beige pants and black shoes, male white 5'6, 125 lbs.

c) male white, tanned complexion, red hair, 5'9, 135 lbs, wearing a brown leather jacket, beige pants and black shoes.

d) male white, tanned complexion, red hair with grey strands, 5'6, 125 lbs, wearing a jacket, beige pants and black sandals.

Question 46

Which of the following witness statements is the most likely description of the fight? Each of the statements is from a different witness.

a) There were two women yelling at each other on the corner of Yonge and Dundas. The woman in the red coat slapped the woman in the blue dress across the face. The woman in the blue dress then swung her purse at the other and knocked her down.

b) Two women were yelling at each other at the corner of Yonge Street. A woman in a red dress slapped another woman in the face. The other woman then swung her purse and knocked the woman in the red dress to the ground.

c) I saw a woman in a blue dress knock a woman in a red dress down by swinging her purse at her. This happened at the corner of Dundas Street and Yonge Street.

d) There was a fight between two women. They were yelling at each other on the corner when a woman slapped the other across the face. The other then proceed to swing her purse and knocked her down. One woman was wearing a red coat and the other was wearing a blue dress.

Question 47

Which of the following witness statements is the most likely description of the suspect? Each of the statements is from a different witness.

a) Male white, light complexion, 6'3, 190 lbs, blonde hair, blue eyes, moustache, 42 years old, wearing green khakis, and a grey sweatshirt.

b) Male white, light complexion, 6'3, 165 lbs, brown hair, green eyes, 35 years old, wearing grey pants and a green sweatshirt.

c) Male white, tanned complexion, 5'9, 190 lbs, blonde hair, blue eyes, moustache, 45 years old, wearing green pants and a sweatshirt.

d) Male Hispanic, 6'4, 195 lbs, blonde hair, 42 years old, wearing green khakis, and a grey sweatshirt.

Question 48

What is the fastest legal route from Queen St west of Baker St to position 5?

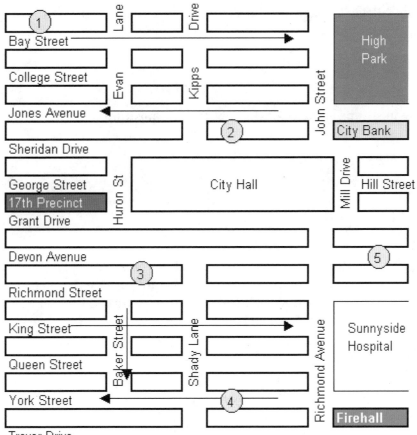

a) Queen to Shady Lane, Shady Lane to Devon, Devon to #5

b) Queen to Baker, Baker to King, King to Richmond, Richmond to Devon, Devon to #5

c) Queen to Richmond, Richmond to Devon, Devon to #5

d) Either A or C

Question 49

You receive a radio call that there is a fire in High Park. You receive the call while you are driving by the 17th Precinct. What is the quickest route there?

a) George to Huron, Huron to Sheridan, Sheridan to John, John to location

b) George to Huron, Huron to Grant, Grant to Mill, Mill to Sheridan, Sheridan to John, John to location

c) George to Huron, Huron to Sheridan, Sheridan to Kipps, Kipps to Jones, Jones to Evan, Evan to College, College to location

d) Either A or B

Question 50

While at position 1 you receive a radio call for a child in danger, hanging from a 4th floor window at position 2 on Jones Ave. Which route would you take?

a) Bay to John, John to Jones, Jones to location

b) Bay to Evan, Evan to College, College to John, John to Jones, Jones to location

c) Bay to Kipps, Kipps to Jones, Jones to location

d) Either A or B

Question 51

Which of the following locations is the easiest to get to from position 4?

a) Huron and George

b) Kipps Dr and Bay

c) City Bank

d) Mill and Hill

Question 52

There are 4 fathers with their children at the mall. The children are ages 1, 2, 3 and 4. It is John's child's birthday. Brian is not the oldest child. Billy welcomed Anne just over a year ago. Ryan's child will be 3 next birthday. Daniel is older than Charlie. Jay's child is the oldest. Charlie is older than Ryan's child. How old is John's child?

a) 1 year old.   b) 2 years old.

c) 3 years old.   d) 4 years old.

Question 53

There are 4 fathers with their children at the mall. The children are ages 1, 2, 3 and 4. It is John's child's birthday. Brian is not the oldest child. Billy welcomed Anne just over a year ago. Ryan's child will be 3 next birthday. Daniel is older than Charlie. Jay's child is the oldest. Charlie is older than Ryan's child. How old is Ryan's child?

a) 1 year old.   b) 2 years old.

c) 3 years old.   d) 4 years old.

Question 54

You are in charge of giving time off to employees in your department. Junior staff members get two weeks off, regular staff members get three weeks off, and senior level members get four weeks off. Team 1 has three regular staff member, one junior staff member and two senior staff members. Team 2 has four regular staff members, two junior staff members and three senior staff members. Which team has more than 20 weeks of time off available?

a) Team 2

b) Team 1.

c) Both Team 1 and 2

d) Neither team.

Question 55

Four types of plants grow in the garden, all during different seasons of the year. Lilies bloom in a season after roses. Ferns bloom before daffodils. Just as roses are dying off for the year, ferns are beginning to grow. All plants have a life span of two seasons. What is the order that the plants grow?

a) Lilies - Daffodils - Roses - Ferns

b) Daffodils – Ferns - Roses – Lilies

c) Roses - Daffodils – Lilies - Ferns

d) Daffodils – Roses – Lilies - Ferns

Question 56

You need to move a head of cabbage, a sheep and a wolf across the river. You can only move one at a time. The sheep will eat the head of cabbage and the wolf will eat the sheep if they are left alone. Which would be the most effective method to move these three across the river?

a) Move in this order: sheep, cabbage, sheep back across, wolf and sheep again.

b) Move in this order: sheep, cabbage and then wolf.

c) Move in this order: wolf, sheep, wolf back across, cabbage and then wolf again.

d) Move in this order: cabbage, sheep and then wolf.

Question 57

You are a new officer, have been working for a week and are assigned to work under a training officer that has 20 years experience. You receive a radio call toward the end of the night for an assault at a local nightclub. Upon arriving at the club, both the complainant and the suspect are on scene. You begin talking to the complainant while your partner speaks to the suspect. There are no visible signs of injury on the complainant. He states that the suspect pushed him and threatened to punch him. Both parties had been drinking. The complainant states that he wants to lay charges.

Which of the following is the best option?

a) Speak with your partner to get further information on the situation.

b) Based on the complaint you received you arrest the suspect for assault and uttering threats.

c) Advise the male to go home, sleep on it, and if he wants to lay charges when he wakes up he can call the police then.

d) Dismiss the allegations as drunken stupor and tell the male to go home.

Question 58

Upon discussing the situation with your partner, he determines that there is no need for police involvement and that the two of you are leaving. You are uncertain and feel that the more aggressive suspect may cause problems when you leave. Your training officer disagrees and begins to leave.

What is your next action?

a) Argue the choice of action while you are still at the nightclub.

b) Make a decision to arrest the suspect on your own, regardless of your partner's opinion.

c) Go along with the more senior officer and leave.

d) Request a sergeant to attend the scene.

Question 59

Upon leaving the nightclub you head into the station for the end of your shift. On the way you hear another radio call come over for the same location of an assault involving the same parties. Another car is dispatched and you are unsure and confused of whether your actions tonight were appropriate.

How would you resolve this uncertainty?

a) Go back to the station and complain to the sergeant about the incident.

b) Let the situation go, and forget about it.

c) Ask your training officer to explain the situation as he saw it, and explain to you why his actions were taken.

d) Insist that you both re-attend the scene to handle the call.

Question 60

While patrolling the neighbourhood in the wintertime you come across a vehicle that has parked in a manner that blocked the street. You have just ordered a tow truck to remove the vehicle and finished writing a parking ticket when a male comes running out the door of a local restaurant. He said that he was just running in to get a coffee quickly.

What is your best option?

a) Yell at the male and point out how inconsiderate he is to other motorists.

b) Allow the male to move the car and apologize for inconveniencing him.

c) Advise the male that his car is going to be impounded and he can pick it up later.

d) Give the male the ticket and instruct him to move his vehicle immediately.

Question 61

You attend a domestic assault call. A neighbour reported that she heard a woman screaming for help, a man yelling very loudly and the sound of furniture being smashed. When officers arrive they discover a woman with visible cuts on her face and blood splatters in the kitchen. The husband states she fell down the stairs and tells you to leave. The woman remains silent and says nothing.

What is the best course of action?

a) Separate the two parties and speak to the woman in private.

b) Leave, as you do not have a warrant to be on their property.

c) Ask the woman in front of the husband if she wants charges laid.

d) Advise the couple that they should not make so much noise and caution them for disturbing the peace.

Question 62

Identify which of the following words is misspelled.

a) incapabel

b) honesty

c) fulfilment

d) engagement

e) none of the above

Question 63

Identify which of the following words is misspelled.

a) distressed

b) whisper

c) vocale

d) licensing

e) none of the above

Question 64

Identify which of the following words is misspelled.

a) municipel

b) monotonous

c) nearby

d) noisy

e) none of the above

Question 65
Identify which of the following words is misspelled.
a) allocate

b) comment

c) peculiar

d) luxurius

e) none of the above

Question 66
Identify which of the following words is misspelled.
a) recommendation

b) mechanecal

c) metropolitan

d) temperature

e) none of the above

Question 67
Identify which of the following words is misspelled.
a) rationale

b) verssion

c) foreseeable

d) accidentally

e) none of the above

Question 68
Identify which of the following words is misspelled.
a) absolute

b) balance

c) composure

d) double

e) none of the above

Question 69
Identify which of the following words is misspelled.
a) furneture

b) independent

c) knocking

d) merit

e) None of the above

Question 70
Identify which of the following words is misspelled.
a) offence

b) petrol

c) propertie

d) recurrence

e) none of the above

Question 71
Identify which of the following words is misspelled.
a) scheme

b) superior

c) unreliable

d) accesory

e) none of the above

Question 72

Identify which of the following words is misspelled.

a) observation

b) mediation

c) justification

d) income

e) none of the above

1)	A		26)	C		53)	B
2)	D		27)	A		54)	A
3)	A		28)	B		55)	D
4)	C		29)	D		56)	A
5)	C		30)	B		57)	A
6)	C		31)	A		58)	C
7)	B		32)	B		59)	C
8)	D		33)	B		60)	D
9)	C		34)	B		61)	A
10)	D		35)	C		62)	A
11)	E		36)	A		63)	C
12)	C		37)	B		64)	A
13)	B		38)	A		65)	D
14)	C		39)	C		66)	B
15)	E		40)	C		67)	B
16)	B		41)	D		68)	E
17)	A		42)	B		69)	A
18)	B		43)	C		70)	C
19)	D		44)	D		71)	D
20)	D		45)	B		72)	E
21)	B		46)	A			
22)	A		47)	A			
23)	C		48)	D			
24)	D		49)	A			
25)	D		50)	C			
			51)	D			
			52)	C			

Percentage	Mark Required
60%	44
65%	47
70%	51
75%	54
80%	58
85%	62
90%	65
95%	69
100%	72

FOR MORE PRACTICE EXAMS, VISIT OUR WEBSITE

Referral Code: ppdc1320   **WWW.POLICEPREP.COM**   1-866-POLICEPREP

Detailed Solutions

Question 26
"Place" should be in the past tense in A. B is missing punctuation marks. D does not make sense.

Question 27
B has a misplaced comma. "Is" should be plural in both C and D.

Question 28
A requires the word "went" instead of "gone". C is missing "and" in the first list. D is missing the word "are".

Question 29
"Bringed" should be "brought" in A. "Come" should be "came" in B and C.

Question 30
"Been" should be "being" in A. C and D do not make sense.

Question 31
"When" is the best answer. If you selected "while", "since" or "although", the sentence wouldn't make sense as the movie could not start if the projector broke down.

Question 32
"Although" is the best answer. The sentence would not make sense if you used any of the other words.

Question 33
The correct answer is the word "but". "Therefore" would be inappropriate because he couldn't make an educated guess because he wasn't certain. "While" and "indeed" would be inappropriate as the sentence would not make sense.

Question 34
A period is required after "in".

Question 35
A period is required after "considered."

Question 36
The 6 hours completed represents 2/6 of the journey. To determine the entire trip you have to multiply the part of the trip completed to the denominator. This number then has to be divided by the numerator. The result is the total length of the trip.

$$\frac{2}{6} = 6 \qquad\qquad 6 \times 6 = 36 \qquad\qquad 36 / 2 = 18 \text{ hours}$$

Question 37
Step 1 – The number or requests processed in June is calculated by multiplying the number of requests in May by the percent that the number dropped. Afterward subtract the two numbers.

1322 x 0.15 = 198   1322 – 198 = 1124 requests in June

Step 2 – To determine the July requests processed, multiply the number of requests in June by the percentage that the number increased. Then add the two numbers.

1124 x 0.17 = 191   1124 + 191 = 1315 requests in July

Question 38
There are 12 babies (4 children x 3 babies = 12). If each baby has 4 toys, then the total number of toys is 12 x 4 = 48.

Question 39
The customer gave the store $40 (2 x $20). Subtract the cost of the product from the amount paid by the customer. $40.00 – 24.07 = $15.93.

Question 40
First determine how much Carlene makes in a week (45 x 8 = $360 / week).Next divide the amount she makes by the total amount she needs for the trip (1440/360 = 4 weeks).

Question 41

First determine the volume of the three containers [3 x 20L = 60L].
Then convert fill rate from mL/s to L/min.
Recall 1L = 1000 mL and 60s = 1 minute.
100 / 1000 x 60 = 6L/min.
Then divide total volume by fill rate [60 / 6 = 10 minutes]

Question 42
Step 1: Determine the total length of the 7-minute per mile run by multiplying a 7-minute per mile pace x 7 miles. (7 x 7 = 49 minutes)

Step 2: Subtract the time of the first two miles from the total, for the amount of time he has left to run. (49 – 12 = 37 minutes remain)

Step 3: Divide 37 minutes by the amount of miles remaining. (37 / 5 = 7.4 minutes per mile)

Question 43
Of the four accounts, Answer C shares more in common with the other three statements. Other witnesses confirm the statements in Answer C.

Question 44
Of the four accounts, Answer D shares more in common with the other three statements. Other witnesses confirm the statements in Answer D.

Question 45
Of the four accounts, Answer B shares more in common with the other three statements. Other witnesses confirm the statements in Answer B.

Question 46
Of the four accounts, Answer A shares more in common with the other three statements. Other witnesses confirm the statements in Answer A.

Question 47
Of the four accounts, Answer A shares more in common with the other three statements. Other witnesses confirm the statements in Answer A.

Question 48

Question 49

Question 50

Question 51

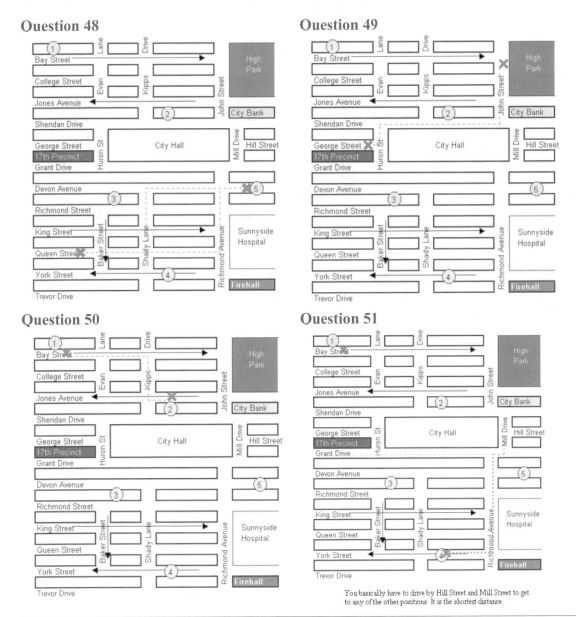

You basically have to drive by Hill Street and Mill Street to get to any of the other positions. It is the shortest distance.

Question 52 and 53
The children are the following ages with the following fathers.

Age	Father	Child
1	Billy	Anne
2	Ryan	Brian
3	John	Charlie
4	Jay	Daniel

Question 54
Team 1 calculations: $(3 \times 3) + (1 \times 2) + (2 \times 4) = 19$ weeks
Team 2 calculations: $(4 \times 3) + (2 \times 2) + (3 \times 4) = 28$ weeks.

Question 55
As roses are dying off, ferns are beginning to grow, so there is a season between roses and ferns: (Ferns - ? - Roses - ? - Ferns). Lilies bloom after roses, and because every plant blooms during a different season, the final order is: (Ferns - Daffodils - Roses - Lilies)

Question 56
Since the sheep cannot be alone with the cabbage and the wolf cannot be alone with the sheep, you must keep them apart. Take the sheep over first, then bring over the cabbage. Because those two cannot be left alone, bring the sheep back over when you go to get the wolf. Take the wolf back since it will not eat the cabbage and can be left alone with it. Then get the sheep.

Question 57
Before making any quick decisions, you should gather as much information as possible about the situation. You have no idea what the other party said to your partner. Talking to your partner would be the most appropriate answer.

Question 58
These situations can be very difficult for new officers. In this case your partner is not doing any illegal activity, but you personally feel that there is a better alternative. Because of your inexperience it would be more prudent to go along with your training officer. The training officer is in a position of responsibility for you and should have more say in how it is handled. By ignoring him, you undermine his credibility and create a less positive working environment. He may be less willing to assist you in the future if you have a poor attitude at the start.

Question 59
Your training officer is there to assist you and help you learn practical aspects of the job. If you are confused about the situation, ask him to explain it. You may have to be diplomatic in this situation so you don't come across as someone who is challenging his decision. Just say you didn't understand it, and ask him to explain it to you so you can learn from him. Letting a confusing situation go unresolved will not benefit you in any way. Asking for help improves his ability to do his job as a training officer and demonstrates that you are capable of asking for help when you need it. Going above his

head to complain to a sergeant should be an absolute last resort, as it will cause major problems with a fellow officer whom you have to work closely with.

Question 60

Part of your duties as a police officer is enforcing the law. The ticket should suffice. Waiting for a tow truck would delay traffic more than allowing him to move the vehicle. It would be unprofessional to begin yelling at the male.

Question 61

The woman may be afraid to speak in front of her husband. Your duty is to protect her from physical harm and continue investigating suspicious circumstances.

Alberta Practice Exam

The APCAT test is divided into two books. You will be required to answer both books at once during actual testing, so it is recommended that you practise both books in one sitting. Questions in Book 2 are based on information in Book 1. The tests are timed and have the following format:

Book 1
no questions – 30 minutes
Book 2
120 questions – 2 hours

You will also be required to take a Written Communication Test. The only materials allowed are pencils and scrap paper. Calculators, books, or counting devices are not allowed. Use a clock or stopwatch to keep track of the time.

Detach the answer key to take the test.

Alberta APCAT Answer Key

Memory Component ✔

	A	B	C	D	
1	○	○	○	○	_____
2	○	○	○	○	_____
3	○	○	○	○	_____
4	○	○	○	○	_____
5	○	○	○	○	_____
6	○	○	○	○	_____
7	○	○	○	○	_____
8	○	○	○	○	_____
9	○	○	○	○	_____
10	○	○	○	○	_____

Reports

	A	B	C	D	
11	○	○	○	○	_____
12	○	○	○	○	_____
13	○	○	○	○	_____
14	○	○	○	○	_____
15	○	○	○	○	_____
16	○	○	○	○	_____
17	○	○	○	○	_____
18	○	○	○	○	_____
19	○	○	○	○	_____
20	○	○	○	○	_____

Spatial Orientation ✔

	A	B	C	D	
21	○	○	○	○	_____
22	○	○	○	○	_____
23	○	○	○	○	_____
24	○	○	○	○	_____
25	○	○	○	○	_____
26	○	○	○	○	_____
27	○	○	○	○	_____
28	○	○	○	○	_____
29	○	○	○	○	_____
30	○	○	○	○	_____

Judgment Section

	A	B	C	D	
31	○	○	○	○	_____
32	○	○	○	○	_____
33	○	○	○	○	_____
34	○	○	○	○	_____
35	○	○	○	○	_____
36	○	○	○	○	_____
37	○	○	○	○	_____
38	○	○	○	○	_____
39	○	○	○	○	_____
40	○	○	○	○	_____
41	○	○	○	○	_____
42	○	○	○	○	_____
43	○	○	○	○	_____
44	○	○	○	○	_____
45	○	○	○	○	_____

Problem Solving ✔

	A	B	C	D	
46	○	○	○	○	_____
47	○	○	○	○	_____
48	○	○	○	○	_____
49	○	○	○	○	_____
50	○	○	○	○	_____
51	○	○	○	○	_____
52	○	○	○	○	_____
53	○	○	○	○	_____
54	○	○	○	○	_____
55	○	○	○	○	_____
56	○	○	○	○	_____
57	○	○	○	○	_____
58	○	○	○	○	_____
59	○	○	○	○	_____
60	○	○	○	○	_____

Memory Component _____ / 10

Report Component _____ / 10

Spatial Orientation _____ / 10

Judgment Component _____ / 15

Problem Solving _____ / 15

Alberta APCAT Answer Key

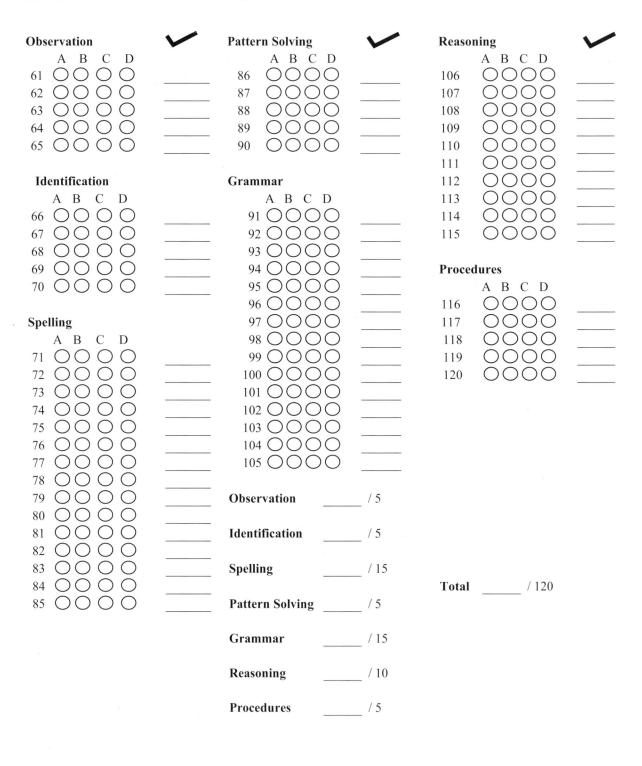

Observation ✔

	A	B	C	D	
61	○	○	○	○	___
62	○	○	○	○	___
63	○	○	○	○	___
64	○	○	○	○	___
65	○	○	○	○	___

Identification

	A	B	C	D	
66	○	○	○	○	___
67	○	○	○	○	___
68	○	○	○	○	___
69	○	○	○	○	___
70	○	○	○	○	___

Spelling

	A	B	C	D	
71	○	○	○	○	___
72	○	○	○	○	___
73	○	○	○	○	___
74	○	○	○	○	___
75	○	○	○	○	___
76	○	○	○	○	___
77	○	○	○	○	___
78	○	○	○	○	___
79	○	○	○	○	___
80	○	○	○	○	___
81	○	○	○	○	___
82	○	○	○	○	___
83	○	○	○	○	___
84	○	○	○	○	___
85	○	○	○	○	___

Pattern Solving ✔

	A	B	C	D	
86	○	○	○	○	___
87	○	○	○	○	___
88	○	○	○	○	___
89	○	○	○	○	___
90	○	○	○	○	___

Grammar

	A	B	C	D	
91	○	○	○	○	___
92	○	○	○	○	___
93	○	○	○	○	___
94	○	○	○	○	___
95	○	○	○	○	___
96	○	○	○	○	___
97	○	○	○	○	___
98	○	○	○	○	___
99	○	○	○	○	___
100	○	○	○	○	___
101	○	○	○	○	___
102	○	○	○	○	___
103	○	○	○	○	___
104	○	○	○	○	___
105	○	○	○	○	___

Reasoning ✔

	A	B	C	D	
106	○	○	○	○	___
107	○	○	○	○	___
108	○	○	○	○	___
109	○	○	○	○	___
110	○	○	○	○	___
111	○	○	○	○	___
112	○	○	○	○	___
113	○	○	○	○	___
114	○	○	○	○	___
115	○	○	○	○	___

Procedures

	A	B	C	D	
116	○	○	○	○	___
117	○	○	○	○	___
118	○	○	○	○	___
119	○	○	○	○	___
120	○	○	○	○	___

Observation ___ / 5

Identification ___ / 5

Spelling ___ / 15

Pattern Solving ___ / 5

Grammar ___ / 15

Reasoning ___ / 10

Procedures ___ / 5

Total ___ / 120

You have 30 minutes to study the following material. You are not allowed to write down any of the information.

Name: Sean Brady
Gender: Male
Age: 26
Eye Colour: Blue
Identifying Features: Scar Upper Back
Crime Wanted For: Drinking and Driving

Name: Michael O'Rielly
Gender: Male
Age: 30
Eye Colour: Green
Identifying Features: Birthmark right knee
Crime Wanted For: Theft

Name: Phil McGrady
Gender: Male
Age: 22
Eye Colour: Brown
Identifying Features: Tattoo Heart left shoulder
Crime Wanted For: Failure to Appear in Court

Name: Aran Hommad
Gender: Male
Age: 19
Eye Colour: Brown
Identifying Features: Scar back neck
Crime Wanted For: Fraud

Property

Make: 2002 Dodge Ram
Colour: Red
License: 998 YRE
Crime: Murder

Silver Bracelet
Lost on Balsam Ave.

Hammer
Found on 14th Ave
Crime Scene

Berretta Replica # 2231829
Stolen from Home Hardware

Information:

Partners Name:	Sharmaine Thomas # 89081
Computer Pass Code:	36 JN 3HL
Station Phone Number:	713 – 1413

Police Codes:

10 – 8	Clear
10 – 4	Acknowledged
10 – 66	Officer Needs Assistance
10 – 98	Bomb Threat

Accident Investigation Procedures:

The following procedures must be adhered to while investigating a traffic accident.

1) Secure the safety of the scene.
2) Call for required back up and emergency personnel.
3) Tend to injured parties in order of seriousness.
4) Record and measure vehicle locations.
5) Note damage to vehicles.
6) Locate the area of impact.
7) Record and note any other physical evidence.
8) Take statements from all witnesses.
9) Notify the sergeant and the detective office.

Use of the Baton:

Police have authority to use force in certain situations such as during the course of an arrest or in self-defence. There are guidelines that must be met before the use of a baton would be authorized. Suspects can't be passively resisting arrest; they must be demonstrating assaulting behaviour. The baton can be used in self-defence and to subdue aggressive suspects. Certain areas must be avoided when swinging the baton. Police officers should aim for delivery areas such as legs and arms when they strike suspects with the baton. Officers should avoid strikes to the head area and spinal column as these strikes could cause serious injury and/or death.

Reports:

When submitting reports, information has to be recorded properly. Inconsistencies between reports can lead to confusion and even the suppression of evidence in court. Keep in mind the following information when you are filling out reports.

1) Dates: yy / mm / dd
   75 / 03 / 12
2) Phone Numbers: area codes + 7 digit numbers
   (313) 555 - 2563
3) Addresses: #, Street, Apt #, city, province
   153 Jones Ave #22, Vancouver, B.C.
4) Report numbers: yy – 5 digit number
   98 - 53431
5) Time: 24 hour clock
   15:36 hrs
6) Insurance Numbers: Must include company name.
   Gecko Ins. – AP5542
7) Final Signature – Rank, Name, Badge, Date
   P.C. Jessop, 5073, 98/02/14

All reports have to be signed off by a sergeant after they have been completed.

DO NOT TURN THE PAGE UNTIL YOU ARE READY TO PROCEED TO BOOK 2.

MEMORY SECTION

Question 1
What object is associated with Balsam Avenue?

A) Replica Berretta   B) Silver Bracelet

C) Hammer   D) Phil McGrady

Question 2
What identifying mark does Aran Hommad have?

A) Scar on neck   B) Birthmark on right knee

C) Tattoo of heart on left shoulder   D) Scar upper back

Question 3
What is the license plate of the Dodge Ram?

A) 713 JNH   B) 141 HLJ

C) 413 EYR   D) 998 YRE

Question 4
What is the phone number of the police station?

A) 712 – 1314   B) 898 - 0812

C) 713 – 1413   D) none of the above

Question 5
Which suspect was not wearing a tie?

A) The 22-year-old   B) The male wanted for Drinking and Driving

C) Michael O'Rielly   D) The man wanted for Fraud

Question 6
What is the code to call for assistance?

A) 10 – 8   B) 10 - 4

C) 10 – 66   D) 10 - 98

Question 7
What is your computer pass code?

A) 89081   B) 33 JL 6 LH

C) 36 JL 3 HN   D) 36 JN 3HL

Question 8
What is true about the Dodge Ram?

A) Dark and involved in a robbery   B) 2002 model and involved in a murder

C) White with a scratch down the side   D) none of the above

Question 9

From where was the Berretta stolen?

A) James Hardware

B) 15 Balsam Avenue

C) 14th Avenue Crime Scene

D) none of the above

Question 10

Who is the oldest suspect?

A) The suspect with green eyes

B) Sean Brady

C) The suspect wanted for Failing to Appear at Court

D) The 26-year-old

Questions 11 – 15 are based on the report below

Report: Missing Person Report	Number: 99 - 339519
Victim (last, first initial): Jessop, Danny M.	Birth Date: 74/22/11
Address: 143 Hammersmith Ave. #22 Elora, Ontario	Phone: 1 (416) 649-4752
Insurance Information: N.A.	
Information: On September 2, 1999 at approximately 3:00 am the victim, Danny Jessop went missing from his home address. There are no suspects or witnesses to the event.	
Completed By: P.C. Rathod #2715 99/09/05	Supervisor: Sgt. Grant #8732 99/09/04

Question 11

Which of the following are errors on the above report?

A) The Report Number

B) The Report Title

C) The Insurance Information

D) Both A and C

Question 12

How should the birth date be written?

A) 1974 / 22 / 11

B) 74 / 22 / 11

C) 11 / 22 / 1974

D) none of the above

Question 13

Which of the following is incorrect on the report?

A) Victim's name   B) Supervisor's signature

C) Address   D) none of the above

Question 14

How should the phone number be written?

A) 1 (416) 649 – 4752   B) 649 - 4752

C) (416) 649 – 4752   D) 649 - 4752 (area code - 416)

Question 15

What is the problem in the information section?

A) Misspelled words   B) The Date

C) The Time   D) Both B and C

Question 16 – 20 are based on the report below

Report: Theft	Number: 98 - 22534
Victim (last, first initial): Sheldon Rodrigues	Birth Date: 76/25/12
Address: 33 Donald Drive Calgary, Alberta	Phone: 698-2241
Insurance Information: Policy # - 52442	
Information: On 98/04/15 at approximately 12:44 hrs the victim had her purse stolen from her by an unknown suspect.	
Completed By: P.C. Jones #7415 98/04/15	Supervisor: Sgt. Morris #832 98/04/15

Question 16

Which of the following boxes were filled in correctly?

A) Report Box   B) Number Box

C) Completed By Box   D) all of the above

Question 17

What time did the theft occur?

A) Just after midnight

B) Just before 01:00 hrs

C) Around lunchtime

D) Both B and C

Question 18

Which date is written incorrectly?

A) Date of the occurrence in the Information section

B) Date the report was completed

C) Birth Date

D) none of the above

Question 19

How many errors were made while filling out this report?

A) 3

B) 4

C) 5

D) 6

Question 20

If you found out that the victim lived in apartment #21, how would you write the address?

A) 33 Donald Drive # 21 Calgary, Alberta

B) #21 33 Donald Drive Calgary, Alberta

C) #21 Donald Drive, Calgary, Alberta

D) none of the above

SPATIAL ORIENTATION

Questions 21 - 25 are based on the map below.

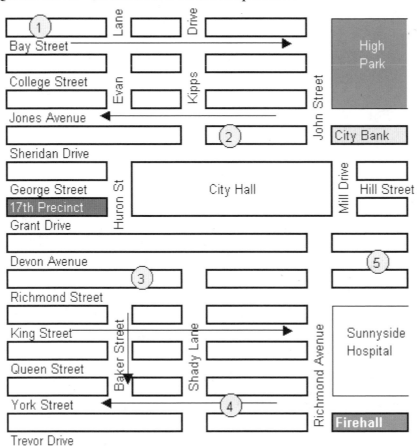

Question 21

You are at the corner of Bay St and John St when you receive a radio call to attend a medical call at a salon located on York Street between Baker St and Shady Lane. What is the fastest legal route to the location?

A) John to Sheridan, Sheridan to Mill, Mill to Grant, Grant to Richmond Ave, Richmond Ave to Richmond St, Richmond St to Baker, Baker to York, York to the location

B) John to Sheridan, Sheridan to Mill, Mill to Grant, Grant to Richmond, Richmond to York, York to the location

C) John to Sheridan, Sheridan to Mill, Mill to Grant, Grant to Richmond, Richmond to King, King to Shady, Shady to York, York to the location

D) John to Sheridan, Sheridan to Mill, Mill to Grant, Grant to Richmond, Richmond to Trevor, Trevor to Shady, Shady to York, York to the location

Question 22

What is the fastest legal route from Queen St west of Baker St to position 5?

A) Queen to Shady Lane, Shady Lane to Devon Ave, Devon Ave to #5

B) Queen to Baker, Baker to King, King to Richmond Ave, Richmond Ave to Devon, Devon to #5

C) Queen to Richmond Ave, Richmond Ave to Devon, Devon to #5

D) Either A or C

Question 23

You receive a radio call that there is a fire in High Park. You receive the call while you are driving by the 17th Precinct. What is the quickest route to High Park?

A) George to Huron, Huron to Sheridan, Sheridan to John, John to the location

B) George to Huron, Huron to Grant, Grant to Mill, Mill to Sheridan, Sheridan to John, John to the location

C) George to Huron, Huron to Sheridan, Sheridan to Kipps, Kipps to Jones, Jones to Evan, Evan to College, College to the location

D) Either A or B

Question 24

While at position 1, you receive a radio call for a child in danger. The child is at position 2 on Jones Ave. Which route should you take?

A) Bay to Evan, Evan to College, College to Kipps, Kipps to Jones, Jones to the location

B) Bay to Evan, Evan to Jones, Jones to the location

C) Bay to Kipps, Kipps to Jones, Jones to the location

D) Either A or B

Question 25

Which of the following locations is the easiest to get to from position 4?

A) Huron St and George St

B) Kipps Dr and Bay St

C) City Bank

D) Mill Dr and Hill St

Question 26

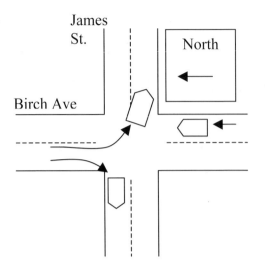

Based on the diagram above, which of the following statements is true?

A) James Street is an east / west street. There are three vehicles travelling near the intersection of Jane Street and Birch Avenue. One vehicle is travelling southbound on Birch Avenue while the other two vehicles are making left and right turns from Birch Avenue to James Street

B) Birch Avenue is a north / south street. There is one vehicle making a left turn from southbound Birch Avenue to eastbound James Street. Another vehicle is travelling northbound on Birch Avenue and the last vehicle is now heading west after turning from Birch Avenue

C) James Street crosses over Birch Avenue and is an east / west street. Birch Avenue is a busier street than James Street and there is one northbound vehicle currently on Birch Avenue. One other vehicle just made a turn from southbound Birch Avenue to eastbound James Street while the last vehicle just completed a right turn from southbound Birch Avenue to westbound James Street

D) James Street crosses over Birch Avenue and is an east / west street. Birch Avenue is a busier street than James Street and there is one northbound vehicle currently on Birch Avenue. One other vehicle just made a turn from southbound Birch Avenue to eastbound James Street while the last vehicle just completed a right turn from southbound Birch Avenue to eastbound James Street

Question 27

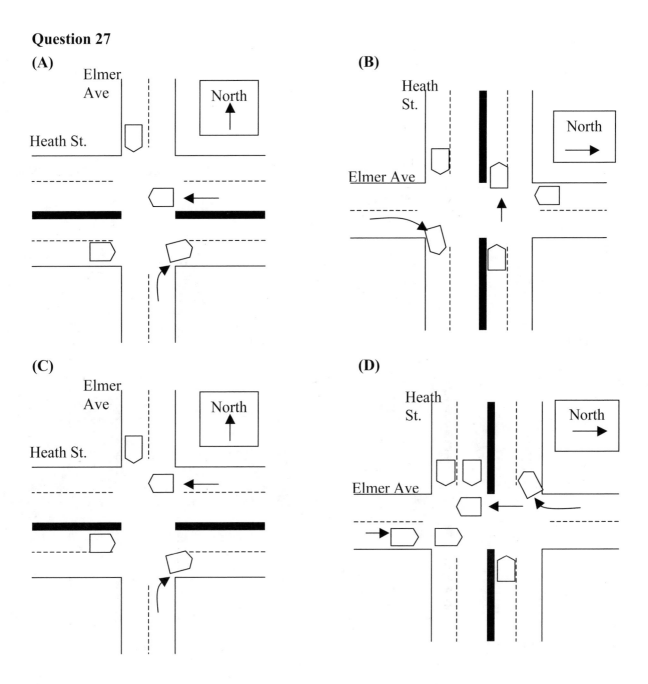

Which of the diagrams above best describes the following scenario?

There is a vehicle travelling westbound on Heath Street in the inside lane. There is a vehicle making a right turn from northbound Elmer Avenue onto Heath Street. There are two stopped vehicles. One is in the southbound lane of Elmer Avenue, while the other is in the outside lane on eastbound Heath Street.

Question 28

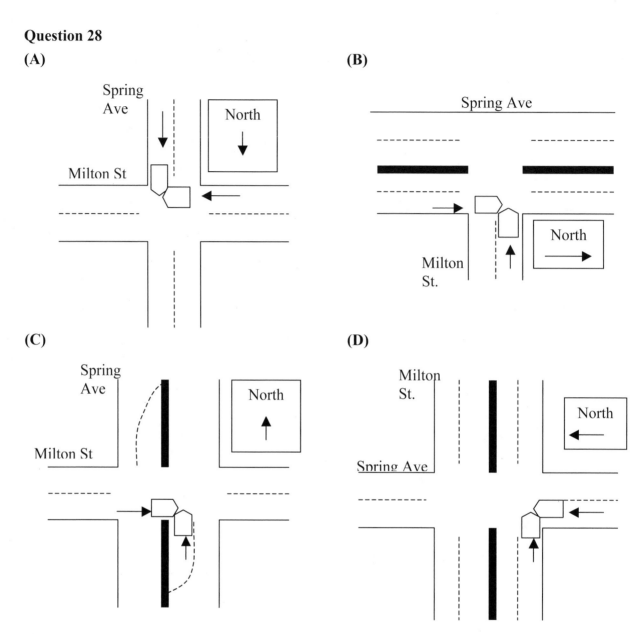

Which of the diagrams above best describes a collision involving a northbound and a westbound vehicle?

Question 29

(A) **(B)**

(C) **(D)**

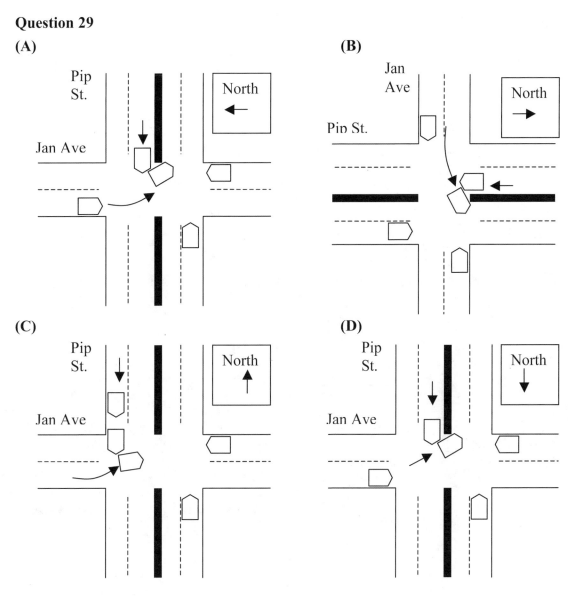

Which of the diagrams above best displays the following scenario?

There is a vehicle stopped northbound on Jan Avenue and eastbound on Pip Street in the outside lane. There is a collision in the northeast intersection of Pip Street and Jan Avenue.

Question 30

(A)

(B)

(C)

(D)

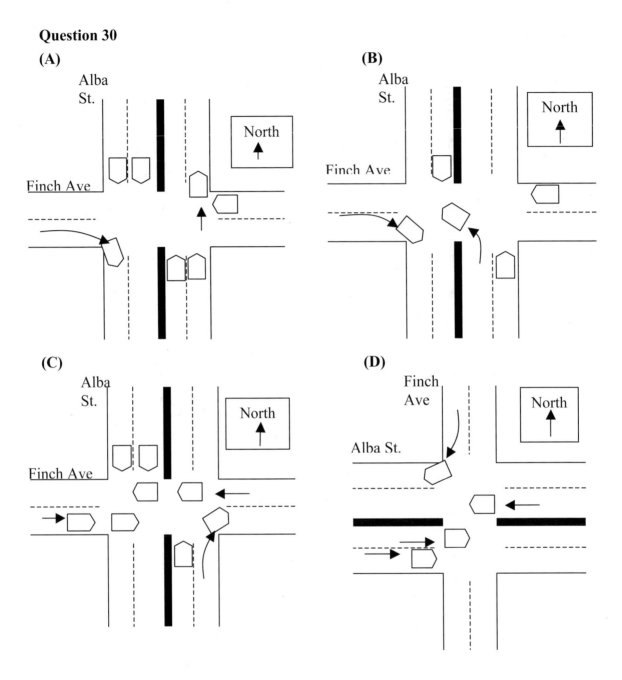

Which of the diagrams above best displays the following scenario?

There is a vehicle turning into the outside lane of Alba Street from Finch Avenue. There is a vehicle travelling in the inside lane of Alba Street going the same direction as the vehicle making the turn.

JUDGEMENT SECTION

Question 31

You have just begun working your day shift and a fellow officer approaches you asking for help with a report that he has to fill out. You are very familiar with the report that the officer needs help with. You were planning on going out on the road to monitor a stop sign at which cars haven't been stopping. Which of the following options should you choose?

A) Delay your activities to assist the officer with the report.

B) Advise the officer that you have to go out now and can't be of assistance at the moment.

C) Do the report yourself as this would be quicker than instructing the officer on how it is done.

D) Inform the sergeant that the officer needs more training.

Question 32

While filling out the report with the officer a call comes over the radio that an officer needs assistance. The location is a thirty second run from the police station. Several units are responding. What decision would you make?

A) Ask the sergeant if you can attend the radio call.

B) Disregard the report for the moment and attend the radio call.

C) Remain in the station with the report, as there are already units on way to the scene.

D) Finish the report quickly and then attend the scene.

Question 33

After the situation has been brought under control several officers on your shift are forced to attend the station to deal with several arrests. There are now fewer officers working on the road. You are back at the station. What should you do?

A) Disregard the report and make yourself available in case another emergency arises.

B) Continue instructing the other officer how to handle the report.

C) Suggest to the officer that both of you should go out for duty and that you will assist with the report before the end of your shift.

D) Offer to help the officers with the paperwork from the arrest.

Question 34

You are working as a police officer on the night shift. While investigating a local drug dealer he provides information to you about a stolen vehicle. You promise that if the information is accurate then you will not charge him. Your partner is watching him while you inspect the vehicle, which is located in an adjacent parking lot. The information is accurate, but there is no one around the vehicle at the moment. You should:

A) Disregard the vehicle, as recovering a stolen vehicle is nothing without an arrest.

B) Charge the drug dealer despite the promise you made to him.

C) Charge the drug dealer with the possession of stolen property as well.

D) Focus your efforts on apprehending the person in possession of the stolen vehicle. Release the drug dealer after you are finished with the investigation.

Question 35

You come across several youths throwing numerous ice cream bars from their car trunk at passing motorists. One of them says he doesn't want to speak to you without a lawyer. The youths have offered no explanation for throwing the ice cream. What should you do?

A) Tell the youth he has no right to a lawyer and force him to talk.

B) Hold the youths and ask dispatch if there had been any thefts in relation to ice cream.

C) Confiscate the ice cream and send the youths on their way. Take down their licence plate number and their personal information.

D) Allow the youths to leave with no action. You have no authority to do anything.

Question 36

You arrive on the scene of a major accident. Paramedics are tending to a female who is severely injured and about to be rushed to the hospital. You are the lead investigator and need a great deal of information. What is the most important action to be taken?

A) Have the injured parties transported to the hospitals immediately for medical aid.

B) Delay the transport of the injured parties to obtain their driving information.

C) Take statements from the injured parties before they are transported.

D) Begin removing the vehicles to clear the roadway and allow traffic flow to resume.

Question 37

You are off-duty at a mall when you observe a woman walking around with money sticking out of her pocket. She doesn't seem to know this and the mall is very crowded. She is speaking to a cashier at the time. What is the most appropriate action?

A) Keep a close eye on the woman to ensure that nothing is stolen from her.

B) Ask the cashier to mention to the lady that her money is visible.

C) Do nothing at all.

D) Inform the woman that her money is hanging out of her pocket.

Question 38

You are investigating a sexual assault from which the suspect has fled. However, he is still believed to be in the area. While preparing a description to broadcast over the air, what are the most important identifying features you should mention?

A) The suspect's habit of heavy drinking.

B) The suspect's height, race, hair colour, weight, and any identifiable facial marks.

C) The suspect's tattoo on his lower left thigh.

D) The victim's information.

Question 39

You are the lead investigator of a failure to remain at the scene of an accident in which the driver was charged with drinking and driving. In order to prepare for trial, you feel that the victim should be put through a photo line-up to identify the suspect. The only opportunity to do this with the victim is at a time when you are scheduled to appear in court for a minor traffic offence. The victim is 8 months pregnant, lives out of town, and is coming out of her way to see you. Your should:

A) Attend court, as it is part of your job, and forget the photo line-up.

B) Order the victim to come in at another time to perform the line-up.

C) Fail to appear at court and see the victim to do the photo line-up.

D) Ask another officer to attend to the victim and perform the photo line-up.

Question 40

During cross-examination at court, the defence attorney asks you a question about an action of yours, which you know was incorrect. How should you respond?

A) Evade the question and give an alternate answer.

B) Refuse to admit your mistake and make up a story to justify your action.

C) Admit your mistake and take accountability for your actions.

D) Ask for a recess to talk to the crown attorney.

Question 41

After the trial the defendant is found not guilty. The victim had testified earlier that week and wasn't in court for the verdict. As a result, she is unaware of the outcome of the trial. What action is most appropriate?

A) Call the victim and inform her of the result of the trial.

B) Wait and see if the victim calls you with interest in the trial; otherwise, leave her alone.

C) Disregard the victim and don't provide any further information.

D) Send a note to the victim accusing the defence attorney of inappropriate actions during the trial, which resulted in the not guilty verdict.

Question 42

You are working as a police officer when a man approaches you stating that his daughter is missing. She was supposed to meet him for lunch an hour ago and failed to show up. She was taking the subway and has never missed an appointment before. The man is visibly upset. How should you respond?

A) Check with the local hospitals and police stations.

B) Tell the man to wait a few hours and call the police if his daughter fails to show up.

C) Obtain a description of the female so that it can be broadcast.

D) Ask the man where he thinks his daughter could be.

Question 43

While performing general patrol you notice that the snow hasn't been cleared from the front of Mrs. Fields' house in a few days. Speaking to her neighbours, you find that they haven't seen her in a few days. She is an elderly woman who doesn't travel and lives alone. Normally, kids in the neighbourhood are paid to remove her snow, but she hasn't been answering the door. What actions are appropriate?

A) Disregard the snow, and follow up later in the week if it hasn't changed.

B) Shovel the sidewalk for Mrs. Fields.

C) Investigate the house. If there is no response enter to make sure she is all right.

D) Knock on the door of the house. If there is no response, leave.

Question 44

While directing traffic at a minor intersection a young woman approaches you stating that there is a man suffering from an apparent heart attack around the corner. What should you do?

A) Inform the woman that you are too busy to leave your station.

B) Leave your traffic point and attempt to verify the health problem around the corner. Notify emergency personnel as required.

C) Remain at your points, but notify dispatch and ask them to send an ambulance.

D) Get information from the woman before proceeding.

Question 45

You pull a vehicle over for failing to stop and the driver of the vehicle alleges that you are only pulling him over because of his race. What is the best response?

A) Let the man off to prove that you are not a racist.

B) Tell the man off and issue him several tickets for his attitude.

C) Ignore the man's response.

D) Inform the man of the reason you are pulling him over and tell him it has nothing to do with his race.

PROBLEM SOLVING

Equipment	1998	1999	2000
Cruisers	14	16	17
Motorcycles	2	3	3
Bicycles	10	14	20

Annual upkeep costs:
Cruisers: $1,400
Motorcycles: $1,500
Bicycles: $ 120

Question 46

What is the total cost of upkeep in the year 2000 for all equipment?

A) $27,600   B) $32,500

C) $30,700   D) $35,400

Question 47

By what percent did the budget for cruisers increase from 1998 to 1999?

A) 15.8%   B) 13.4%

C) 12.9%   D) 14.3%

Question 48

If the number of bicycles increased in 2001 by 50% from the 2000 number, what would be the new annual cost for bicycles?

A) $4,800   B) $3,600

C) $3,000   D) $4,200

Question 49

Constable Jordan arrested a woman for shoplifting outside a department store. The woman was searched and the following property was found.

Item	Value
3 sweaters	$45 each
2 Pairs of Jeans	$50 each
4 T-shirts	$15 each
3 Necklaces	$ 7 each

Which of the following formulas would Constable Jordan use to calculate the total value of the property?

A) 3 + 45 + 2 + 50 + 4 + 15 + 3 + 7

B) 3(45) x 2(50) x 4(15) x 3(7)

C) 3(2) + 4(3) + 45(50) + 15(7)

D) 3(45) + 2(50) + 4(15) + 3(7)

Question 50

Jeff was loading a pallet that could hold up to 250 lbs. He placed 6 balls weighing 20 lbs. each on the pallet followed by 8 cases weighing 15 lbs. each. What percentage of the pallet's capacity has been reached?

A) 87%

B) 90%

C) 93%

D) 96%

Question 51

A man drove for 6 hours. In that time, he managed to complete 2/6 of his journey. What is the total length of his journey?

A) 12 hours

B) 18 hours

C) 24 hours

D) 30 hours

Question 52

There are 24 pizza slices. Mike ate 1/2 of the pizza. Jim ate 4/12 of the pizza. Daren ate the remaining slices. How many slices did Daren eat?

A) 6

B) 8

C) 4

D) 5

Question 53

Sergeant Greaves was tallying the total number of arrests his officers made during the last week of June.

Officer	# of Arrests
Chan	4
Empey	5
Searles	3
McConnel	7
Grant	6

Which of the following formulas would be used to calculate the total number of arrests?

A) 4 x 5 x 3 x 7 x 6   B) 4 + 5 - 3 + 7 - 6

C) 4 + 5 + 3 + 7 + 6   D) 4(5) + 3(7) + 6

Question 54

The President has 48 statues in the White House. Each shelf holds 6 statues. How many shelves are needed to hold all the statues?

A) 8   B) 7

C) 6   D) 5

Question 55

Doug is responsible for filling out insurance requisitions at his office. In May, he was able to process 1,322 requisitions. In June, the number of requisitions completed fell by 15%. In July, he was able to improve on his June numbers by 17%. How many requisitions did Doug complete in July?

A) 1,300   B) 1,315

C) 1,348   D) 1,412

Question 56

Solve for "y". $15 + 3 - 2y = 7y + 3$

A) 1.67   B) 1.85

C) 2.14   D) 3.14

Question 57

Water flows through a damn at a rate of 550 gallons in 12 seconds. How much will flow through in 3 seconds?

A) 137.5 gallons   B) 142.6 gallons

C) 153.8 gallons   D) 170.4 gallons

Question 58

The capacity of a women's shelter is 130. On the coldest night of the year a police officer comes across 6 homeless women. While speaking to the shelter, police are informed that they are at 96.2% occupancy. What will their new occupancy rate be if they accept the 6 women?

A) 97.5%   B) 98.5%

C) 99.5%   D) Over 100%

Question 59

Qlinx spent $36 million on an oil refinery and a transport tanker. The price of the refinery was twice the price of the tanker. How much did Qlinx pay for the refinery?

A) $12 million   B) $18 million

C) $24 million   D) $30 million

Question 60

Cadet Johnson was ordered to retrieve 150 arrest information books, 4 boxes containing 50 summons books, and 2 boxes containing 20 parking ticket books. Which of the following formulas would Johnson use to calculate the total number of books that he needed to retrieve?

A) 100 + 50 + 2 + 20 + 50 + 4   B) 2(150) + 2(20) + 4(50)

C) 2(20) + 150 + 4(50)   D) 150 + 20 + 50 x 2 x 4

OBSERVATION

Question 61

How many differences are there between the following pictures?

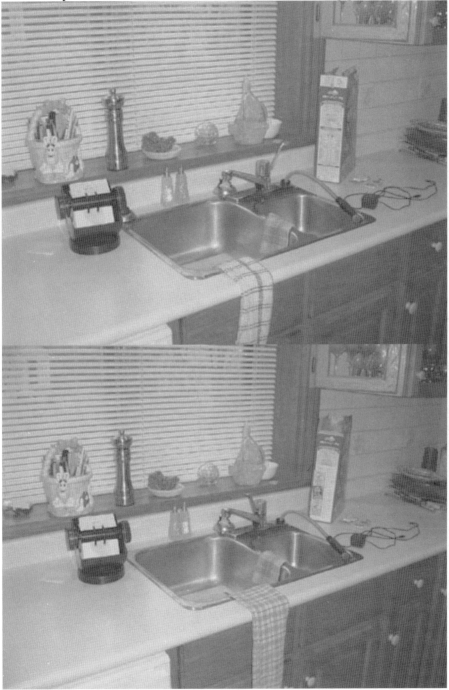

A) 3   B) 4

C) 5   D) 6

Question 62

How many differences are there between the following pictures?

A) 4   B) 5

C) 6   D) 7

Question 63

How many differences are there between the following pictures?

A) 1   B) 3

C) 5   D) 7

Question 64

How many differences are there between the following pictures?

A) 6

B) 7

C) 8

D) 9

Question 65

How many differences are there between the following pictures?

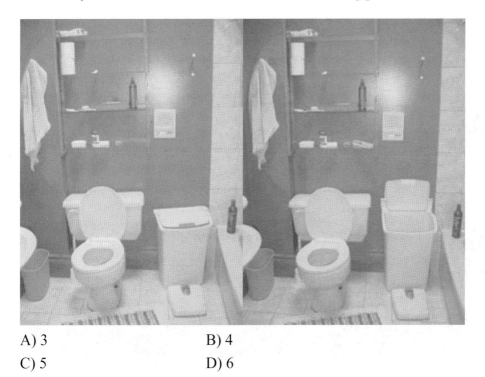

A) 3

B) 4

C) 5

D) 6

Question 66

Which of the following people matches this suspect?

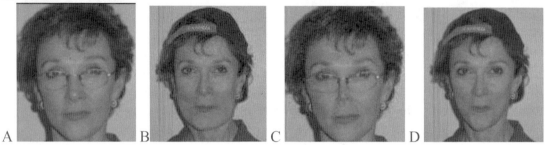

Question 67

Which of the following people matches this suspect?

Question 68

Which of the following people matches this suspect?

A   B   C   D

Question 69

Which of the following people matches this suspect?

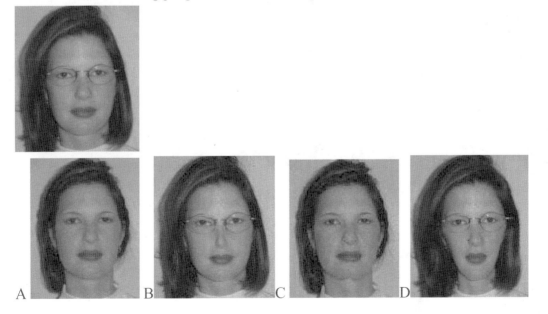

A   B   C   D

Question 70

Which of the following people matches this suspect?

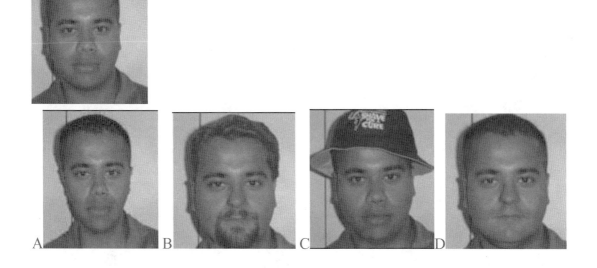

SPELLING

Question 71

Which of the following words is misspelled?

A) Reduction

B) Synthisise

C) Conversion

D) Definition

Question 72

Which of the following words is misspelled?

A) Inferior

B) Maintenance

C) Bigotry

D) Substenance

Question 73

Which of the following words is misspelled?

A) Recieve

B) Regime

C) Nocturnal

D) Nourishment

Question 74

Which of the following words is misspelled?

A) Comrade

B) Presure

C) Celebrations

D) Dependence

Question 75

Which of the following words is misspelled?

A) Coincidense

B) Deception

C) Remarkable

D) Occurrence

Question 76

Which of the following words is misspelled?

A) Aggression

B) Indifferent

C) Malevolant

D) Sequence

Question 77

Which of the following words is misspelled?

A) Preposition

B) Modifiing

C) Character

D) Description

Question 78

Which of the following words is misspelled?

A) Downsized

B) Oust

C) Compenssation

D) Rationalize

Question 79

Which of the following words is misspelled?

A) Transferred   B) Nuatical

C) Undergo   D) Competencies

Question 80

Which of the following words is misspelled?

A) Multicultural   B) Ethnisities

C) Emergencies   D) Prevalent

Question 81

Which of the following words is misspelled?

A) Zealus   B) Patient

C) Obsession   D) Passive

Question 82

Which of the following words is misspelled?

A) Platonic   B) Incestuous

C) Cultivate   D) Pasionate

Question 83

Which of the following words is misspelled?

A) Psychiatrists   B) Counseling

C) Inherrent   D) Encountering

Question 84

Which of the following words is misspelled?

A) Liason   B) Awe

C) Intermediate   D) Kindergarten

Question 85

Which of the following words is misspelled?

A) Paramilitary   B) Specialized

C) Millitia   D) Separation

PATTERN SOLVING

Question 86

Solve the following pattern by choosing the next three letters or numbers.

B, G, E, J, H, M ...

A) K, P, O

B) L, Q, O

C) K, P, N

D) N, L, R

Question 87

Solve the following pattern by choosing the next two letters or numbers.

E, J, O, ...

A) T, Y

B) V, Z

C) R, Z

D) S, X

Question 88

Solve the following pattern by choosing the next two letters or numbers.

1, 2, 4, 8, 16, ...

A) 24, 32

B) 18, 22

C) 32, 64

D) 30, 60

Question 89

Solve the following pattern by choosing the next three letters or numbers.

A, F, D, B, G, E, C, H, ...

A) D, F, J

B) F, D, I

C) M, K, I

D) K, I, M

Question 90

Solve the following pattern by choosing the next two letters or numbers.

1, 2, 4, 7, 11, 16, ...

A) 20, 27

B) 22, 29

C) 25, 35

D) 23, 30

In the following fifteen questions, choose the sentence that is most clearly written.

Question 91

A) The two police officers searched the building and than headed out back to investigate the surrounding area for clues to the crime.

B) The two police officers searched the building, than headed out back to investigate the surrounding area for clues to the crime.

C) The two police officers searched the building and then headed out back to investigate the surrounding area for clues to the crime.

D) The two police officers searched the building. Then headed out back to investigate the surrounding area for clues to the crime.

Question 92

A) Since he was arrested for assault he had been having a hard time convincing his wife that he wasn't a violent man.

B) He was arrested for assault since he had been having a hard time convincing his wife that he wasn't a violent man.

C) Since he was arrested for assaulting he had been having a hard time convincing his wife that he wasn't a violent man.

D) He had been having a hard time convincing his wife that he wasn't a violent man; since he was arrested for assault.

Question 93

A) Judge Winters was definitely the fairer judge between the five Supreme Court justices.

B) Judge Green was the fairest of the five Supreme Court Justices.

C) Of the five Supreme Court Justices, judge Green was the fairest.

D) Both B and C are correct.

Question 94

A) I couldn't believe how quickly the gang of thieves broke into the house. My partner and I was absolutely shocked.

B) I couldn't believe how quickly the gang of thieves broke into the house. We were absolutely shocked.

C) I could not believe how quickly the gang of thieves broke into the house. My partner and I, we were absolutely shocked.

D) I couldn't believe how quickly the gang of thieves broke into the house. My partner and I were absolutely shocked.

Question 95

A) It's going to be really hard to get the evidence admitted into court. The bag and all of its contents were seized without a warrant.

B) Its going to be really hard to get the evidence admitted into court. The bag and all of its contents were seized without a warrant.

C) Its going to be really hard to get the evidence admitted into court. The bag and all of it's contents were seized without a warrant.

D) It's going to be really hard to get the evidence admitted into court. The bag and all of it's contents were seized without a warrant.

Question 96

A) Two of the witnesses were to frightened to testify against the suspect.

B) Two of the witnesses were to frightened too testify against the suspect.

C) To of the witnesses were to frightened too testify against the suspect.

D) Two of the witnesses were too frightened to testify against the suspect.

Question 97

A) When the officers arrived at the complainants house, a woman was yelling very loud.

B) When the officers arrived at the complainants house, a woman was yelling very loudly.

C) A woman was yelling very loudly when the officers arrived at the house of the complainant.

D) Both B and C are correct.

Question 98

A) "You and me should consider going to the hockey game tonight, if we can get tickets," Steve said to John.

B) Sergeant Stevens assigned the shoplifting call to John and me, as I was the only clear unit.

C) Sergeant Stevens assigned the shoplifting call to John and I, as we were the only clear unit.

D) None of the phrases are grammatically correct.

Question 99

A) I collected the papers that were required for court from the legal clerk.

B) From the legal clerk, I collected the papers, from that clerk that I required for court.

C) I collected off the legal clerk, the papers that I required for court.

D) None of the phrases are grammatically correct.

Question 100

A) Who is to say, which test tube contains the greater number of liquid nitrogen?

B) The amount of jackets in the coat check greatly exceeded fifty.

C) The amount of people at the board meeting was ten.

D) The number of beer bottles in the case was twenty-four.

Question 101

A) Jamal was extremely upset when the witness recanted her testimony at court, he went back the prosecutor's office and asked that she be charged with perjury.

B) Jamal went back the prosecutor's office and asked that she be charged with perjury, he was extremely upset when the witness recanted her testimony at court.

C) Jamal was extremely upset when the witness recanted her testimony at court, so he went back the prosecutor's office and asked that she be charged with perjury.

D) Jamal was extremely upset when the witness recanted her testimony at court, although he went back the prosecutor's office and asked that she be charged with perjury.

Question 102

A) Kalpesh was waiting to hear from the suspect, but didn't expect to get much information from him.

B) While Darlene was waiting to testify but having a difficult time recollecting the events in the proper order.

C) Shayna, chasing the fleeing suspect down a dark alley in the middle of the night.

D) Kevin, while driving through a dark alley looking for suspects, he thought the suspect was nearby.

Question 103

A) Michael will tend to the victims of the bank robbery, before canvassing surrounding businesses to see if they witnessed anything.

B) Michael will attend to the victims of the bank robbery. Afterward he will canvas surrounding businesses to see if they witnessed anything.

C) Michael will attend to the victim's of the bank robbery, before canvassing surrounding businesses to see if they witnessed anything.

D) Michael will tend to the victims of the bank robbery. Afterwards, he will canvas surrounding businesses to see if they witness anything.

Question 104

A) Officer Cooper was about to loose his patience with the driver of the vehicle. Only one of the driver's three children had a seatbelt on, and that belt was very loose.

B) Officer Cooper was about to lose his patience with the driver of the vehicle. Only one of the driver's three children had a seatbelt on, and that belt was very loose.

C) Officer Cooper was about to lose his patience with the driver of the vehicle. Only one of the driver's three children had a seatbelt on, and that belt was very lose.

D) Officer Cooper was about to loose his patience with the driver of the vehicle. Only one of the driver's three children had a seatbelt on, and that belt was very lose.

Question 105

A) One aspect of the job that officers find hard to bare, are domestic violence, wife assault and child abuse.

B) One aspect of the job that officers find hard to bear is domestic violence, such as wife assault and child abuse.

C) One aspect of the job that officers find hard to bare is domestic violence such as wife assault and child abuse.

D) One aspect of the job that officers find hard to bear, are domestic violence, wife assault and child abuse.

Reasoning

Question 106

Police officers are required to investigate matters and question suspects, witnesses and victims. Below is a list of acceptable and unacceptable questions.

Acceptable	Unacceptable
What happened?	Did you see him steal the wallet?
Where were you going?	Were you going home at the time?
How did you feel?	Did you feel angry?

The primary reason why questions are categorized this way is because:

A) The acceptable ones are less personal and intrusive.

B) The acceptable ones are more powerful.

C) The unacceptable ones lead the interviewee to conclusions that they may not otherwise be thinking.

D) The unacceptable ones may anger the interviewee.

Question 107

While operating a radar speed-measuring device the following elements are required for court testimony:

1) Perform checks on the unit prior to use to ensure accuracy.
2) Perform checks periodically while operating the machine.
3) Perform a check at the end of use.

Which of the following generalities can be inferred from the information above?

A) Courts need to ensure that the unit was functioning properly at the time that the speed was measured.

B) Courts are too demanding on police officers.

C) Courts do not trust radar manufacturers.

D) Courts do not trust officers.

Question 108

Police are trained to investigate all of the factors below when in charge of a motor vehicle collision investigation.

1) Pre-Driving events – events prior to the beginning of the trip.
2) Events during the trip – any situations that arose while driving before the accident.
3) Point of possible sighting – when a normal person may perceive a hazard.
4) Point of actual sighting – when the driver actually witnessed the hazard.
5) The Reaction Point and Time – how the driver reacted to the situation.

Which of the following generalities can be inferred from the information above?

A) Police need more training on accident investigation.

B) Police have been performing inadequate investigations prior to this course.

C) Police need to consider events prior to the accident as relevant to the investigation.

D) All of the above.

Question 109

There can be several parties to an offence. They can include:

1) **Committer** – the person who commits the offence.
2) **Aider** – this person doesn't have to be present at the time of the offence, but has to do something that assists the committer perform the act. (an example would be leaving a safe unlocked)
3) **Abettor** – has to be present and encourages or instigates the offence.
4) **Counsellor** – talks another person into committing an offence.

Which of the following generalities can be inferred from the information above?

A) As an officer you have to determine all parties of the offence before laying charges.

B) You may lay charges against more than one party when you investigate an offence.

C) Abetting is a more serious offence than counselling.

D) Both B and C.

Question 110

While being trained on how to operate a radar speed-measuring device you are told the following can interfere with obtaining an accurate reading.

1) Other vehicles in the area.
2) Your own heater or air conditioner fan.
3) Hydro lines.
4) Water (rain, snow, etc).
5) Mobile radio transmissions.

Which of the following generalities can be inferred from the information above?

A) These are precautions you should take before selecting a site to set.

B) Your instructor is pointing out the limitations of radar and doesn't support its use.

C) There are other factors that will also interfere with radar speed-measuring units.

D) Both A and C.

Question 111

Police officers are required to investigate matters and question suspects, witnesses and victims. Below is a list of acceptable and unacceptable questions.

Acceptable	Unacceptable
What happened?	Did you see him steal the wallet?
Where were you going?	Were you going home at the time?
How did you feel?	Did you feel angry?

Which of the following is an acceptable question?

A) Did Johnny cut you with a kitchen knife?

B) Was it Billy that stole your computer?

C) What happened when you entered the apartment?

D) None of the above

Question 112

Police have a variety of tools at their disposal, including pepper spray. Police are taught to use pepper spray to:

      1) Distract suspects.
      2) Disorient suspects.
      3) Disrupt activities of suspects.
      4) Disperse illegal groups or gatherings.
      5) Disable violent suspects.

Which of the following is an appropriate use of pepper spray?

A) Officer Gordon was interrogating a suspect who was refusing to cooperate. Officer Gordon sat his pepper spray down on the table in a threatening gesture and continued the interrogation.

B) Constable Glen was working an illegal poverty protest when he came across some unattended sleeping bags. He took out his pepper spray and used it on the sleeping bags.

C) Constable Johnson got a call to attend a dispute involving two neighbours. Arriving to find the neighbours arguing, he took out his pepper spray to break up the fight.

D) Officer Jones was investigating a suspect when the suspect raised his hands as if to fight. Jones immediately pepper sprayed him in the face.

Question 113

Hearsay evidence is any evidence that another person tells a witness. It is generally inadmissible in court, but there are exceptions to the hearsay rule.

      1) If it was said during the offence by anyone closely connected to the offence.
      2) If the statement was said within earshot and in the presence of the accused.
      3) If it is a statement by the accused.
      4) If the evidence is proven reliable, it may be admissible if there is an extenuating circumstance (example: witness dies, very young children, etc.).

Which of the following statements would be admissible in court?

A) Jill Kennedy screamed "Die you bastard" as she stabbed the victim in the chest. Two witnesses heard the statement.

B) In the middle of a bank robbery two witnesses say they heard the deceased victim scream out "Please don't kill me!" as the robbers shot her.

C) A 4-year-old child told her teacher that her father beat her. A doctor's examination later revealed evidence that the child was beaten.

D) All of the above.

Question 114

As a police officer, you must follow special rules when dealing with young people. If you arrest a juvenile you have to:

    1) Notify a parent as soon as possible either verbally or in writing.
    2) When a juvenile is released with a court date you must provide information to the parent about the court date.
    3) Provide information to another adult relative if the parent isn't available.
    4) Inform the young person's spouse if he or she is married.

Which of the following actions would be appropriate as a police officer?

A) Constable Chase arrested a 15-year-old woman for shoplifting and released her on the scene. When he got back to the station he mailed a letter to her parents with the relevant court date.

B) Mail a letter to a parent about the arrest of a 13-year-old suspect for robbery.

C) When you arrest a 14-year-old suspect for arson, you are unable to contact his parents. You leave a message with his high school friend.

D) An officer brings in a 15-year-old for assault. The youth tells the officer that he doesn't want to call anyone, including his parents. The officer respects his wishes.

Question 115

As a police officer, you cannot arrest someone unless you have grounds to believe that any one of the following conditions is met:

    1) Concern the offender will repeat the offence.
    2) The suspect's identity is unknown.
    3) The accused may not appear in court.
    4) You are attempting to preserve or secure evidence.

Which of the following is a legal arrest?

A) Constable Starling brought Sean Colvin into the station on a charge of theft because he was verbally abusive and rude.

B) Kalpesh was arrested and brought back to the station because he refused to provide his last name to the officers.

C) James Cagney was arrested for heroin trafficking and brought back to the station because of a neighbourhood clean up project.

D) None of the above.

Procedures

Question 116

What is your primary task when you arrive at an accident scene?

A) Treat injured parties

B) Talk to witnesses

C) Ensure the safety of the area

D) All of the above

Question 117

Which of the following is not a listed procedure for accident investigations?

A) Note damage to vehicles

B) Take witness statements

C) Relay information to your sergeant

D) Impound suspect vehicles

Question 118

Which action should be taken first?

A) Treat injured parties

B) Locate the impact area

C) Take statements

D) Record vehicle locations

Question 119

Which of the following actions would be justified according to the information on the "Use of the Baton"?

A) Striking a suspect in the arm who raises his fists and prepares to fight.

B) Striking a protester in the arm at a university sit-in.

C) Striking a suspect in the leg who is attempting to kick you.

D) Both A and C.

Question 120

Given the tone of the "Use of the Baton" article, which of the factors below would have to be considered before using the baton on a suspect?

A) The age of the suspect

B) Any disabilities the suspect has

C) The actions of the suspect

D) All of the above

Memory Component	
1)	B
2)	A
3)	D
4)	C
5)	A
6)	C
7)	D
8)	B
9)	D
10)	A
Reports	
11)	A
12)	D
13)	B
14)	C
15)	D
16)	D
17)	C
18)	C
19)	B
20)	A
Spatial Orientation	
21)	B
22)	D
23)	A
24)	C
25)	D
26)	B
27)	A
28)	B
29)	A
30)	D

Judgement Section	
31)	A
32)	B
33)	C
34)	D
35)	B
36)	A
37)	D
38)	B
39)	D
40)	C
41)	A
42)	D
43)	C
44)	B
45)	D
Problem Solving	
46)	C
47)	D
48)	B
49)	D
50)	D
51)	B
52)	C
53)	C
54)	A
55)	B
56)	A
57)	A
58)	D
59)	C
60)	C

Observation	
61)	C
62)	D
63)	A
64)	C
65)	A
Identification	
66)	D
67)	B
68)	C
69)	A
70)	C
Spelling	
71)	B
72)	D
73)	A
74)	B
75)	A
76)	C
77)	B
78)	C
79)	B
80)	B
81)	A
82)	D
83)	C
84)	A
85)	C
Pattern Solving	
86)	C
87)	A
88)	C
89)	B
90)	B

Grammar	
91)	C
92)	A
93)	B
94)	D
95)	A
96)	D
97)	C
98)	D
99)	A
100)	D
101)	C
102)	A
103)	B
104)	B
105)	B
Reasoning	
106)	C
107)	A
108)	C
109)	B
110)	A
111)	C
112)	D
113)	D
114)	A
115)	B
Procedures	
116)	C
117)	D
118)	A
119)	D
120)	D

Mark	Percentage		Mark	Percentage
85	70.1%		105	87.5%
90	75%		110	91.7%
95	79.2%		115	95.8%
100	83.3%		120	100%

Detailed Solutions

Reports

Question 11 – 15

Report: Missing Person Report	Number: **99 - 339519** 5 digit max
Victim (last, first initial): Jessop, Danny M.	Birth Date: 74/22/11 **74 / 11 / 22**
Address: 143 Hammersmith Ave. #22 Elora, Ontario	Phone: **1 (416) 649-4752** (416) 649-4752
Insurance Information: N.A.	
Information:

On **September 2, 1999** at approximately **3:00 am** the victim, Danny Jessop went missing from his home address. There are no suspects or witnesses to the event. | |
| **The date and time aren't written correctly.** | |
| Completed By: P.C. Rathod #2715 99/09/05 | Supervisor: Sgt. Grant #8732 **99/09/04** |

Can't sign before completed

(A,D,B,C,D)

Question 16 - 20

Report: Theft	Number: 98 - 22534
Victim (last, first initial): **Sheldon Rodrigues**	Birth Date: **76/25/12**
Address: 33 Donald Drive **#21** Calgary, Alberta	Phone: **698-2241**
Insurance Information: Policy # - 52442	
Information:

On 98/04/15 at approximately **12:44 hrs** the victim had her purse stolen from her by an unknown suspect. | |
| **12:44 hrs is 12:44 in the afternoon.** | |
| Completed By: P.C. Jones #7415 98/04/15 | Supervisor: Sgt. Morris #832 98/04/15 |

(D,C,C,B,A)

Spatial Orientation

Question 21

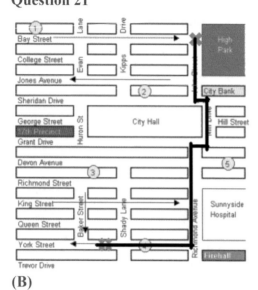

(B)

Question 22

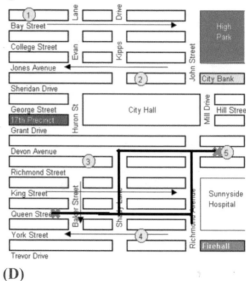

(D)

Question 23

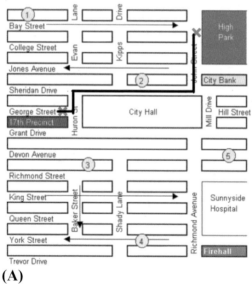

(A)

Question 24

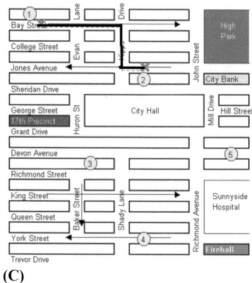

(C)

Question 25

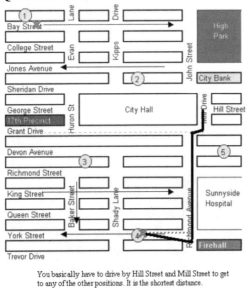

You basically have to drive by Hill Street and Mill Street to get to any of the other positions. It is the shortest distance.

(D)

Question 26

B – Option A is incorrect because it states there is a vehicle travelling southbound on Birch Avenue when there clearly is not. Option C and D are both incorrect because it makes an assumption not supported by the diagram. There is no evidence that Birch Avenue is a busier street than James Street. You cannot reach that conclusion from the diagram above. Option D is also incorrect about the right turn from southbound Birch Avenue to eastbound James Street. Option B is the best answer.

Question 27

A – Answer B is not the best answer because there are actually five cars in the diagram, while only four are mentioned in the scenario. Option C is incorrect because the vehicle travelling westbound would be in the wrong lane (outside lane) and the vehicle stopped on Heath Street would also be in the wrong lane (inside lane). Option D also contains too many vehicles and fails to match the description of the scenario on several levels. Option A is the best choice.

Question 28

B – Option A is inaccurate as the vehicle on Spring Avenue is heading north, but the vehicle on Milton Street is heading east. Option C is incorrect because the vehicle on Spring Avenue is heading north, but the vehicle on Milton Street is heading east. Option D is also incorrect as the vehicle on Spring Avenue is heading north, but the vehicle on Milton Street is heading east as well. Option B is the only correct answer.

Question 29

A – Options B and C are incorrect as the accidents in these cases would be in the northwest corner of the intersection. Option D is incorrect as the accident takes place in the southeast corner of the intersection. Option A is the answer.

Question 30
D – Option C can be eliminated immediately as there are no vehicles making a turn onto Alba Street. Options A and B can be eliminated as the remaining vehicles on Alba Street going in the same direction are not moving. Option D is the answer.

Judgement Section

Question 31
Delay your activities to assist the officer with the report. **(A)**

Developing others is one of the key competencies of a police officer. By failing to help the officer, or by doing the report yourself, the other officer will not learn how to complete the task. If you take the time now, the officer will become self-reliant and will also be in a position to assist other officers if the need arises. Cooperation is another key competency. Police officers require each other not just in emergencies but also to understand other important aspects of the job through information sharing and mentoring. Work Organization is also a key competency, and although it is not an option here, another good answer is to provide the officer with a copy of your report that you have personally stored for future reference, along with instructions on how it should be filed. (Developing your own personal procedural manual is very effective.).

Question 32
Disregard the report for the moment and attend the radio call. **(B)**

Concern for safety is a key competencies for a police officer. This includes your safety, the safety of your fellow officers, and the public. Although there are other units responding, the scenario specifically says that the location is extremely close and you may be the first person to get there. Initiative is also a key competency and, in emergency situations like this, initiative would be required.

Question 33
Suggest to the officer that both of you should go out for duty and that you will assist with the report before the end of your shift. **(C)**

This answer demonstrates several key competencies.
1) Concern for safety - with so many officers tied up in the station, there is a lack of manpower if something else happens.
2) Initiative - it is highly that a supervisor who found you working on the report would order you out on the road. As an officer, you must be able to make the proper decisions without supervision.
3) Cooperation and Developing Others – this would also apply for the same reasons outlined in answer # 1.

Question 34
Focus your efforts on apprehending the person in possession of the stolen vehicle. Release the drug dealer after you are finished with the investigation. **(D)**

When attaining information from informants it is important that you keep your word. If you don't it will be difficult to get information later. The stolen vehicle is more important to you than the original drug charge, otherwise you wouldn't have made the deal. You should keep the dealer until the investigation is over to prevent him from alerting the car thief.

Question 35
Hold onto the youths and ask dispatch if there have been any thefts lately involving ice cream. **(B)**

This scenario is difficult without an understanding of police powers. The situation should be investigated immediately, and you should seek more information before making any major decisions such as releasing suspects or forcing confessions. The next best source of information is your dispatcher.

Question 36
Have the victims transported to the hospitals immediately for medical aid. **(A)**

Your number one priority is the preservation of life.

Question 37
Inform the woman that her money is hanging out of her pocket. **(D)**

This is the most direct and efficient means of alerting the woman that she has exposed money that could be easily stolen.

Question 38
The suspect's height, race, hair colour, weight, and any identifiable facial marks. **(B)**

Officers will be looking for the male in the area. If you provide the above description they will have a greater chance of apprehending the male. Identifying marks that are covered are useless, description of the victim is irrelevant, and habits may not be quickly observable.

Question 39
Ask another officer to attend to the victim and the photo line-up. **(D)**

Work Organization and Cooperation are both exhibited with this decision. Policing is about working together as a team. You are required for court and should attend. There is no reason another officer can't perform the photo line-up. This allows you to perform all the tasks that are required.

Question 40
Admit your mistake and take accountability for your actions. **(C)**

Integrity is an important component of being a police officer. If you made a mistake and admit to it there is nothing that a defence lawyer can do to you. Lying under oath should not be considered.

Question 41
Call the victim and inform her of the result of the trial. **(A)**

Work Organization and Initiative competencies are demonstrated by taking the time to call the witnesses and inform them of the situation. This event impacted their life, and they have a right to know the outcome.

Question 42
Ask the man where he thinks his daughter could be. **(D)**

You must not act too hastily in this situation. The daughter has only been absent an hour. You should make sure she is missing before obtaining a description or beginning a search.

Question 43
Investigate the house and, if there is no response, enter the house to make sure she is all right. **(C)**

Police are required to investigate suspicious incidents and preserve life. An elderly woman living alone could be in serious danger if she fell and hurt herself. This warrants immediate action on your part to ensure that she is safe inside.

Question 44
Leave your traffic point and attempt to verify the health problem around the corner. Notify emergency personnel as required. **(B)**

Your number one priority is the preservation of life. Once you attend the scene and confirm there is a man in need of medical attention you would begin to assist and call for the paramedics.

Question 45
Inform the man of the reason you are pulling him over and tell him it has nothing to do with his race. **(D)**

Allegations such as this are best handled by immediately confronting them and should not impair you in the course of your duties. Once you explain why you stopped the vehicle, you should continue your duties.

Problem Solving
Question 46
This question requires multiplication and addition. Multiply the number of vehicles by their costs and add them together for the total.

Cruisers	17 x $ 1,400	= $ 23,800
Motorcycles	3 x $ 1,500	= $ 4,500
Bicycles	20 x $120	= $ 2,400
		$30,700 **(C)**

Question 47
Step 1: Determine the size of the increase in budget between 1998 and 1999 for cruisers.

1998	14 x $1,400 = $19,600	$ 2 2, 4 0 0
1999	16 x $1,400 = $22,400	- $ 1 9, 6 0 0
		$ 2, 8 0 0

Step 2: To determine the percentage of the increase, divide the amount of the increase ($2,800) by the original budget ($19,600).

$$1 9 6 0 0 \overline{) 2 8 0 0.0 0 0 0} \quad 0.1 4 2 8 \text{ rounds to } 0.143 \text{ or } 14.3\% \textbf{ (D)}$$

Question 48
Step 1: Calculate the number of bicycles there would be with a 50% increase. Multiply the current number of bicycles by 50% and add this number to the existing number of 20.

$$20 \times 0.50 = 10 \qquad \text{then} \qquad 10 + 20 = 30$$

Step 2: Multiply the projected number of bicycles in 2001 (30) by the costs allocated to them ($120).

$$\$120 \times 30 = \$3,600 \textbf{ (B)}$$

Question 49
To answer these questions correctly it is extremely important to understand the order of operations. If you have any problems with these types of questions, review the math teaching material and focus on the order of operation.

To find the total value of the stolen property, add all of the articles together. There are several ways this can be stated mathematically. One option is to individually add up all articles (remember there are 3 sweaters, 2 pairs of jeans, etc.).

$$45 + 45 + 45 + 50 + 50 + 15 + 15 + 15 + 15 + 7 + 7 + 7 = \$316$$

Another option is to group like terms and multiply. Once the like terms are multiplied together, add all of the like terms to get the solution. There are three $45 value items, which can be written 3 x 45, or 3 (45).

$$3(45) + 2(50) + 4(15) + 3(7) = \$316 \textbf{ (D)}$$

Question 50

This is a two-step problem solved by determining the total weight that has been placed on the pallet, followed by determining what percentage of the capacity that weight represents.

Step 1 is to determine the total weight on the pallet. This is a multiplication and addition process.

$$6 \text{ balls} \quad \times \quad 20 \text{ lbs} \quad = 120 \text{ lbs}$$

$$8 \quad \times \quad 15 \quad = 120 \text{ lbs}$$

$$120 + 120 = 240 \text{ lbs}$$

Step 2 is to determine the percentage this weight represents. This is accomplished with long division.

$$250 \overline{)240.00} \quad \frac{0.96}{} \quad = 96\% \textbf{ (D)}$$

Question 51

You must understand how fractions work to solve this problem. The 6 hours completed represents 2 / 6 of the journey. To determine the length of the entire trip, multiply the part of the trip completed by the denominator (bottom portion of the fraction).

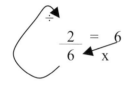

This number is then divided by the numerator (top portion of the fraction). The result is the total length of the trip (18 hours).

$$6 \times 6 = 36$$

$$36 / 2 = 18 \textbf{ (B)}$$

Question 52

This question involves multiplication, division, addition and subtraction. The first step is to determine how many slices Mike and Jim ate.

24 total slices
1 / 2   Mike
4 / 12   Jim

To determine the number of slices each had you must multiply the fraction by the total number. This is a two-stage process.

$$24 \times \frac{1}{2} = \frac{24}{2} \qquad\qquad 24 \times \frac{4}{12} = \frac{96}{12}$$

Multiply 24 by the numerator in both equations. The denominator remains the same.

$$\frac{24}{12} = 12 \qquad\qquad \frac{96}{12} = 8$$

After this, divide the numerator by the denominator. Mike had 12 slices and Jim had 8. By adding them together, you find that 20 slices have been eaten. This is now a subtraction problem.

24 total slices $24 - 20 = 4$ slices **(C)**
20 slices eaten

Question 53

To calculate the total number of arrests in this problem, add each individual officer's arrest number together.

$4 + 5 + 3 + 7 + 6 = 26$ **(C)**

In an equation where all numbers are added to each other, the order in which they appear doesn't matter. This equation can be restated any of the following ways:

$4 + 3 + 7 + 6 + 5 = 26 \qquad\qquad 3 + 5 + 4 + 6 + 7 = 26$
$5 + 3 + 4 + 7 + 6 = 26$ etc.

Question 54

This question is a straight division problem. You are asked to determine how many shelves holding 6 statures are required to hold 48 statues. Dividing 48 by 6 will solve the problem.

$$6 \overline{)48} = 8 \quad \textbf{(A)}$$

Question 55

Step 1: Determine the number of requests that were processed in June. This is accomplished by multiplying the number of requests in May by the percentage that the number dropped and then subtracting the two numbers from the May number.

```
  1 3 2 2            1 3 2 2
x   0 . 1 5        -   1 9 8
  ────────          ──────────
    1 9 8            1 1 2 4  requests in June
```

Step 2: Determine the number of requests processed in July. This is accomplished by multiplying the number of requests in June by the percentage that the number increased. Then add the two numbers.

```
  1 1 2 4            1 1 2 4
x   0 . 1 7        +   1 9 1
  ────────          ──────────
    1 9 1            1 3 1 5  requests in July (B)
```

Question 56

Step 1: Subtract 3 from both sides of the equation.

$$15 + 3 - 3 - 2y = 7y + 3 - 3 \qquad \text{or} \qquad 15 - 2y = 7y$$

Step 2: Add 2 y to both sides of the equation.

$$15 - 2y + 2y = 7y + 2y \qquad \text{or} \qquad 15 = 9y$$

Step 3: Isolate "y" by dividing both sides by 9.

$$\frac{15}{9} = \frac{9y}{9} \qquad \text{or } 1.67 = y \text{ (A)}$$

Question 57

The will require the use of fractions. Start by setting up an algebraic equation. In 12 seconds, 550 litres will flow. By assuming that the flow rate will not change, you can establish a relationship between the time and the water flow.

$$\frac{3}{12} = \frac{y}{550}$$

3 / 12 can be rewritten as 1/4 .
This makes the calculations easier.

$$\frac{1}{4} = \frac{y}{550}$$

Isolate "y" by multiplying both sides of the equation by 550.

$$\frac{550}{4} = y$$

550 / 4 = 137.5 litres **(A)**

Question 58

Step 1: Use multiplication to determine the current number of people in the shelter before the six new women are included.

```
   0.9 6 2
x    1 3 0
   1 2 5
```

There are 126 people before the police drop off 6 more. Then there will be 131.

Step 2: Take the new occupant number and divide it by the capacity of 130 women that can stay at the shelter.

```
          1.0 0 7
1 3 0 | 1 3 1.0 0 0
```
rounds up to 1.01

The new occupancy rate is 101%, which exceeds capacity. **(D)**

Question 59

This question is solved using algebra. If "y" represents the cost of the tanker, the price of the refinery must equal 2 (y). Adding the two prices together will equal $36 million.

Step 1: You have to create an algebraic equation and solve it.

$y + 2 (y) = 36$ Add the "y's" together
                          $1 y + 2 y = 3 y$
$3 (y) = 36$ Isolate "y" by dividing both sides by 3.
$y = 12$

Step 2: Now that you know the price of the tanker, determine the price of the refinery by multiplying the price of the refinery by two.

$12 \times 2 = 24$

The price of the refinery is $24 million. **(C)**

Question 60

There are several ways to state this equation mathematically. Basically, you are adding all of the books together. There are three groups in this problem:

150 arrest books   this can only be stated as 150

4 boxes of 50 summons   this can be stated several ways:

$50 + 50 + 50 + 50$ or like terms can be grouped:
$4 (50) = 4 \times 50$

2 boxes of 20 parking   this can be stated the same as the
ticket books   example above

$20 + 20$ or $2 (20)$

Add up the different elements. It doesn't matter which of the options are used, so long as only one of each element is included.

The answer can be any of the following:

$150 + 50 + 50 + 50 + 50 + 20 + 20$ or

$150 + 4(50) + 2 (20)$ or

$150 + 4(50) + 20 + 20$ or

$150 + 50 + 50 + 50 + 50 + 2(20)$

It doesn't matter which order the terms are in, so long as the terms being multiplied remain together. **(C)**

Observation
Question 61

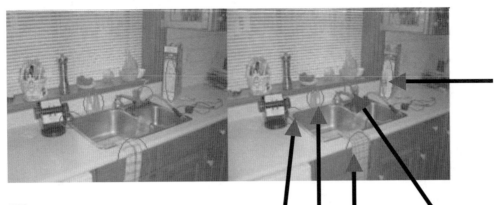

(C)

Question 62

(D)

Question 63

(A)

Question 64

(C)

Question 65

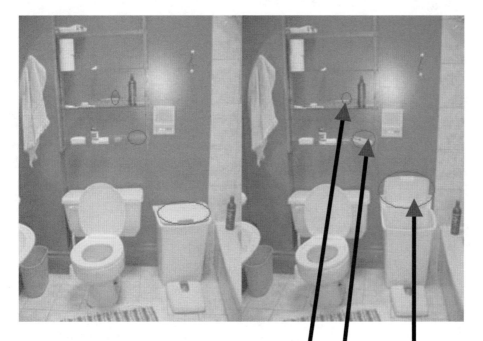

(A)

Pattern Solving
Question 86
The best way to solve these problems is to write out the alphabet and determine how the letters relate to each other.

A B C D E F G H I J K L M
B G E J H M K P N **(C)**
+5 -2 +5 –2 +5 -2 +5 -2

Question 87
E, J, O, T, Y
+5 +5 +5 +5 **(A)**

Question 88
1, 2, 4, 8, 16, 32, 64 **(C)**
 x2 x2 x2 x2 x2 x2

Question 89
A, F, D, B, G, E, C, H, F, D, I **(B)**
+5 -2 -2 +5 -2 -2 +5 -2 -2 +5

Question 90
1, 2, 4, 7, 11, 16, 22, 29 **(B)**
+1 +2 +3 +4 +5 +6 +7

Grammar
Question 91
"**Then**" is used while discussing a sequence of events. It has the same meaning as "afterwards", "subsequently" or "followed by". "**Than**" is used as a means of comparison. It is often used with or near the word "rather". The final sentence in the fourth option is a fragment. **(C)**

Question 92
Be careful with subordinate clauses. If a clause cannot stand on its own it will have to be linked to the rest of the sentence with a comma. **(A)**

Question 93
To form the comparative adjective or adverb for most single syllable words you add "-*er*" to the end of the word to compare two objects. If there were three or more to compare you would use the ending *-est*. A person can't be the fairer of three or more parties. Option C is incorrect, because Judge Green should be capitalized (proper name). **(B)**

Question 94
The subject and verb must agree with each other (My partner and I requires a *were*). Option B is wrong because the pronoun "*We*" is undefined. You don't know whom "*we*" is referring to. The third option is wrong because the 'we' is redundant (My partner and I, we...) **(D)**

Question 95
"It's" is a contraction for "it is". "Its" conveys possession. **(A)**

Question 96
<u>To</u>: in the direction of, towards, near, in order to.
<u>Too</u>: also, as well, in addition, besides, excessively.
<u>Two</u>: is a number. **(D)**

Question 97
Adverbs are used to modify or compliment verbs, adjectives or other adverbs. They generally explain how (gently), when (soon), or where (fully). They often end in "-*ly*". Apostrophes are required to denote ownership (the complainant's house). **(C)**

Question 98
All of the phrases have problems with subject / object noun agreement. Sentence A requires the subject "I" not "me". Sentence B requires the pronoun 'we'. In sentence C, the "I" is an object and should be "me". **(D)**

Question 99
Option B contains redundant information. Option C is incorrect because when receiving objects, goods or information, it is correct to use the word 'from'. "Off of" is redundant and awkward. **(A)**

Question 100
Generally speaking, use "amount" for things that are general or abstract and cannot be counted (furniture). Use "number" for things that can be counted (3 chairs). **(D)**

Question 101
The first two examples are run-on sentences. Both of C and D use a comma and a coordinating conjunction between the two clauses. However, the "although" in D implies that the second action was less important. This is wrong because the relationship between the two clauses is not correct. **(C)**

Question 102
Examples B and C are both sentence fragments. The final sentence doesn't make sense and has redundancies (Kevin… he). **(A)**

Question 103
Attend - to be present at, serve, wait on
Tend - be inclined, be likely, have a tendency
C uses an apostrophe inappropriately with the word "victim's" and D has an incorrect verb tense with "witness". **(B)**

Question 104
Lose - misplace, to be unable to find, to be defeated
Loose - unfastened, wobbly, slack, movable **(B)**

Question 105

Bear - an animal, to tolerate, put up with

Bare - to expose, naked, uncovered

Subject / object agreement also has to occur. The *One aspect... is* domestic violence. **(B)**

Question 106

Leading questions can be answered simply with a "yes" or "no". All of the acceptable questions can't be answered in this manner, while all of the unacceptable questions can. Options A and D are incorrect, as both sets of questions may lead to very personal information and may anger the interviewee. Option B is incorrect because there is no explanation of what is meant by 'powerful'. You can make an assumption that the unacceptable questions are leading in this case. **(C)**

Question 107

Option A is based on the data in the question and is the best answer. Option B is inappropriate as there is no evidence that the courts are too demanding of the officers. Option C is incorrect because if courts didn't trust radar manufacturers they would not allow officers use the devices. Option D is also incorrect because courts are relying on officers to testify as to what they saw. There is no evidence in the question that the courts do not trust the officers. **(A)**

Question 108

Options A, B and D are incorrect as they assume facts that aren't included in the question. There is no information about the amount of training officers have received or how thorough their investigations have been to date. **(C)**

Question 109

Option A is incorrect because there is no mention of how investigations have to be handled and when charges can be laid. Options C and D are also incorrect as there is no mention in the question as to which party to an offence is more responsible. **(B)**

Question 110

Option B is incorrect as the instructor is informing you of the proper use of the equipment, not passing a judgment on it. Options C and D are also incorrect because they assume facts that aren't evident in the question. There may be other factors that interfere with radar speed-measuring units, but you can't infer this from the question. **(A)**

Question 111

The major difference between acceptable and unacceptable questions is the element of leading the people you are interviewing to a conclusion. Often, leading questions can be answered with a simple yes or no. Acceptable questions cannot be answered this way and require more explanation, or a description of events. Option C is the only choice that falls into this category. **(C)**

Question 112

The actions that take place in option A are not covered by the guidelines provided in the question. They could be viewed as coercing a statement and may be illegal. Option B is also not covered in the question. Option C is inappropriate as the two neighbors involved in the dispute are not suspects, and should not be sprayed. **(D)**

Question 113

Option A is correct as the statement was made during the offence by the perpetrator. Option B is acceptable because two witnesses prove the statement reliable, and the victim who made the statement is dead. Option C is also acceptable. **(D)**

Question 114

Option A is inappropriate as there are faster means of notifying a parent than mailing a letter. The child is in custody and phone calls would be necessary. Option B is inappropriate, as a reliable adult was not contacted. Option C is inappropriate as well because the rules dictate that a parent or adult has to be called. There is no option of waiving that right. **(A)**

Question 115

Option A is inappropriate, as the guidelines do not support officers making an arrest for simply being abusive. Option C is inappropriate for the same reasons. If a suspect only provides a first name to the officers he has failed to properly identify him or herself and the arrest can continue. **(B)**

B.C. Practice Exam

This practice exam is divided into three books. You will be required to answer all questions at once during the actual testing, so it is recommended that you practise all three books in one sitting. Questions in Book 2 are based on information in Book 1. The tests are timed and have the following format:

Book 1
no questions – 5 minutes
Book 2
79 questions – 60 minutes
Book 3
79 questions – 60 minutes

Do each test in order (Book 1, Book 2, Book 3). The only materials allowed are pencils and scrap paper. No calculators, books, or counting devices are allowed. Use a clock or stopwatch to keep track of the time. You cannot make any notes while studying Book 1.

Detach the answer key to take the test.

JIBC Answer Key Book 2

Sample A ○ B ● C ○ D ○ ✓

Memorization

	A	B	C	D	
1	○	○	○	○	___
2	○	○	○	○	___
3	○	○	○	○	___
4	○	○	○	○	___
5	○	○	○	○	___
6	○	○	○	○	___
7	○	○	○	○	___
8	○	○	○	○	___
9	○	○	○	○	___
10	○	○	○	○	___

Total ___ /10

Reading Comprehension

	A	B	C	D	
11	○	○	○	○	___
12	○	○	○	○	___
13	○	○	○	○	___
14	○	○	○	○	___
15	○	○	○	○	___
16	○	○	○	○	

Total ___ /6

Mathematics

	A	B	C	D	
17	○	○	○	○	___
18	○	○	○	○	___
19	○	○	○	○	___
20	○	○	○	○	___
21	○	○	○	○	___
22	○	○	○	○	___
23	○	○	○	○	___
24	○	○	○	○	___
25	○	○	○	○	___
26	○	○	○	○	___
27	○	○	○	○	___
28	○	○	○	○	___
29	○	○	○	○	___
30	○	○	○	○	___
31	○	○	○	○	___
32	○	○	○	○	___
33	○	○	○	○	___
34	○	○	○	○	___
35	○	○	○	○	___
36	○	○	○	○	___

Total ___ /20

Grammar

	A	B	C	D	
37	○	○	○	○	___
38	○	○	○	○	___
39	○	○	○	○	___
40	○	○	○	○	___
41	○	○	○	○	___
42	○	○	○	○	___
43	○	○	○	○	___
44	○	○	○	○	___
45	○	○	○	○	___
46	○	○	○	○	___
47	○	○	○	○	___
48	○	○	○	○	___
49	○	○	○	○	___
50	○	○	○	○	___
51	○	○	○	○	___
52	○	○	○	○	___
53	○	○	○	○	___
54	○	○	○	○	___
55	○	○	○	○	___
56	○	○	○	○	___

Total ___ /20

Spelling

	A	B	C	D	
57	○	○	○	○	___
58	○	○	○	○	___
59	○	○	○	○	___
60	○	○	○	○	___
61	○	○	○	○	___
62	○	○	○	○	___
63	○	○	○	○	___
64	○	○	○	○	___
65	○	○	○	○	___
66	○	○	○	○	___

	A	B	C	D	
67	○	○	○	○	___
68	○	○	○	○	___
69	○	○	○	○	___
70	○	○	○	○	___
71	○	○	○	○	___
72	○	○	○	○	___
73	○	○	○	○	___
74	○	○	○	○	___
75	○	○	○	○	___
76	○	○	○	○	___

Total ___ /20

Judgement

	A	B	C	D	
77	○	○	○	○	___
78	○	○	○	○	___
79	○	○	○	○	___

Total ___ /79

The Judgment Section should be answered in paragraph format. Review the chapter on Essay Writing in the Preparation section and ensure that you are using the proper format. Be sure to review the detailed solutions for the rationale behind each answer.

JIBC Answer Key Book 3

Sample A ○ B ● C ○ D ○ ✓

Spelling

	A	B	C	D			A	B	C	D	
1	○	○	○	○	___	16	○	○	○	○	___
2	○	○	○	○	___	17	○	○	○	○	___
3	○	○	○	○	___	18	○	○	○	○	___
4	○	○	○	○	___	19	○	○	○	○	___
5	○	○	○	○	___	20	○	○	○	○	___
6	○	○	○	○	___	21	○	○	○	○	___
7	○	○	○	○	___	22	○	○	○	○	___
8	○	○	○	○	___	23	○	○	○	○	___
9	○	○	○	○	___	24	○	○	○	○	___
10	○	○	○	○	___	25	○	○	○	○	___
11	○	○	○	○	___	26	○	○	○	○	___
12	○	○	○	○	___	27	○	○	○	○	___
13	○	○	○	○	___	28	○	○	○	○	___
14	○	○	○	○	___	29	○	○	○	○	___
15	○	○	○	○	___	30	○	○	○	○	___

Total ___ /30

Problem Solving

	A	B	C	D	
31	○	○	○	○	___
32	○	○	○	○	___
33	○	○	○	○	___
34	○	○	○	○	___
35	○	○	○	○	___
36	○	○	○	○	___
37	○	○	○	○	___
38	○	○	○	○	___
39	○	○	○	○	___
40	○	○	○	○	___
41	○	○	○	○	___
42	○	○	○	○	___
43	○	○	○	○	___
44	○	○	○	○	___
45	○	○	○	○	___

Total ___ /15

Logic

	A	B	C	D	
46	○	○	○	○	___
47	○	○	○	○	___
48	○	○	○	○	___
49	○	○	○	○	___
50	○	○	○	○	___
51	○	○	○	○	___

Total ___ /6

Vocabulary

	A	B	C	D	
52	○	○	○	○	___
53	○	○	○	○	___
54	○	○	○	○	___
55	○	○	○	○	___
56	○	○	○	○	___
57	○	○	○	○	___
58	○	○	○	○	___

	A	B	C	D	
59	○	○	○	○	___
60	○	○	○	○	___
61	○	○	○	○	___
62	○	○	○	○	___
63	○	○	○	○	___
64	○	○	○	○	___
65	○	○	○	○	___
66	○	○	○	○	___
67	○	○	○	○	___
68	○	○	○	○	___
69	○	○	○	○	___
70	○	○	○	○	___
71	○	○	○	○	___
72	○	○	○	○	___
73	○	○	○	○	___
74	○	○	○	○	___
75	○	○	○	○	___
76	○	○	○	○	___

Total ___ /25

Judgement

	A	B	C	D	
77	○	○	○	○	___
78	○	○	○	○	___
79	○	○	○	○	___

Total ___ /3

Total ___ /79

_____ + _____ = _____ / 158

Ex: 68 + 65 = 133 / 158 = 84%

Divide your final mark by 158 to get your percentage on the exam. Aim for a mark higher than 80% for complete confidence prior to the exam. Review specific areas you are having difficulty with in the Preparation section.

You have 5 minutes to memorize the information on the following two pages. You will be questioned about it at the beginning of Book 2. You are not allowed to write down any of the information.

Wanted: Theft

Name:	Shane Cort	Height:	5'8
Age:	35	Weight:	170 lbs
Hair:	Red	Eyes:	Green
Complexion:	Light		

Identifying Marks: Freckles Across Back

Wanted: Failure to Appear in Court

Name:	Sam Ramadori	Height:	5'9
Age:	33	Weight:	175 lbs
Hair:	Brown	Eyes:	Brown
Complexion:	Dark		

Identifying Marks: Stab Wound Stomach

Wanted: Aggravated Assault

Name:	Narish Hahn	Height:	5'8
Age:	25	Weight:	160 lbs
Hair:	Black	Eyes:	Brown
Complexion:	Dark		

Identifying Marks: Missing Left Index Finger

Wanted: Possession of Cocaine

Name:	Calvin Borda	Height:	6'1
Age:	37	Weight:	220 lbs
Hair:	Brown	Eyes:	Blue
Complexion:	Light		

Identifying Marks: Missing Left Index Finger

Book 2

Do not turn the page until you are ready to begin Book 2. Give yourself 60 minutes to complete Book 2, including the time you need to write 3 short essays at the end.

You have 60 minutes to answer the following 79 questions. You are not allowed to use a dictionary or any other aids.

MEMORIZATION COMPONENT

The following 10 questions are based on the pictures you studied for the last 5 minutes.

Question 1

What objects were on the sidewalk in the bottom picture?

a) Two bicycles

b) Two black garbage bags

c) A propped-up store sign.

d) Both B and C.

Question 2

Which of the following people had a hand in their pocket?

a) A man wearing a coat and carrying a briefcase.

b) A man wearing blue jeans and a vest.

c) A man wearing shorts.

d) A bald man.

Question 3

Which store was directly beside Millennium Nails?

a) Mad cd's

b) CD Replay

c) Flight Centre

d) Hydro Body

Question 4

Which of the following statements is accurate?

a) The people in the top picture are walking the same direction the bicycles are pointing.

b) In each picture there is only one person carrying an item in their hands.

c) In the top picture there are five people walking towards the CD store.

d) None of the above.

Question 5

Which store has a person stopped in front to look into the window?

a) Millennium Nails

b) CD Replay

c) Hydro Body

d) Flight Centre

Question 6

Which of the four suspects is the tallest?

a) The suspect wanted for possession of cocaine

b) Shane Cort

c) The suspect wearing glasses

d) Both A and C

Question 7

Which suspect was wearing a checkered shirt?

a) Narish Hahn   b) Shane Cort

c) Calvin Borda   d) Sam Ramadori

Question 8

Which suspect had a stab wound to his stomach?

a) The suspect with red hair   b) The suspect wanted for theft

c) The suspect wearing a suit   d) The suspect missing his left index finger

Question 9

Which suspects had brown hair?

a) The suspect weighing 220 lbs.   b) The suspect who is 35-years-old

c) The suspect wanted for assault   d) Both A and C

Question 10

Which of the following descriptions apply to Shane Cort?

a) 25-years-old   b) 5'8

c) Blue eyes   d) None of the above

READING COMPREHENSION

The next three questions are based on the paragraph below.

The pace of growth in Ontario this year will only be half of what Finance Minister John Smith predicted in last spring's budget. Next year, it will remain at a meagre 1.3%. Smith painted that bleak picture as the backdrop for yesterday's statement to the Legislature. He then added a few small drops of bright pigment to the dreary canvas, saying, "We have a duty to reach out to those who need our help". Smith announced a welcome Christmas present for 220,000 low-income working families in the province — a one-time tax-free payment of $100 for each child under age 7. But he made it hard to applaud the $37 million initiative. He could not bring himself to show the same compassion for children whose parents are on welfare, even though the economy isn't creating any new jobs. For the kids on welfare, Smith had only a piece of coal. The finance minister also listed a number of infrastructure projects that the province was undertaking to give the economy a boost. "Details on these initiatives," he said, "as well as hundreds of other sport, culture, tourism, transportation and clean water projects will be announced by year end." Again, we would cheer were it not for the fact that Smith's estimate for capital spending is only $5 million higher than it was in the spring budget, and $130 million lower than capital spending last year. Smith then threw in a number of small measures to increase security and promote tourism. But his basic message was a warning of spending cuts to come. What makes these threatened cuts especially galling is Smith's dogged insistence on proceeding with tax reductions that will drive the budget into deficit next year.

Question 11

According to the above passage, which one of the following statements is true?

a) Estimate for capital spending is $5 million lower than it was in the spring budget.

b) There has been a one-time tax-free payment of $100 to 220,000 welfare families.

c) Growth in Ontario is predicted to be 1.3 per cent.

d) Welfare recipients will receive a 1.3 per cent increase in benefits.

Question 12

What is the general message of the article?

a) The Ontario Government has their priorities mixed up regarding funding allocation.

b) The economy is going to suffer over the next several years.

c) Tax cuts will benefit the economy as a whole over the next several years.

d) Spending on cultural events is prudent at this time.

Question 13

What is the Christmas present announced by Finance Minister John Smith?

a) Total capital spending of $130 million.

b) An increase in capital spending of $5 million.

c) A one-time tax-free payment of $100 for each child under age 7 to 220,000 low-income working families

d) A one-time tax-free payment of $100 to 220,000 welfare families.

The next three questions are based on the paragraph below.

An RCMP officer who picked up a vacationing judge in Washington State and drove him around before the judge approved a wiretap authorization involving former premier Peter Salk created an apprehension of bias, Salk's lawyer suggested Tuesday at a pre-trial hearing. "It doesn't look right," Don Jackson told Alberta Supreme Court Justice Elizabeth Hauchglaube during the defence lawyer's second day of legal argument on the issue of whether the wiretap evidence should be ruled inadmissible. "It is said that not only should justice be done, but justice should be seen to be done," said the lawyer, who will continue his legal argument today. Jackson is trying to convince the judge that the wiretap authorization was illegally obtained and should be excluded. He contends that the judge vacationing in Washington did not have the jurisdiction to hold a hearing outside the country and should not have offered police legal advice about whether it would permissible to issue an authorization in the U.S. "Judges are not meant to give legal advice," Jackson told Hauchglaube. "The courts should be held to the highest standards of impartiality." He said the conduct of the officers of the Crown, including police, created a reasonable apprehension of bias. "What happened in Washington is not in the best interests of the administration of justice." Jackson was referring to the fact that police investigators, a special prosecutor and an agent for the attorney-general of Alberta flew to Seattle aboard an RCMP jet to visit Alberta Supreme Court Associate Chief Justice Steven Thurston in Seattle on Feb. 14, 1999.

Question 14

According to the above passage, which one of the following statements is true?

a) The officer who gained permission for the wiretap was a member of the Vancouver Police Service.

b) The judge held the hearing for the wiretap outside of Canada.

c) Don Jackson is the premier of B.C.

d) The wiretap authorization was illegally obtained.

Question 15

What is the legal argument the defence is using to exclude the wiretap evidence?

a) The Supreme Court did not authorize the wiretap.

b) The judge who authorized the tap had given police advice on the matter

c) The judge who authorized the tap did not have the jurisdiction to hold a hearing outside the country.

d) Both b and c.

Question 16

Where was the judge when the wiretap was granted?

a) Seattle   b) Los Angeles

c) Vancouver   d) San Francisco

Mathematics

Question 17

Solve for "y": $-2/y + 6(4) = 6$

a) – 9   b) 9

c) 1/9   d) None of the above

Question 18

– 12.21 x 0.8 =

a) - 9.768   b) 9.321

c) - 8.752   d) None of the above

Question 19

– 17.7 - 2.1 + 8.3 =

a) 23.9   b) - 11.5

c) - 28.1   d) None of the above

Question 20

Solve for "y": $(24 - y) / 4 = 4$

a) 8   b) - 4

c) 4   d) None of the above

Question 21
511.21 - (-202.91) =
a) 308.3

b) - 714.12

c) - 308.3

d) None of the above

Question 22
21.01 - 12 + 5 x 3.5 =
a) 49.035

b) - 8.49

c) 26.51

d) None of the above

Question 23
15/18 + 1/2 - 1/3 - 2/6 =
a) 1/3

b) 1 1/3

c) 11/18

d) None of the above

Question 24
Solve for "y":   **4y + 14(2) = 28**
a) 0

b) 14

c) –9

d) None of the above

Question 25
- 12.621 - 4.698 + 2 =
a) - 15.319

b) - 11.319

c) - 19.319

d) None of the above

Question 26
- 12.39 (5.54) =
a) 68.406

b) - 68.406

c) - 68.4606

d) None of the above

Question 27
Solve for "y":   **5 - (2y)6 + 6/3 = 15(3)**
a) - 19/6

b) - 3 1/6

c) Both A & B

d) None of the above

Question 28
101.806 (- 3.5) =
a) - 356.213

b) - 356.321

c) - 365.321

d) None of the above

Question 29

Solve for "y": $3y + 6(4) = 2y$

a) – 12   b) 24

c) – 24   d) None of the above

Question 30

$1/4 + 0.387 + 2 =$

a) 2 3/5   b) 2.637

c) 2.736   d) None of the above

Question 31

$- 100 - 10 - 1 - 0.1 =$

a) - 111.1   b) - 110.9

c) - 88.9   d) None of the above

Question 32

$5/8 + 3/4 ÷ 1/2 =$

a) 2   b) 17 / 8

c) 1   d) None of the above

Question 33

Solve for "y": $3y - 12 = 128$

a) 45   b) 25.32

c) 46 2/3   d) None of the above

Question 34

$- 101.086 (- 3.5) =$

a) - 353.1   b) - 353.801

c) - 104.586   d) None of the above

Question 35

$16 \times 24 ÷ 2 \times 5 =$

a) 384   b) 960

c) 38.4   d) None of the above

Question 36

Solve for "y": $5 - (2y) 6 + 7 (6) = 15 ÷ 3$

a) 2.6   b) 3

c) 3.5   d) None of the above

Grammar

For the following 8 questions, choose the words that correctly complete the sentences

Question 37

My friends and I _____ going to the movies.

a) am

b) should

c) will

d) are

Question 38

One member of the Vancouver Canucks _____ waiting at the airport to catch a plane when he was asked for an autograph.

a) were

b) was

c) have

d) has

Question 39

Jamie was concerned about the _____ of criminals that were being released on parole who were still considered by police to be potentially violent.

a) number

b) amount

c) amounts

d) many

Question 40

Jamie eagerly went to the hockey try-outs _____ a group of 15 boys all wanting to make the team.

a) as part of

b) as opposed to

c) instead of

d) rather than

Question 41

Once elected, the Member of Parliament had to give _____ his anonymity.

a) about

b) up

c) into

d) instead

Question 42

We _____ going to the store when out of nowhere a thunderstorm _____ out.

a) were, break

b) are, break

c) were, broke

d) are, broke

Question 43

An index, such as standardized test scores, _____ quantified and supposedly objective, are used by business schools to help assess applicants.

a) that are

b) who are

c) that is

d) who is

Question 44

James passed the notes onto Bill and _____. _____ needed them to study for our exam.

a) I, Bill and I

b) I, Bill and me

c) me, Bill and I

d) me, Bill and I

Question 45

To deal with the upcoming fire drill on Monday, the principle ordered kindergarten teachers _____ fire drills during the preceding week.

a) should practice

b) practicing

c) would do the practices

d) to practice

Question 46

Children often learn by imitating adults, but psychologists don't know how they learn to adapt _____ how they develop imagination.

a) or

b) but

c) nor

d) also

Pick the best selection below to replace the underlined passage in the following questions. Selection A is the same as what is written above.

Question 47

The rugby player, <u>having trained long and hard</u>, finally achieved his aim to win a match.

a) having trained long and hard

b) trained long and hard

c) training long and hard

d) had long and hard training

Question 48

Tomorrow, <u>it will be announced by the Prime Minister the new tax policy.</u>

a) it will be announced by the Prime Minister the new tax policy.

b) the Prime Minister will announce the new tax policy.

c) it is to be announced by the Prime Minister, the new tax policy.

d) the Prime Minister is announcing the new tax policy.

Question 49

<u>After Sheila had failed her assignment,</u> she realized the importance of deadlines.

a) After Shiela had failed her assignment,

b) Failing her assignment,

c) While Shiela failed her assignment,

d) Shiela having failed her exam,

Question 50

Warming herself by <u>the fire, was a beautiful girl which was burning brightly,</u> with blonde hair.

a) the fire, was a beautiful girl which was burning brightly

b) the fire, which was burning brightly, was a beautiful girl

c) the fire was a beautiful girl and it was burning brightly

d) the fire, a beautiful girl which was burning brightly

Question 51

The U.S. Military is able to find their way through the desert with the aid of a global positioning system.
Rewrite, beginning with: With the aid of a global positioning system…
The next words will be:

a) through the desert

b) finding their way through the desert

c) the U.S. Military is able

d) the U.S. Military being able to

Question 52

For the following 5 questions, choose the sentence that is most clearly written.

a) Captain Gordon did not think the victim could be capable of revenge against her attacker.

b) Captain Gordon did not think the victim could be capable to revenge against her attacker.

c) Captain Gordon did not think the victim, against her attacker, capable to revenge.

d) Captain Gordon did not think the victim, against her attacker, could be capable of revenge.

Question 53

a) A judge's rulings on sex offenders were sometimes harsh, and she is advised to review some of her decisions.

b) A judge's rulings on sex offenders were sometimes harsh, and she advised to review some of her decisions.

c) A judge's rulings on sex offenders are sometimes harsh, and she is advised to review some of her decisions.

d) A judge's rulings on sex offenders were sometimes harsh, and she was advising to review some of her decisions.

Question 54

a) The greatest danger a police officer faces should he relax and lets his guard down.

b) The greatest danger a police officer faces is when he relaxes and lets his guard down.

c) The greatest danger a police officer faces occurs when he relaxes and lets his guard down.

d) The greatest danger a police officer faces are when he relaxes and lets his guard down.

Question 55

a) The collision happened on account of the brakes were faulty.

b) The collision happened because the brakes were faulty.

c) The collision happened from the brakes were faulty.

d) The collision happened besides the brakes were faulty.

Question 56

a) Since you began training; you have been able to work the entire shift without rest.

b) Since you began training, you have been able to work the entire shift without rest.

c) Since you began training and you have been able to work the entire shift without rest.

d) Since you began training because you have been able to work the entire shift without rest.

Spelling

For the following 20 questions pick out the word which is spelled incorrectly.

Question 57
a) Fluke   b) Flunk   c) Flury   d) Floor

Question 58
a) Penny   b) Pepper   c) Penthouse   d) Pandent

Question 59
a) Prostate   b) Prosperus   c) Subway   d) Succour

Question 60
a) Original   b) Origen   c) Organism   d) Ginger

Question 61
a) Event   b) European   c) Ureka   d) Untrue

Question 62
a) Europe   b) Untie   c) Ethnic   d) Unisan

Question 63

a) Submit b) Stygian c) Concer d) Concrete

Question 64

a) Concieve b) Concourse c) Sturdy d) Stunner

Question 65

a) Retrospective b) Revalation c) Inhabitant d) Inherit

Question 66

a) Wicketkeeper b) Inhale c) Inflation d) Yeild

Question 67

a) Zoollogy b) Zygote c) Fight d) Flaunt

Question 68

a) Concrete b) Conclusive c) Naked d) Namless

Question 69

a) Napalm b) Nature c) Languag d) Friend

Question 70

a) Fijian b) Feind c) Trifle d) Trilateral

Question 71

a) Triten b) Trite c) Schnapps d) Scholarship

Question 72

a) Troll b) Tropic c) Trucking d) Trouph

Question 73

a) Parabola b) Papaya c) Aptatude d) Approve

Question 74

a) Briliant b) Brighten c) Par d) Panic

Question 75

a) Relay b) Relent c) Brimfull d) Breeding

Question 76

a) Spleen b) Splash c) Coulomb d) Counsal

Judgement

Prepare a short written answer for the following three questions.

Question 77

While on patrol, you notice a couple arguing in the vehicle beside you. It is a very heated argument and you can hear yelling. The woman in the passenger seat glances over at you and ignores you. The vehicle begins to pull away. What action should you take?

a) Notify your supervisor about the incident.

b) Check the licence plate on the computer, and if nothing comes back move on to other business.

c) Pull the vehicle over and charge the couple with disturbing the peace.

d) Pull the vehicle over and arrest the male for verbal assault.

Question 78

While patrolling your precinct you observe one of the local drug dealers running down the street and continually looking behind him. You know that he normally works on the corner and are surprised to see him moving so quickly. He is heading in your direction. What should you do?

a) Let him go, as he is not performing any apparent illegal activity.

b) Take note of his actions and follow up next time you speak to him.

c) Tackle him as he is running by.

d) Stop him and talk to him to get information on his behaviour.

Question 79

You attend a domestic assault call. A neighbour reported that she heard a woman screaming for help, a man yelling very loudly and the sound of furniture being smashed. When officers arrive they discover a woman with visible cuts on her face and blood splatters in the kitchen. The husband states she fell down the stairs and tells you to leave. The woman remains silent and says nothing. What is the best course of action?

a) Leave, as you do not have a warrant to be on their property.

b) Ask the woman in front of the husband if she wants charges laid.

c) Separate the two parties and speak to the woman in private.

d) Advise the couple that they should not make so much noise and caution them for disturbing the peace.

You have 60 minutes hours to answer the following 79 questions. You are not allowed to use a dictionary or any other aids.

Spelling
For each of the following questions pick out the word below which is spelled incorrectly.

Question 1

a) Interceede   b) Plankton   c) Kinetic   d) Tentative

Question 2

a) Object   b) Kindergartten   c) Reserve   d) Serial

Question 3

a) Guest   b) Corporate   c) Recquisite   d) Particle

Question 4

a) Gratefull   b) Compliment   c) Ascribe   d) Granary

Question 5

a) Pungent   b) Magnolia   c) Horroscope   d) Gradient

Question 6

a) Martian   b) Heredity   c) Jewellary   d) Fibreglass

Question 7

a) Experement   b) Innocuous   c) Nominal   d) Compensate

Question 8

a) Kernel   b) Passage   c) Savoury   d) Tradding

Question 9

a) Ligament   b) Educate   c) Classice   d) Procedure

Question 10

a) Equivocal   b) Cinnamon   c) Blunder   d) Anual

Question 11

a) Proporty   b) Genie   c) Crystal   d) Aerial

Question 12

a) Famous   b) Aniversary   c) Rotary   d) Paisley

Question 13

a) Computer   b) Whiskey   c) Practical   d) Benifit

Question 14

a) Forgetfull   b) Editor   c) Prohibit   d) Draught

Question 15

a) Braille   b) Delivery   c) dezigner   d) Liberty

Question 16

a) Agrement   b) Progress   c) Continental   d) Serving

Question 17

a) Pathway   b) Emotion   c) Colision   d) Pallor

Question 18

a) Pamper   b) Usefull   c) Foundation   d) Oblong

Question 19

a) Spouse   b) Compozition   c) Navigate   d) Reader

Question 20

a) Ilegal   b) Scaffolding   c) Sweetener   d) Wholemeal

Question 21

a) Compressor   b) Brake   c) Cardigan   d) Ofence

Question 22

a) Fixture   b) Botulism   c) Punkture   d) Chestnut

Question 23

a) Enginering   b) Leisure   c) Commuter   d) Harmonic

Question 24

a) Trophy   b) Allele   c) Parliment   d) Sedentary

Question 25

a) Fluctuation   b) Mountainer   c) Pitcher   d) Ruminant

Question 26

a) Consensus   b) Rotiserie   c) Examination   d) Conservatory

Question 27

a) Teritory   b) Conquer   c) Seminar   d) Roughen

Question 28

a) Terrace   b) Conflict   c) Consarvation   d) Ruffle

Question 29
a) Preface   b) Curfew   c) Atmosfere   d) Debatable

Question 30
a) Locality   b) Scrible   c) Traditional   d) Weather

Problem Solving

Arrested Person	Amount of Cocaine	# of $100 bills	# of $50 bills	# of $20 bills
Yang	2.9 kgs	137	115	31
Sharma	1.7 kgs	132	39	30
Hatch	0.8 kgs	43	116	79

After a drug investigation, police officers seized the above items from three involved parties. 1 gm of cocaine is worth: $80

Question 31
How much cash did the officers take from suspect Sharma?

a) $15,750   b) $201   c) $151,750   d) $14,750

Question 32
What is the total value of the products seized from all involved parties?

a) $480,500   b) $479,600   c) $479,500   d) $479,400

Question 33
What percentage of the total cash was Hatch's?

a) 29.6%   b) 24.6%   c) 19.6%   d) 34.6%

Question 34
There are 4 children in the Yang family. Each child is married and has 3 babies. We must give 4 stuffed animals to each baby. How many stuffed animals do we need to buy?

a) 48   b) 52   c) 50   d) 54

Question 35
If there are 250 electoral votes and they are equally divided between the 50 states, how many does each state have?

a) 50   b) 4   c) 6   d) 5

Question 36

Customs Agent Arquet was involved in a major drug bust at the airport. She arrested three suspects. Each of the suspects had two suitcases, each containing 5 kilograms of cocaine. Which of the following formulas would Arquet use to calculate the total number of kilograms seized during the arrest?

a) 3 (2) (5)   b) 5 x 3 x 2   c) 3(5+5)   d) Any of the above

Question 37

There are 18 slices in a pizza. Mike ate 1/2 of the pizza. Jim ate 2/6 of the pizza. Daren ate the leftover slices. How many slices did Daren eat?

a) 5   b) 4   c) 3   d) 2

Question 38

Illio put change in a bottle. He put in 2 pennies, 5 quarters, 3 dimes and 1 nickel. What is the probability of picking out a penny?

a) 18%   b) 42%   c) 35%   d) 8%

Question 39

Constable Gordon arrested a drug dealer for trafficking. He had to submit the suspect's property including the following money.

Denomination	# of Bills
$50	10
$20	8
$10	4
$5	3
$1	6

Which of the following formulas would Gordon use to calculate the total value of money seized?

a) 50(10) + 1(6) + 10(4) + 5(3) + 20(8)

b) 50 + 10 + 5 + 3 + 10 + 4 + 1 + 6 + 20 + 8

c) (50 + 20 + 10 + 5 + 1) x (10 + 8 + 4 + 3 + 6)

d) Both A and C

Question 40

Natasha Kaya worked 5 hours a day, 35 hours a week. She earns $6 an hour. How much will she earn in 3 weeks?

a) $590   b) $606   c) $620   d) $630

Question 41

If you get 4 eggs per day, how many weeks will it take to get 364 eggs?

a) 13   b) 6   c) 18   d) 8

Question 42

Jane Green bought 4 tapes at $6 each. She then found $9 on the street corner. She now has $59. How much money did Jane have before she bought the tapes?

a) $74   b) $89   c) $90   d) $56

Question 43

Billy was making a pen for his puppies. He had four pieces of wood. Two of the pieces of wood were 9 yards long. The other two pieces of wood were 3 yards long. After Billy has built the pen, what will its perimeter be in yards?

a) 19   b) 17   c) 24   d) 28

Question 44

Constable James is organizing equipment for the annual police charity picnic. Below is a list of all of the prize equipment he is responsible for.

Equipment	Quantity
Bicycles	20
Pairs of roller-skates	15
Barbie Dolls	100
Toy Cars	100

What formula would James use to calculate the total number of prizes available?

a) 20 + 15 + 100   b) 15 + 100(2) + 20

c) 20 + 15 + 100 + 100   d) Both B and C

Question 45

Rebecca needs to save $1,250 in order to take a trip. She works 50 hours a week and earns $5 an hour. How many weeks will she have to work to save for the trip?

a) 3   b) 2   c) 5   d) 4

Logic Section

The next three questions refer to the following information.

Question 46

You are retracing your steps though an earlier police vehicle pursuit in order to fill out your report. You originally spotted the vehicle on Bloor Street heading westbound. As you attempted to pull the vehicle over, the driver accelerated and made a right turn onto Davis Street. Along Davis Street there was too much traffic and the suspect managed to turn around and head in the opposite direction before you could box him in. You continued the pursuit and followed as he made a left on to Thompson Avenue, followed by a right on to Jones Street, and then another right on to Carling Avenue. As the driver attempted to make a left onto Appleby Line you managed to box him in and apprehend the suspect.

What direction was the suspect heading on Thompson Avenue?

a) North   b) South   c) East   d) West

Question 47

What direction was the suspect attempting to head on Appleby Line?

a) North   b) South   c) East   d) West

Question 48

What streets did the suspect drive North on?

a) Davis & Jones   b) Jones & Carling

c) Jones   d) Davis

Question 49

Arrange the following sentences into the most logical sequence of events.
1) A neighbour heard a woman screaming for help at the house next door, 39 Elmer Avenue.

2) Police attended 39 Elmer Avenue to deal with the emergency.

3) Police showed up at the neighbour's house in order to take a statement of what she heard.

4) An intruder was located in 39 Elmer Avenue and arrested for break and enter and assault.

5) An intruder broke into 39 Elmer Avenue to find a woman alone in the kitchen of the house.

a) 5, 1, 3, 2, 4   b) 1, 5, 3, 2, 4   c) 1, 5, 2, 4, 3   D) 5, 1, 2, 4, 3

The next two questions refer to the following information.

You arrive on a scene of a stabbing at a local high school. There are four people who you encounter during the investigation: Bill, Todd, Raju and Nigel. The first person you encounter is a firefighter who advises that you speak with Bill and Todd, who are being looked after by the ambulance attendant. Leaving the firefighter you next speak to Raju. The victim was rushed to the hospital, so you speak to the witness before heading to the hospital to take a statement from Todd.

Question 50

Who is the witness to the stabbing?

a) Bill   b) Todd   c) Raju   d) Nigel

Question 51

What role does Nigel play in this investigation?

a) Victim   b) Witness   c) Firefighter   d) Ambulance

Vocabulary

For the following 25 questions choose the two words that are linked as either synonyms or antonyms.

Question 52

a) diverse	**b) smart**	**c) intelligent**	**d) bungle**
a) a & b	b) a & c	c) a & d
d) b & c	e) b & d	f) c & d

Question 53

a) attack	**b) soar**	**c) retreat**	**d) introduce**
a) a & b	b) a & c	c) a & d
d) b & c	e) b & d	f) c & d

Question 54

a) damp	**b) moist**	**c) arrest**	**d) history**
a) a & b	b) a & c	c) a & d
d) b & c	e) b & d	f) c & d

Question 55

a) entrance	**b) knowledge**	**c) pregnant**	**d) exit**
a) a & b	b) a & c	c) a & d
d) b & c	e) b & d	f) c & d

Question 56

a) birth	**b) entire**	**c) yell**	**d) scream**
a) a & b	b) a & c	c) a & d
d) b & c	e) b & d	f) c & d

Question 57

a) forget	b) busy	c) remember	d) shot
a) a & b	b) a & c	c) a & d	
d) b & c	e) b & d	f) c & d	

Question 58

a) require	b) need	c) limb	d) desperate
a) a & b	b) a & c	c) a & d	
d) b & c	e) b & d	f) c & d	

Question 59

a) forbid	b) allow	c) career	d) popular
a) a & b	b) a & c	c) a & d	
d) b & c	e) b & d	f) c & d	

Question 60

a) dine	b) gigantic	c) nervous	d) enormous
a) a & b	b) a & c	c) a & d	
d) b & c	e) b & d	f) c & d	

Question 61

a) sweet	b) fresh	c) capture	d) release
a) a & b	b) a & c	c) a & d	
d) b & c	e) b & d	f) c & d	

Question 62

a) excite	b) morose	c) gloomy	d) create
a) a & b	b) a & c	c) a & d	
d) b & c	e) b & d	f) c & d	

Question 63

a) unite	b) problem	c) before	d) divide
a) a & b	b) a & c	c) a & d	
d) b & c	e) b & d	f) c & d	

Question 64

a) melody	b) possible	c) lazy	d) tune
a) a & b	b) a & c	c) a & d	
d) b & c	e) b & d	f) c & d	

Question 65

a) deter	b) ill	c) healthy	d) annual
a) a & b	b) a & c	c) a & d	
d) b & c	e) b & d	f) c & d	

Question 66

a) yearly	b) attend	c) decisively	d) annually
a) a & b	b) a & c	c) a & d	
d) b & c	e) b & d	f) c & d	

Question 67

a) broad	b) advise	c) narrow	d) settle
a) a & b	b) a & c	c) a & d	
d) b & c	e) b & d	f) c & d	

Question 68

a) honour	b) awful	c) terrible	d) special
a) a & b	b) a & c	c) a & d	
d) b & c	e) b & d	f) c & d	

Question 69

a) pretence	b) early	c) polite	d) rude
a) a & b	b) a & c	c) a & d	
d) b & c	e) b & d	f) c & d	

Question 70

a) appear	b) distrust	c) write	d) seem
a) a & b	b) a & c	c) a & d	
d) b & c	e) b & d	f) c & d	

Question 71

a) teach	b) sample	c) slow	d) fast
a) a & b	b) a & c	c) a & d	
d) b & c	e) b & d	f) c & d	

Question 72

a) extreme	b) relate	c) sever	d) cut
a) a & b	b) a & c	c) a & d	
d) b & c	e) b & d	f) c & d	

Question 73

a) sell	b) insist	c) devise	d) buy

a) a & b	b) a & c	c) a & d
d) b & c	e) b & d	f) c & d

Question 74

a) relax	b) balance	c) rest	d) counsel

a) a & b	b) a & c	c) a & d
d) b & c	e) b & d	f) c & d

Question 75

a) muster	b) modern	c) procedure	d) ancient

a) a & b	b) a & c	c) a & d
d) b & c	e) b & d	f) c & d

Question 76

a) elementary	b) basic	c) patriot	d) post

a) a & b	b) a & c	c) a & d
d) b & c	e) b & d	f) c & d

Judgement

Question 77

Prepare a short written answer to the following three questions.

You are a new officer and are working under a training officer with 20 years experience. Toward the end of the night you receive a radio call for an assault at a nightclub. Upon arriving at the club, you find both the complainant and the suspect on scene. You begin talking to the complainant while your partner addresses the suspect. There are no visible signs of injury on the complainant. He states that the suspect pushed him and threatened to punch him. Both parties have been drinking. The complainant states that he wants to lay charges.

Which of the following is the best option?

a) Talk to your partner and see what information he has on the incident.

b) Based on the complaint received, arrest the suspect for assault and uttering threats.

c) Advise the complainant to go home, sleep on it, and call the police if he wants to lay charges when he wakes up.

d) Dismiss the allegations as drunken stupidity and tell the complainant to go home.

Question 78

Upon discussing the situation with your partner, he determines that there is no need for police involvement and that the two of you are leaving. You are uncertain and feel that the more aggressive suspect may cause problems when you leave. Your training officer disagrees and tells you that you are leaving.

What is your next action?

a) Go along with the more senior officer and leave.

b) Argue the choice of action while you are still at the nightclub.

c) Decide to arrest the suspect on your own, regardless of your partner's opinion.

d) Request a sergeant to attend the scene.

Question 79

Leaving the nightclub, you head into the station for the end of your shift. On the way in you hear another radio call come over for the same location of an assault involving the same parties. Another car is dispatched and you are unsure and confused about whether or not your actions tonight were appropriate.

How would you resolve this uncertainty?

a) Go back to the station and complain to the sergeant about the incident.

b) Let the situation go and forget about it.

c) Ask your training officer to explain the situation as he saw it, and explain to you why his actions were taken, as you are confused.

d) Insist that you both re-attend the scene to handle the call.

B.C. Answer Key – Book 2

Memorization	
1	D
2	B
3	A
4	C
5	C
6	D
7	A
8	C
9	A
10	B

Reading Comp.	
11	C
12	A
13	C
14	B
15	D
16	A

Mathematics			
17	C	27	C
18	A	28	B
19	B	29	C
20	A	30	B
21	D	31	A
22	C	32	B
23	D	33	C
24	A	34	D
25	A	35	B
26	D	36	C

Grammar			
37	D	47	A
38	B	48	B
39	A	49	A
40	A	50	B
41	B	51	C
42	C	52	A
43	C	53	C
44	D	54	C
45	D	55	B
46	A	56	B

Spelling			
57	C	67	A
58	D	68	D
59	B	69	C
60	B	70	B
61	C	71	A
62	D	72	D
63	C	73	C
64	A	74	A
65	B	75	C
66	D	76	D

Judgement	
77	B
78	D
79	C

Spelling			
1	A	16	A
2	B	17	C
3	C	18	B
4	A	19	B
5	C	20	A
6	C	21	D
7	A	22	C
8	D	23	A
9	C	24	C
10	D	25	B
11	A	26	B
12	B	27	A
13	D	28	C
14	A	29	C
15	C	30	B

Prob. Solving	
31	A
32	C
33	B
34	A
35	D
36	D
37	C
38	A
39	A
40	D
41	A
42	A
43	C
44	D
45	C

Logic	
46	C
47	B
48	D
49	D
50	A
51	C

Vocabulary					
52	D	60	E	68	D
53	B	61	F	69	F
54	A	62	D	70	C
55	C	63	C	71	F
56	F	64	C	72	F
57	B	65	D	73	C
58	A	66	C	74	B
59	A	67	B	75	E
				76	A

Judgement	
77	A
78	A
79	C

FOR MORE PRACTICE EXAMS, VISIT OUR WEBSITE

Referral Code: ppdc1320   WWW.POLICEPREP.COM   1-866-POLICEPREP

DETAILED SOLUTIONS

BOOK 2 – Grammar Section

Question 52
Captain Gordon did not think the victim could be capable of revenge against her attacker. **(A)**
The sentence requires the preposition **_of_** to begin the clause 'revenge against her attacker'. Sentences three and four are wordy and unclear.

Question 53
A judge's rulings on sex offenders are sometimes harsh, and she is advised to review some of her decisions. **(C)**
Watch out for consistency between verb tenses. All of the other sentences shift tenses between the first verb (are / were) and the second verb (is advised / advised / is advised / was advising). The verbs should be consistent.

Question 54
The greatest danger a police office faces occurs when he relaxes and lets his guard down. **(C)**
Sentence A doesn't make sense. The verb "to be" (is when, are when) is inappropriate in this circumstance.

Question 55
The collision happened because the brakes were faulty. **(B)**
Sentence one is grammatically incorrect. The proper preposition is "because". If "from" or "besides" are used the sentence fails to make sense.

Question 56
Since you began training, you have been able to work the entire shift without rest. **(B)**
Sentence A is incorrect, because it uses a semi-colon incorrectly. Sentences C and D are incorrect because a conjunction is not required.

BOOK 2 – Judgement Section (Sample answers)

Question 77
The role of police officers in society is to protect the public and maintain public order. That being said, police should exercise discretion before becoming unnecessarily involved in a citizen's private life. Neither party is disturbing the peace in any way, nor are they posing any threat to safety. If either party wanted police involvement, they would have used the opportunity to request assistance. Because neither party sought assistance and there was no evidence of any other wrongdoing, there is no need to involve a supervisor or pull the vehicle over. A computer check would be a non-invasive means of gathering further information about any possible problems the owner may have had with the police and may reveal further information that may warrant action. Doing a license check and allowing the couple to leave would be the best solution. **(B)**

Question 78

Investigating suspicious circumstances is part of a police officer's duty. Unusual activities, especially when performed by known criminals, warrant action. Police can talk to citizens even if they are not in the process of performing illegal acts. A conversation with the individual may reveal information that needs to be acted on. There is no evidence to suggest that physical force is required to detain the individual. Simply approaching the male and questioning him about any problems would be the most suitable action a police officer could take in this situation. **(D)**

Question 79

Domestic situations are unpredictable and can be very dangerous to both officers and the parties involved. Due to the nature of the call, it would be inappropriate to leave without providing protection for the victim. There are obvious signs of an assault and the male is clearly lying. Asking the female if she needs help in front of her attacker would not be appropriate. The first step would be to separate the two parties and ensure that she feels safe before gathering more information. Once all the facts have been gathered, and there is enough evidence to make an arrest, one should be made. The male could be arrested on the spot. **(C)**

BOOK 3 – Problem Solving Section

Question 31

This question involves straight multiplication and addition.

Step 1: Multiply out all of the cash flows for each dollar denomination.

$100 x 132 = $ 13,200
$50 x 39 = $ 1,950
$20 x 30 = $ 600

Step 2: Add the total cash together from the separate bills.

$13,200 + $1,950 + $900 = $15,750 **(A)**

Question 32

This question involves straight addition and multiplication. Multiply the values of the bills by the number of bills. Remember to include the value of the drugs as well. If you run into any difficulties solving this problem, review the addition and multiplication sections of the teaching material. Remember that there are 1,000 grams in a kilogram. The answer is $470,500. **(C)**

Question 33

This solution will require division, addition and multiplication. First, reach a total for all the cash that was confiscated. Then divide the amount of cash that Hatch has by the total value of the money seized.

Total Value of Cash Seized =	$47,500
Value of Hatch's Cash =	$11,680

$$\frac{0.2\ 4\ 5\ 8}{47500\ |\ 11680.0000}\quad\text{or}\ 24.6\%\ \textbf{(B)}$$

```
                  0 . 2 4 5 8   or  24.6% (B)
4 7 5 0 0 | 1 1 6 8 0 . 0 0 0 0
          - 9 5 0 0 0 0
            2 1 8 0 0 0 0
          - 1 9 0 0 0 0 0
              2 8 0 0 0 0 0
            - 2 3 7 5 0 0 0
                4 2 5 0 0 0
              - 3 8 0 0 0 0
                4 5 0 0 0
```

Question 34

This question is a two-stage multiplication problem. The first step is to determine how many babies there are. This is accomplished by multiplying the number of babies by the number of children. After this is determined, multiply the number of babies by the number of toys needed for each baby.

4 children   4 x 3 = 12

3 babies each

4 toys each   12 x 4 = 48 **(A)**

Question 35

This question is a division problem. You are being asked to break the total number of electoral votes into 50 small groups. Divide 250 by 50 for the answer.

```
              5 (D)
5 0 |   2 5 0
      - 2 5 0
            0
```

Question 36

Multiplying all the numbers to determine the total number of kilograms seized. If you have a hard time visualizing this, use the diagram below.

(3 people) x (2 suitcases) x (5 kilograms) **(D)**

This equation can be written any of the following ways:

$$3 (2) (5) \qquad 3 \text{ x } 2 \text{ x } 5 \qquad 3 (2 \text{ x } 5)$$

Like addition, it doesn't matter what order the numbers are in when they are all multiplied together. The above could be restated:

$$2 (3) (5) \qquad 5 \text{ x } 2 \text{ x } 3 \qquad 2 (3 \text{ x } 5)$$

The equation could also add up all of the kilograms individually and be written:

$$5 + 5 + 5 + 5 + 5 + 5$$

Also, remember that a combination can occur in the equations.

(5 x 2) can also be restated (5 + 5)

3 (5 + 5) is an additional form of the equation.

Question 37

This question involves multiplication, division, addition and subtraction. The first step is to determine how many slices Mike and Jim ate.

18 total slices	To determine the number of slices each had, multiply the fraction by the total number. This is a two-stage process.
1 / 2 Mike	
2 / 6 Jim	

$$18 \text{ x } \frac{1}{2} = \frac{18}{2} \qquad 18 \text{ x } \frac{2}{6} = \frac{36}{6}$$

Multiply the numerator in both equations by 18. The denominator remains the same.

$$\frac{18}{2} = 9 \qquad \frac{36}{6} = 6$$

After this is done, divide the numerator by the denominator. Mike had 9 slices and Jim had 6 slices. Adding them together reveals that 15 slices have been eaten. Subtract 15 from 18 for the answer.

18 total slices $18 - 15 = 3$ **(C)**
15 slices eaten

Question 38

For this problem, determine the total number of coins and divide by the number of pennies.

2 pennies	The total coins are:
5 quarters	
3 dimes	$2 + 5 + 3 + 1 = 11$
1 nickel	(remember you have to include the pennies)

```
          0 . 1 8 1
   1 1 | 2 . 0 0 0
        - 1 1
            9 0
          - 8 8
            2 0
          - 1 1
              9
```

Ignore any number after 8. If the number is 5 or greater, round the 8 up to a 9.

To express this number as a percentage, multiply the number by 100.

$0 . 1 8 \times 100 = 18 \%$ **(A)**

Question 39

In order to get the total value of the cash, add all of the money together. There are several ways this can be stated mathematically. One option is to individually add up all of the cash. However, this results in an unwieldy equation.

An alternate method is to group like terms and multiply. Once the like terms are multiplied together, add them to reach the solution. There are four $10 bills, which is written 4 (10) or 4 x 10. LIKE TERMS MUST ALL HAVE THE SAME VALUE.

$$10 (50) + 8 (20) + 4 (10) + 3 (5) + 6 (1) \quad \textbf{(A)}$$

It doesn't matter in what order the numbers are added or which number comes first, so long as the proper numbers are multiplied together (10 has to be multiplied by 50).

There can also be a combination of multiplied like terms, and added terms, so long as each unit is accounted for.

$$10 (50) + 8 (20) + 10 + 10 + 10 + 10 + 3 (5) + 6 (1)$$

The tens that are in bold could be written 4 (10).

Question 40

Many word problems try to fool you with irrelevant information. Determine what information is necessary to solve the problem and discard the rest.

5 hours per day
35 hours per week
$6 an hour
3 weeks total

Here, the number of hours per day is not needed to solve the problem. It is a distraction.

This is a multi-step multiplication problem. Determine how much money is made in one week and then multiply by the number of weeks worked.

1) 35 x $6 = $210

2) $210 x 3 = $630 **(D)**

Question 41

This problem involves both multiplication and division skills. The first step is to determine how many eggs are received in a week. This is accomplished by multiplying the number of eggs per day by 7 days.

$$4 \times 7 = 28$$

Next, divide the number of eggs per week by the total number of eggs. The result is the solution to the problem.

```
            1 3 (A)
  2 8 ⌐ 3 6 4
      -2 8
        8 4
      - 8 4
          0
```

Question 42

To solve this problem, work backwards using subtraction and multiplication.

$59   money now (at the end of the question)
$9   money found on corner
$24   money spent on tapes ($6 x 4 = $24)

Starting with the $59, subtract the $9 that Jane found because she did not have it before she bought the tapes.

$$\$59 - \$9 = \$50$$

Then add back the money spent on the tapes. This will give you the answer.

$$\$50 + \$24 = \$74 \textbf{ (A)}$$

Question 43

To answer this question, you will need to calculate perimeter. Perimeter is the border around a given area. To calculate a perimeter, add up all the sides of the area. The perimeter is represented by the dotted line below.

9 m

3 m

$$9 + 9 + 3 + 3 = 24 \text{ meters } \textbf{(C)}$$

Question 44

This problem requires basic addition skills. To calculate the total number of prizes, add the numbers of each prize together.

$$20 + 15 + 100 + 100 = 235 \textbf{ (D)}$$

It doesn't matter in which order the numbers appear. This equation could be restated any of the following ways:

$$20 + 100 + 15 + 100 = 235$$

$$100 + 15 + 20 + 100 = 235$$

There are also two like terms in this problem (100). It is possible to restate the formula in this manner:

$$20 + 15 + 2 (100) = 235$$

Again, it doesn't matter in what order the numbers appear, so long as the like terms are multiplied together.

$$15 + (100 \times 2) + 20 \quad \checkmark \qquad 2 \times 100 + 15 + 20 \quad \checkmark$$

$$2 \times 15 + 100 + 20 \quad \times \qquad 2 (100 + 15 + 20) \quad \times$$

Question 45

This is a two-step problem involving multiplication and division. First, determine how much Rebecca makes in a week.
$$50 \times \$5 = \$250$$

Next, determine the number of weeks. This is found by dividing $1,250 by $250.

$$\begin{array}{r} 5 \ \text{(C)} \\ 250 \overline{\smash{)}1250} \\ -1250 \\ \hline 0 \end{array}$$

BOOK 3 – Judgment Section (Sample answers)
Question 77

Working as a member of a team is extremely important as a police officer. In this situation you should consult with your fellow officer, so that you know all of the facts before making a decision. You have no idea what the other party's side of the story is. Speaking to your coworker is especially important in this scenario because your partner has 20 years seniority and is responsible for you. Making a decision without consulting your partner could lead to an error in judgment as well as a reputation for not respecting the seniority of fellow officers. **(A)**

Question 78

Discretion is an important part of policing and learning when to act in questionable situations is learned through experience. In this situation, your partner has a great deal more experience and if he is confident with the decision then that decision should be respected. As a new officer, it would be inappropriate to overrule a senior officer. Arguing in front of the public about a decision should never occur, as it is unprofessional. If you have an issue with a decision that a more senior officer is making, you should address it at a later time. Following the instincts of a senior officer is the most appropriate decision to make in this circumstance. **(A)**

Question 79

The role of a training officer is to help you learn the practical aspects of the job. Because there was a disagreement on a course of action does not mean that the training officer acted inappropriately. Before taking any action it is your responsibility to seek assistance from the training officer. It is their job to clarify any confusion. They might explain that there wasn't enough evidence to take action during your first visit, but now the police are required. It would be inappropriate and unprofessional not to ask for help from your training officer at this stage. Never leave confusing situations unresolved. Going above his head to complain to a sergeant should be an absolute last resort, as it would cause problems with fellow officers with whom you have to work closely. **(C)**

Vancouver Practice Exam

This practice exam is divided into several books. You will be required to answer all questions at once during actual testing, so it is recommended to practise all books in one sitting. Questions in Book 1 are based on information in the bulletin. The tests are timed and have the following format:

Police Bulletin
No questions – 5 minutes
Book 1
10 questions – 5 minutes
Book 2
Passage – 60 minutes
Book 3
30 questions – 45 minutes

Do each test in order (Book 1, Book 2, Book 3). The only materials allowed are pencils and scrap paper. No calculators, books, or counting devices are allowed. Use a clock or stopwatch to keep track of the time. You cannot make any notes while studying Book 1.

Detach the answer key to take the test.

Vancouver Police Answer Sheet

Book 1

	A	B	C	D
1)	○	○	○	○
2)	○	○	○	○
3)	○	○	○	○
4)	○	○	○	○
5)	○	○	○	○
6)	○	○	○	○
7)	○	○	○	○
8)	○	○	○	○
9)	○	○	○	○
10)	○	○	○	○

_____ / 10

Book 3

	A	B	C	D
1)	○	○	○	○
2)	○	○	○	○
3)	○	○	○	○
4)	○	○	○	○
5)	○	○	○	○
6)	○	○	○	○
7)	○	○	○	○
8)	○	○	○	○
9)	○	○	○	○
10)	○	○	○	○
11)	○	○	○	○
12)	○	○	○	○
13)	○	○	○	○
14)	○	○	○	○
15)	○	○	○	○

Book 3

	A	B	C	D
16)	○	○	○	○
17)	○	○	○	○
18)	○	○	○	○
19)	○	○	○	○
20)	○	○	○	○
21)	○	○	○	○
22)	○	○	○	○
23)	○	○	○	○
24)	○	○	○	○
25)	○	○	○	○
26)	○	○	○	○
27)	○	○	○	○
28)	○	○	○	○
29)	○	○	○	○
30)	○	○	○	○

_____ / 30

Vancouver Police Marking Scheme

The actual Vancouver Police Exam has a slightly different format that requires written answer as opposed to multiple choice answers for certain components. There is also a video element to the memory component. The exam contains the following:

Memory
Multiple-choice questions based on a short video and a bulletin that you have to review prior to the exam.

15 marks based on a video
5 marks based on a bulletin

Writing / Editing
You must review 4 passages discovering 10 errors in each of the passages relating to spelling, grammar and punctuation. Each error that is discovered receives 1/2 a mark. The second stage is to rewrite the paragraph correcting all of the errors that were discovered. A total of 5 marks are received for each passage, but marks are deducted for additional mistakes created, or errors that were not discovered.

Discovering errors = 5 marks x 4 passages = 20 marks
Rewriting the passage = 5 marks x 4 passages = 20 marks

Reading Comprehension
Questions based on a passage involving reading comprehension and mathematical ability (addition, subtraction, division, multiplication, fractions, percentages, etc.). Answers are to be written in sentence, paragraph or point form depending on the question.

30 marks total

Summarizing
Writing a summary of a passage / story eliminating needless information and covering the important / relevant points. The summary must be a maximum of 6 sentences and 125 words. Marks are deducted for spelling, grammar and punctuation mistakes.

15 marks

Criminal Suspects

Wanted:	Assault with a Weapon
Name:	Sean Bezic
Age:	33
Weight:	190 lbs
Height:	5'11
Eyes:	Blue
Hair:	Brown
Complexion:	Light
Identifying Marks:	Birthmark Forehead

Wanted:	Drug Trafficking
Name:	Greg Palmos
Age:	28
Weight:	210 lbs
Height:	6'1
Eyes:	Brown
Hair:	Black
Complexion:	Medium Tan
Identifying Marks:	Burn Across Chest

Wanted:	Assault
Name:	Kelly Smith
Age:	30
Weight:	125 lbs
Height:	5'8
Eyes:	Blue
Hair:	Blonde
Complexion:	Light
Identifying Marks:	Pierced Belly Button

Wanted:	Fraud
Name:	Cam White
Age:	22
Weight:	150 lbs
Height:	5'7
Eyes:	Brown
Hair:	Brown
Complexion:	Light
Identifying Marks:	Missing Left Middle Toe

Crime Scene

Do not flip the page until your 5 minutes is up and you are ready to answer the questions in Book 1.

Book 1 – Memory   5 minutes

These questions are based on the Police Bulletin and street scene.

Questions 1

Which suspect was missing a middle toe?

a) Kelly Smith   b) The 22-year-old suspect

c) The suspect wanted for assault with a weapon   d) Greg Palmos

Question 2

Which of the following facts is true about the suspect with the birthmark on the forehead?

a) His height is 5'11   b) He is 28 years old

c) Wanted for Fraud   d) Has blonde hair

Question 3

Who is the shortest suspect?

a) Sean Bezic   b) Kelly Smith   c) Greg Palmos   d) Cam White

Question 4

Which suspects were wanted for some form of assault?

a) Kelly Smith and Greg Palmos   b) Sean Bezic and Cam White

c) Sean Bezic and Kelly Smith   d) Greg Palmos and Cam White

Question 5

Which of the following statements is true about Kelly Smith?

a) 30-years-old   b) 135 lbs

c) Wanted for Fraud   d) Both A and C

Question 6

What number should you dial for help at the mall?

a) 01   b) 91   c) 07   d) 41

Question 7

What was beside the victim on the ground?

a) 2 keys, a cell phone and a box.   b) A spilled drink and some popcorn.

c) A bag with bread.   d) None of the above.

Question 8

Which of the following people were not in the scene?

a) A man collapsed on the ground.   b) A baby in a stroller.

c) An old lady on a bench.   d) A jewellery sales staff.

Question 9

What was the name of the mall?

a) Hillcrest   b) Crossroads   c) Royz Toyz   d) Sceptical

Question 10

What was beside the garbage can?

a) Grocery Bag   b) Medical Bag   c) Candy Dispenser   d) None of these

You have 1 hour to identify ten mistakes in each of the four passages below. After determining the mistakes, rewrite the passage correcting the errors. During the exam, you will be penalized for new mistakes introduced into the passage.

QUESTION 1

A shortage of ticket's for tomorrow's graduation ceremony at Champlain Regional College have students deciding weather to invite Mom or Dad. Unprecedented demand for tickets by the school's 292 graduats left families scrambbling for a seat at the ceremony, to be held in the theatre at nearby Bishop's University.

"For us, it's a source of distress and delight at the same time," said Melanie Cutting, the CEGEP's directer of student services. "It's a delight there is so much interest, but distressing because we didn't know if we should be able to accomodate everyone." In previus years, the 650-seat theatre at Bishop's University easily accommodated all graduates and guests. The ceremony and wine and chease reception is free.

QUESTION 2

Motherhood may indeed be its own reward, but labur analysts has calculated that stay-at-home mothers are worth an salary of $164,337 a year.

According to a knew report from Salary.com, the anual wage, including overtime pays, would be paid if the workload carried out by stay-at-home mothers was remunerated in market terms.

The estimate takes into account the average stay-at-home moms job responsibilitys, number of hours worked and frequency of time spent on specific tasks during a tipical weak.

QUESTION 3

To many businesses are failing to train staff in how to handle personal information, putting consumer's at risk of identity theft, says Canada's privacy commissionar.

Recent data breaches have reinforce worries about both domestic security issues and how information flow across the border, Shannon Roulston said in her 2006 anual report, tabled Thursday in the House of Commons. Data breaches is becoming more regular occurrences. The privacy office was involved in two major data breach investigations last year.

One was a joint investigation with the information and privacy commission of British Columbia: Victor Tong, into a breach of the database at TJX Companies Inc., the operator of Winners and HomeSense stores across Canada. Hackers alegedly got into the company's database, which contained the personal information of Canadian customers?

QUESTION 4

The neonatal intensive-care-unit that handles some of the sickest, most fragile babys in Vancouver remained closed today after a baby died of serratia — a bactirea that normally doesn't kill adults or healthy children but can be deadly if contracted by premature infants.

Sunnybrook Hospital officials said the two-week old baby, who weighed between 500 and 1,500 grams, dies last weakend. They won't release the name or sex of the infants for privacy reasons.

Four other infants have tested positive for serratia but are showing no sign's of sickness. They have been isolated are being closely watched and tests are under way to see if they all suffer from the same strain.

Until the babies were clear of the bacteria, the level 3 neonatal unit will try not to except any infants, said Dr. Jennifer Stone, Sunnybrook's director of infection control.

Question 1

Ontario outpaced the rest of the country during the strong economic boom of the 90's because it is the most integrated into the US economy of all the provinces. This integration has also led to the current economic slow down. The US has been sliding into a recession and the Canadian job market has lost 10,000 jobs since June. Recessions are cyclical events and Ontario will have to make it through some tough times ahead. While some provinces have gained, Ontario has lost 29,000 jobs. It is against that harsh reality - and forecasts of worse to come - that Finance Minister Jim Flaherty delivers his economic statement tomorrow. Up until now, Flaherty has been emphasizing that the long-term outlook for Ontario is positive. The immediate economic forecast is a problem. Since the only tune the Mike Harris government seems to know is 99 tax cuts and it's off to the mall, Flaherty is probably disposed to add another refrain. Tax cuts are not necessarily the most effective form of stimulus for an economy that is suffering due to a global recession. But tax cuts won't do much for Ontarians who lose their jobs to recession. These are usually the most vulnerable workers - the workers with the fewest skills, the lowest incomes and the most meagre savings to fall back on.

According to the above passage, which one of the following statements is true?

a) The Canadian economy is directly tied to the U.S. economy.

b) The tax cuts to be implemented by the Ontario government will not help the people hurt most by the recession.

c) Jobs have been declining across Canada, steadily in all provinces.

d) The U.S. economy is beginning to correct itself.

Question 2

Which one of the following statements is supported by the above passage?

a) Ontario is the weakest link in the Canadian economy.

b) Since May the total number of jobs in Canada has decreased by 29,000.

c) The recession is localized to the North American economy.

d) Ontario's economy is the most directly linked to the U.S. economy.

Question 3

According to the above passage, which one of the following statements is true?

a) Ontario's economic boom during the 1990's coincided with a U.S. economic boom.

b) Ontario will continue an economic slump, until after the U.S. economy recovers.

c) The other provinces will eventually follow Ontario's economic slump.

d) Tax cuts are the only tools the Ontario government is using to fight a recession.

Question 4

It wasn't long ago that the idea of state legislation to protect the Spruce Valley Conservation would never arrive. A succession of Labour cabinet ministers pointedly said that municipalities themselves had the powers to shield this natural feature from development. Environmentalists disagreed with the cabinet minister about the powers of the municipalities. More importantly, so did tens of thousands of region residents.

They wanted provincial action to protect the conservation and packed town hall meetings to loudly say so. Pushed by this public opinion, the Tasmanian government unveiled legislation yesterday that, if passed, will put most of the conservation beyond the reach of developers. It would create a greenbelt of rolling hills and lakes. And it would signal that there are boundaries to the urban sprawl that pushes relentlessly outward. Municipal Affairs Minister James Jessop called it a monumental occasion. In just a year the government has moved from a stubborn refusal to get involved; to grudging acceptance of its responsibility; to yesterday's introduction of sweeping measures to safeguard the conservation's natural features and its precious water resources. Residents deserve credit for speaking out. Jessop and his cabinet colleagues deserve credit for listening. Three state governments have grappled with this tough issue. Finally, this government has acted.

According to the above passage, which one of the following statements is true?

a) Municipalities have the necessary power to protect the Spruce Valley Conservation.

b) The Tasmanian government has been actively involved in the protection of the Spruce Valley Conservation from the onset.

c) The Tasmanian government has taken the important steps to protect the Conservation.

d) The previous Labour government settled the Conservation issue years before.

Question 5

According to the above passage, which one of the following statements is true?

a) Environmentalists want local governments to be responsible for the Conservation.

b) Residents petitioned the government through town hall meetings.

c) Developers wanted to build housing units and a power plant in the Conservation.

d) The current government doesn't care about the environment.

Question 6

How many governments have grappled with this issue according to the above passage?

a) 1   b) 2   c) 3   d) 4

Question 7

Rita is able to read 30 pages an hour. For an assignment she has two books to read. The first book has 1,350 pages, second book has 2,010 pages. How many hours will it take Rita to finish both books?

a) 75   b) 110   c) 112   d) 121

Question 8

John travels 75 KM to work each way. If he averages 120 KM/Hr, how long (Minutes) does he spend driving to and from work each day?

a) 1.25   b) 75   c) 50   d) 60

Question 9

Constable Smith issued 16 speeding tickets and 5 drinking under influence charges last month. The Police department had a total 64 speeding tickets and 20 DUI charges last month. What percentage of speeding tickets issued last month was made by Constable Smith?

a) 12%   b) 29%   c) 10%   d) 25%

Question 10

Tim needs to fill three 20L barrels with oil. If his oil dispenser flows at 100 mL/s, how long will it take him to fill the 3 containers? (Minutes)

a) 100   b) 75   c) 50   d) 10

Question 11

Julie went shopping with $250 in her purse. She purchased one sweater and a jacket. If she spent $75 on the sweater and returned home with only $15, how much did she spend on the jacket?

a) 160   b) 250   c) 75   d) 80

Question 12

1 in 5 cars in the city of Brampton has visible damage to the body. In a parking lot with 130 cars, how many cars would not be damaged?

a) 26   b) 50   c) 100   d) 104

Question 13

A website receives an average of 15,000 visitors/month. If 1 out of every 5 visits is from a government user, how many government users visit the site in a year?

a) 3,000   b) 15,000   c) 36,000   d) 180,000

Question 14

There are 500 cell phone users in the 1st Bank Office Building. It is known that 55 users subscribe to global text-messaging, 35 users have camera phones, and 400 users subscribe to voice mail. What percentage of the users have voice mail?

a) 20%   b) 40%   c) 60%   d) 80%

Question 15

The average rainfall in Waterloo has increased at an annual rate of 2%. If the total rain fall was 856mm in 2002. What is the expected rainfall in 2005? (mm)

a) 907.4   b) 908.4   c) 873.12   d) 900

Question 16

The state will spend $3.2 million over the next four years to combat domestic violence, but some critics say that doesn't go far enough. Justice Minister Shelley Hayes said Friday the funding will cover hiring four victim-support workers, establishing a training course for police and justice officials and allowing for emergency intervention orders and other initiatives. Queensland's review on their Framework for Action Against Domestic Abuse include more than 50 recommendations. The review was conducted by James Huang, dean of University of Melbourne's law school, and fellow professor Adrian Kinkead. "I think this report has heightened the focus, I guess, of everyone in the justice system, and in the government, on family violence," Mr. Huang said. The deaths of Kelly Anne Toner and Ben James McCaffery and the resulting investigation led Mr. Huang to commission the $70,000 report. Mr. McCaffery shot Ms. Toner and then himself on the second floor of their Jamestown home in July 1999. The two had a history of domestic violence, and government reviews found shortcomings in the response of Jamestown police and the Department of Community Services. The report deals with five areas for people and agencies who deal with domestic violence - training, procedures, working together, victim support and accountability.

According to the above passage, which one of the following statements is true?

a) Domestic violence is the most pressing concern in Queensland policing.

b) The state plans to spend $3.2 million over the next two years to combat domestic violence.

c) The funding will cover four victim-support workers, establishing a training course for police and allowing for emergency intervention orders and other initiatives.

d) Queensland's framework Action Against Domestic Abuse has 60 recommendations.

Question 17

The report deals with five areas for people and agencies that deal with domestic violence. These areas are:

a) Victim support, accountability, training, procedures and working together.

b) Training, procedures, enforcement, victim support and accountability.

c) Procedures, working together, victim support, accountability and punishment.

d) Accountability, victim support, working together, procedures and prosecution.

Question 18

What event initiated the $70,000 report into domestic violence?

a) The murder of Ms. Toner.

b) The suicide of James McCaffery.

c) The murder suicide of Mr. Toner and Ms. McCaffery.

d) The murder suicide of Mr. McCaffery and Ms. Toner.

Question 19

Gas leaks are extremely dangerous situations. Especially in large urban areas where populations are extremely concentrated and any explosion could cause massive damage and a large number of personal injuries. Firefighters are trained to evacuate any area affected when a suspected flammable gas leak occurs. This would include evacuating a building or all occupants.

If the gas leak's location is determined firefighters will open all possible doors and windows in order to create greater ventilation. One of the main priorities in these emergency situations is to eliminate the threat. Once the location of the leak is determined the main valve should be shut off outside the building, or if that isn't possible a valve inside the building feeding the leaking pipe should be closed. By checking the flow of the meter firefighters will be able to determine if the leak has been terminated. If there is no gas flow registering than it is safe to assume the leak has stopped.

Sources of ignition have to be contained. If there is a major gas leak out in public firefighters will have motorists turn their vehicles off and order them not to start them up again. The ignition process of starting car causes some sparking which could ignite gas that exists in the area due to a leak. Preventing smoking is another obvious precaution that should be made by emergency personnel. Inside buildings lights should neither be turned on, nor turned off if they are already on. The act of flipping a light switch can cause a small electrical spark, which is all that is required to detonate the gas.

Once ignited it is very difficult to put out a fire until the source of the gas has been cut off. One major concern that firefighters may encounter is boiling liquid expanding vapour explosions (BLEVE). A BLEVE can occur if there is gas tanker or cylinder is on fire due to a faulty relief valve or even if there is a fire in the vicinity which is heating the contents of the tank. The heat causes the gas inside to expand rapidly, increasing pressure, which eventually has to be released, through a massive explosion. Firefighters will aim a water stream at the tank, not to extinguish the fire escaping from the tank, but to cool the tank to prevent the gas from expanding and eliminate the threat of a BLEVE.

Fire departments around the world have procedures in place to handle the dangerous situation of gas related fires. Not all gases are easily detectable. Some are odourless and colourless, which require special instruments to detect.

What is the general theme of this passage?

a) Methods to extinguish gas fires.

b) Outline of several procedures when encountering gas leaks and gas fires.

c) Dangers of BLEVEs.

d) A description of different types of fires involving several materials.

Question 20

What is a method outlined to determine whether a gas flow has been stopped?

a) Shutting off all motor vehicle engines.

b) Opening windows to improve ventilation.

c) Checking the external meter for flow.

d) Checking the external valve for flow.

Question 21

What is not recommended according to the article above?

a) Evacuating a building where a gas leak has been confirmed.

b) Turning off motor vehicles in a gas leak area.

c) Cooling a gas cylinder with water if it is in fire, or near a heat source.

d) Shutting off all lights in a suspected gas leak.

Question 22

Why would ventilation be important in an area affected by a gas leak?

a) Allows gas concentrations to grow in other areas.

b) Ventilation should only be used in urban areas.

c) Reduces the concentration of gas in the affected areas.

d) Both B and C.

Question 23

A firefighter sees a fire escaping from gas pipe in a basement of a warehouse. The room has a large propane tank located near the fire. What strategy should be used in this case?

a) Water should be aimed at the tank to reduce the temperature of the gas inside.

b) An attempt should be made to shut off the valve feeding the pipe.

c) Both A and B.

d) Neither A nor B.

Question 24

During the course of your training you are taught the procedures you should follow when you encounter a major accident scene, or dangerous situation.
1) Get appropriate backup and emergency personnel en route to assist you
2) Create a safe work environment to perform your duties
3) Assist people in immediate life threatening situations
4) Treat victims in order of emergency priority
5) Transport victims in need of medical attention to the hospital
6) Collect evidence on scene
7) Clear the area for normal use
Which of the following is the most important step to take when you arrive at an emergency scene?

a) Transport injured parties to the hospital

b) Treat an injured woman who is bleeding from her head

c) Assist a man who is trapped in a vehicle, which is on fire

d) Preserve evidence proving that the driver was under the influence of alcohol

Question 25

	Murders	Thefts	Robberies
1998	4	359	64
1999	3	376	66
2000	6	412	72

Above are important crime statistics for the Town of Surrey. Below are the estimated costs to investigate each crime.

    Murder: $3,000

    Theft: $200

Robbery: $600

What was the total budget in 1999 for these three crimes?

a) $115,600   b) $123,800   c) $109,400   d) $140,500

Question 26

By what percent did the number of robberies increase from 1998 to 2000?

a) 12.5%   b) 11.1%   c) 6.6%   d) 88.9%

Question 27

What percentage of the budget of 2000 was used toward investigating thefts?

a) 75.6%   b) 84.1%   c) 62.5%   d) 57.4%

Question 28

James ran 2 miles in 12 minutes. He has to run another 5 miles and wants to average a 7-minute mile over the entire run. What will James have to run the remaining 5 miles in on average to accomplish this?

a) 6.3 min / mile   b) 7.4 min / mile   c) 8.6 min / mile   d) 10.2 min / mile

Question 29

Shane and Indervir were digging a hole in the yard. They were required to remove 1000 lbs of dirt to complete the job. Shane was capable of removing 125 lbs of dirt per hour and Indervir was capable of removing 100 lbs of dirt per hour. How long would it take the two working together to complete the whole?

a) 3.45 hours   b) 4.45 hours   c) 5.40 hours   d) 5.75 hours

Question 30

A man drove for 7 hours. In that time he managed to complete 1/3 of his journey. How many more hours is he going to drive for?

a) 10   b) 18   c) 14   d) 22

Vancouver Answer Key

Book 1

1	2	3	4	5	6	7	8	9	10
B	A	D	C	A	C	A	D	B	A

Book 2 - Passage

Question 1

A shortage of **tickets** for tomorrow's graduation ceremony at Champlain Regional College **has** students deciding **whether** to invite Mom or Dad. Unprecedented demand for tickets by the school's 292 **graduates** left families **scrambling** for a seat at the ceremony, to be held in the theatre at nearby Bishop's University.

"For us, it's a source of distress and delight at the same time," said Melanie Cutting, the CEGEP's **director** of student services. "It's a delight there is so much interest, but distressing because we didn't know if we **would** be able to **accommodate** everyone." In **previous** years, the 650-seat theatre at Bishop's University easily accommodated all graduates and guests. The ceremony and wine and **cheese** reception is free.

Question 2

Motherhood may indeed be its own reward, but **labour** analysts **have** calculated that stay-at-home mothers are worth **a** salary of $164,337 a year.

According to a **new** report from Salary.com, the **annual** wage, including overtime **pay**, would be paid if the workload carried out by stay-at-home mothers was remunerated in market terms.

The estimate takes into account the average stay-at-home **mom's** job **responsibilities**, number of hours worked and frequency of time spent on specific tasks during a **typical week**.

Question 3

Too many businesses are failing to train staff in how to handle personal information, putting **consumers** at risk of identity theft, says Canada's privacy **commissioner**.

Recent data breaches **have reinforced** worries about both domestic security issues and how information **flows** across the border, Shannon Roulston said in her 2006 **annual** report, tabled Thursday in the House of Commons. Data breaches **are** becoming more regular occurrences. The privacy office was involved in two major data breach investigations last year.

One was a joint investigation with the information and privacy commission of British **Columbia, Victor Tong,** into a breach of the database at TJX Companies Inc., the operator of Winners and HomeSense stores across Canada. Hackers **allegedly** got into the company's database, which contained the personal information of Canadian **customers.**

Question 4

The neonatal **intensive care unit** that handles some of the sickest, most fragile **babies** in Vancouver remained closed today after a baby died of serratia — a **bacteria** that normally doesn't kill adults or healthy children but can be deadly if contracted by premature infants.

Sunnybrook Hospital officials said the two-week old baby, who weighed between 500 and 1,500 grams, **died** last **weekend**. They won't release the name or sex of the **infant** for privacy reasons.

Four other infants have tested positive for serratia but are showing no **signs** of sickness. They have been **isolated, are** being closely watched and tests are under way to see if they all suffer from the same strain.

Until the babies **are** clear of the bacteria, the level 3 neonatal unit will try not to **accept** any infants, said Dr. Jennifer Stone, Sunnybrook's director of infection control.

Book 3

1	B	**6**	C	**11**	A	**16**	C	**21**	D	**26**	A
2	D	**7**	C	**12**	D	**17**	A	**22**	C	**27**	D
3	A	**8**	B	**13**	C	**18**	D	**23**	C	**28**	B
4	C	**9**	D	**14**	D	**19**	B	**24**	C	**29**	B
5	B	**10**	D	**15**	B	**20**	C	**25**	B	**30**	C

Detailed Answers Book 3

Questions 1 – 6 do not have detailed answer explanations.

Question 7

C - First calculate the total number of pages Rita must read [1,350 + 2,010 = 3,360]. Then divide the total number pages by her reading speed [3,360/30 = 112 minutes]

Question 8

B - We need to calculate John's total return trip driving distance [75 + 75 = 150KM]. Then divide total distance by his average driving speed [150/120=1.25hr]. Then convert 1.25 hours to minutes by multiplying by 60, to arrive at 75 minutes.

Question 9

D - Total speeding tickets issued = 64; speeding tickets issued by Constable = 16. Thus percentage = 16/64 x 100% or 25%

Question 10

D - First determine volume of three containers [3 x 20L = 60L]. Then convert fill rate from mL/s to L/min. Recall 1L = 1000mL and 60s = 1 minute;
100 / 1000 x 60 = 6L/min];
Then divide total volume by fill rate [60 / 6 = 10 minutes]

Question 11

A -Simply subtract $75 and $15 from her beginning $250. Answer: $160

Question 12

D - The ratio of damaged cars to to non-damaged cars is 1:50. Thus 4 out of every 5 (80%) is non-damaged. So in a parking of 130 cars 80% or 130*0.8 = 104 cars.

Question 13

C - If 1 in 5 are government users, each month the website receives [1/5 * 15,000] 3,000 government users. Thus in one year the site would receive [3,000 * 12=] 36,000 government users.

Question 14

D - Percentage of voice mail users = 400/500 = 0.8 which converts to 80%.

Question 15

B - The annual increase in rainfall from one year to the next is 2%. Starting at 856mm (2002), begin to calculate the rainfall for the following years: 856 x 1.02 = 873.12mm (2003); Then 873.12 x 1.02 = 890.58mm (2004); Finally, 890.58 x 1.02 = 908.4 mm (2005).

Questions 16 - 24 do not have detailed answer explanations.

Question 25

First determine the total budget for each crime, and then add the total crime budget together. (3 x $3000 = $9,000 + 376 x $200 = $75,200 + 66 x $600 = $39,600). The total is $123,800.

Question 26

There was an increase of 8 robberies between 1998 and 2000 (72 – 64 = 8). This represents a 12.5% increase (8 / 64 = 0.125 or 12.5%).

Question 27

The total budget was $143,600 in 2000. This is determined by totaling all of the cost of the crimes (6 x $3000 + 412 x $200 + 72 x $600 = $143,600). The total spent on thefts was $82,400 (412 x 200) which represents 57.4% of the budget (82,400 / 143,600 = 0.5738 or 57.4%).

Question 28

It would be best to set up an algebraic equation to solve this problem. The total will be 7 miles and the average has to be 7 minutes a mile. There are two components to the run, 2 miles at 6 minutes / mile and 5 miles at "y" minutes / mile. These two components when added together and divided by 7 must result in 7.

$$\frac{2(6) + 5(y)}{7} = 7$$ Now simply solve for "y".

12 + 5 (y) = 49   Multiply both sides by 7.
5 (y) = 37   Subtract both sides by 12.
y = 7.4   Divide both sides by 5 results in 7.4 minutes / mile.

Question 29

Shane and Indervir can dig 225 lbs / hour (100 + 125 = 225). If they have to remove 1000 pounds, simply divide 1000 / 225 = 4.44 hours. In order to make sure all of the dirt is removed you will have to round up to 4.45 hours as 4.4 will only remove 990 lbs of dirt.

Question 30

The total journey will take 21 hours (7 x 3 = 21) which means there are 14 hours left in the journey (21 – 7 = 14).